The problems of american education

The problems of american education

EDITED AND WITH AN
INTRODUCTION BY
BURTON R. CLARK

A NEW YORK TIMES BOOK

New Viewpoints
A Division of Franklin Watts, Inc.
New York
1975

Library of Congress Cataloging
in Publication Data

Clark, Burton R   comp.
   The problems of American education.

   "A New York Times Book."
   Articles reprinted from the New York times.
   CONTENTS: Bush, D. Education for all is ed-
ucation for none.—Hechinger, F. M. Five basic
problems of education.—Gross, D. The Bunker
Hill of desegregation. [etc.]
   1. Education—United States—Addresses, es-
says, lectures. I. New York times. II. Title.
LA217.C5   370'.973   71-190128
ISBN 0-531-05566-3 (pbk.)

I am grateful to Adele Clark for the library
search which made it possible for me to assemble and edit this book.

CONTENTS

The problems of american education

INTRODUCTION

Instruction of the young and the old has always been one of the basic activities of mankind. Indeed, humans inform one another, conveying beliefs, knowledge, and skill, as they raise a family, earn a living, govern a polity, minister a church, nurse the ill, encounter friends, or communicate through the mass media. All social settings, in a broad sense, contain occasions for teaching and learning. What we call education is simply those social systems that are deliberately assembled to promote and concentrate such occasions. We create teaching as a form of adult work and learning as an explicit activity of the young, and we concentrate the teachers and learners in social and geographic space.

It all seems quite necessary when so many have so much to learn, but as soon as we create *Education* we create new problems. We have a new social institution with ways and dynamics of its own. Teaching becomes an occupation with its own definitions of the good, its own interests of career and status. The concentrating of the young in grade and age strata insures that they too will create their own quasi-independent perceptions and will seek to protect and effect them. Systematic coordination of effort is needed, and thus administration is born. As education becomes a separate sphere, its ultimate control becomes an inescapable matter, creating the need for educational politics. The various levels of education need to be articulated with one another and the higher ones linked effectively to the outside world. And so on. As elsewhere in society, problems in the educational realm are created, and solved in whole or in part, in an endless process. To solve one problem is to turn to face another, especially in a rapidly changing world.

The basic social trends of a nation set a general framework for the particular educational problems it faces at any given time. In order to work toward our present situation, we can note certain primary trends in American society. First, the nation has long been in the grasp of an internal migration that has moved its population from small rural places to large metropolitan centers. Second, the changes in the economy that helped to cause that migration have also encouraged rising expectations of how much education and training various individuals must have before they are prepared to work and to participate effectively in a complex society. Third, in response to the rising expectations as well as the economic demand, the American educational system has steadily changed its character from elite to mass—at the elementary level in the nineteenth century, at the secondary level in the first half of the twentieth century, and now in higher education. As a result of these fundamental flows, we have today a structure of prolonged mass education in largely urban settings.

In addition, several other trends have become critical and prominent in their impact during the quarter century since the end of World War II. The most important of these is a growing and appalling concentration of educational inequality. The shift to urban life has concentrated the population in large metropolitan areas. Within these concentrations, the practices of the housing market and the personal choices in housing of the more advantaged social classes have increased rather than decreased the *residential* separation of social classes and races. The middle class has come to live ever farther away from the lower class, increasingly in separate suburban towns served by separate school districts. Whites and blacks grow ever further apart, with the blacks largely concentrated in the heart of the city and the whites either far away from the center or stubbornly clinging to parts of the city that are lower-class and lower-middle-class white. Since American schools historically have been zoned by neighborhood and town, increased segregation in housing has meant increased segregation in the schools.

The effect of these residential patterns on the possibilities of school integration, now so painfully obvious, was for years not observed. Until late in the 1950s and the early 1960s, optimism prevailed. The American comprehensive school would still be the great melting pot, helping to integrate American society across the old and stubborn barriers of social class and race. But it was not to be. As a result of racial attitudes, and particularly of institutionalized discrimination in the assigning of people to housing and neighborhood, the American comprehensive school has become more segregated along lines of social class and race. Thus, the problem of educational inequality—one with us historically —became, objectively, larger and deeper. It only took a rise in black militancy to make it explosive.

The second new trend of the recent past involves the development of "adolescence" as a long, distinctive, and self-conscious stage of life. The nature of this development remains vague, its causes controversial. Increasingly, the young do not relate well to adult functions and responsibilities, largely because of delayed admission to work. Yet, past the age of 12 or 13 they are no longer children, and may have the strength and capacity to function as adults both intellectually and sexually. Delaying the entry into work and marriage puts them in limbo, producing a large population in dire need of purpose and meaning. A distinct stage of adolescence is also promoted by the contraction and weakening of the extended family—that web of aunts, uncles, cousins, and grandparents—which in various societies even today (and in periods past in American society) is spun around the young, sometimes choking them half to death while providing them with a perceivable and palpable role and identity. Then, too, without doubt, a distinct stage of adolescence has been strengthened greatly in

The Problems of
American Education

5

recent years by the mass media and a youth industry
that shapes the thinking and behavior of the young
while serving them for profit. Powerful business interests now seek to separate out the young as a
special consumer market that must be stimulated to
expand its consumption. The AM radio band is adolescent territory, as is a good part of the popular
records industry, concerts, and clothing. The youth-
oriented segments of the mass media and commerce
have moved quickly into contention as the prime
socializers in modern society, directly relating to
the young in ways that are not fully mediated by the
teacher and parent.

The effects of this distinctive stage of adolescence on the schooling of the young are profound.
Here is a large part of the population that is increasingly treated as a stratum and is increasingly conscious of itself as one. Since this self-conscious stratum is assigned to education by law and norm, the
school and college are where they are found for
most of the working hours of the day. It would not
be surprising if the adolescents were to want to
define the school and the college as their "turf."
Even if the territory sometimes seems to be controlled by others and basically unfriendly, it is
where the young must play out most of the adolescent years.

Thus far we have spoken of how the social class
and racial characteristics of the neighborhood dic-
tate school inequalities and how the student has
been caught up in a well-defined adolescent stage
of life. One other trend now stands prominent and
completes a triangle of conflict: the bureau-

6

cratization of educational work. In recent years, educational organizations have increased greatly in scale, paralleling the development of large organizations in other sectors of American life. This trend stems from the concentration of population in large cities and the shift from elite to mass education. We need only imagine the old rural school district, composed of one or two small schools at one end of the continuum of size and complexity and the New York City and Los Angeles districts at the other end, to realize how much we have changed the relationship between pupil and teacher. The gigantic school district and the huge university seek to arrange themselves in a formal pyramid of authority and jurisdiction, to relate their many parts in systematic ways, and to seek fair and equitable, and hence uniform, procedures—in short, to become a mammoth bureaucracy. The casting of education into bureaucratic forms has been hastened by the ideologies of school administration, much influenced by the models of American business, that have amounted to a managerial search for efficiency. Also, the teacher at all levels has become more specialized, replacing the generalist, who bracketed many functions, with an ever more elaborate division of labor in which each person is an expert in a separate specialty. This, too, while appropriate to modern professionalism, contributes to the bureaucratic cause.

If we look at the results of these major social trends we see modern American education as a structure of prolonged and bureaucratically organized mass socialization, located in an urban setting, affecting a population segregated by class and race (and ethnicity), and daily relating to millions of young people much influenced by a self-conscious adolescent stage of life. If we add to this picture the rapidity of modern social change, we have the basis for a series of current major problems.

1. TEACHING THE NEW ADOLESCENT

Teaching, as indicated above, has become more specialized and routinized, defined by bureaucratic and professional patterns. At the same time, conditions outside the school have radically altered the instructional needs of the young toward flexibility and variety in teaching and special sensitivity to the more holistic features of adolescence. For students as a whole, it seems, teaching is now more problematic than at any other time in recent history.

2. TEACHING THE POOR

Teaching is particularly perplexing for the poor—especially poor nonwhites. The bureaucratic and professional molds of modern teaching, together with the inherited traditions of the profession, have blended badly with the values and practices of the lower class, poor blacks, Mexican Americans, and Puerto Ricans. These large minorities among the poor are not only segregated in school but also go to school longer than in the old days, when the poor went to work after only a few years in the schoolhouse.

8

3. THE CONTROL OF THE SCHOOLS

Democratic ideology encourages those in all social strata to enter the political arena, there to influence public policy. This ideology has been particularly strong in American education, since education here was early defined as a state and local (rather than a national) prerogative; as a result, the system of control became centered on the device of citizen-dominated governing boards and the belief that the board member was a trustee of the interests of the public. American doctrine has instructed parents to go out and run the schools. As different groups of parents hew to different values, however, they naturally conflict. On the other hand, the growth of educational bureaucracy pushes for control by the administrator, while the development of professionalism in education dictates that teachers and professors should have much control over the nature of their work. The growing segregation of schools by class and race, and the disjuncture between the system and the poor, has greatly deepened the conflict over who, and whose values, will have greatest influence. Control has become a fundamental problem.

4. PURPOSE AND LEGITIMACY

Finally, the serious strains in education of the postwar period, and especially those of the 1960s in American life, have opened for questioning even the intrinsic legitimacy of schooling. There seems to be a great loss of public confidence in the workings of the educational system from kindergarten to graduate school. The lower social strata claim that

The Problems of
American Education

schools do not supply even the simplest of educational services—decent teachers in decent buildings producing functional literacy in reading, writing, and arithmetic. The intellectual critics of the upper middle class, and some articulate spokesmen among the poor, claim that today's educational services basically fail the young because the subject matter and presentation are archaic, boring, and inappropriate to their present and future needs.

A loss of public confidence must sooner or later affect the self-esteem of teachers. Like all workers, teachers have mechanisms for defending themselves against the criticisms of outsiders: they can pull together and back one another; they can gain moral support from the philosophies and norms of the profession. But on a number of grounds American teachers have been vulnerable. They are supposed to heed the claims of laymen and accept their ultimate control. They are subject to supervision by local lay trustees as well as administrators. They often internalize the expectation of universal accomplishment, which causes them acute discomfort when they cannot reach all the young. They find it difficult to know when they are effective since the goals of their work are ambiguous and lacking in consensus. Their basic vulnerability undercuts their own strategies in defending and reassuring themselves, particularly when outside critics evaluate them in terms of universal benefit and steadily pound away on the theme of failure. Then, discouragement becomes a repetitive motif in the talk of teachers. And, as their confidence erodes, a vicious circle of passive withdrawal from teaching and angry defensive reactions weakens the corps that is finally the central resource of the whole educational enterprise.

The loss of public confidence and the despair of teachers may eventually undercut the resilience of educational institutions. But whatever their defects, schools and colleges normally have an uncommon and even uncanny capacity somehow to get the work done and stagger on to another year. They seem to have some "Thank-God-for-Joe" people— teachers whose hours never end, custodians who get the clutter cleaned up, registrars who get the grades in and the seniors graduated. Distinguished schools and colleges, heavy with mystique, are notably loaded with this resource of devotion. But even those places that operate at the bottom of the barrel, and are often seen as grubby and mean-spirited, seem to possess such cadres—people who still believe in the goodness of education or in the terrible waste and immorality of failing the young. Yet, surely there are limits to the resilience of the devoted group and the institutions that they carry on their backs. If public confidence is chipped away too far and teacher despair deepens too much, large segments of the educational system may fall below the threshold of resilience, measurably worsening the education of millions of young. If confusion in purpose and identity continues in our schools and colleges, we will face increasingly the need to reestablish the fundamental legitimacy of the entire enterprise.

These trends and problems are my definitions, one man's perceptions in the early 1970s. How has

The Problems of
American Education

the educational terrain been seen by others? A review of the flow of articles about education in the
New York Times during the last three decades reveals radical shifts in emphasis.

Before World War II, there was little national
comment. Education was a quiet business of the
local community and the state, rather than a steady
concern of national statesmen and the major political parties. The federal government only occasionally concerned itself with education in such
isolated events as the land-grant legislation in the
mid-nineteenth century that encouraged the states
to start universities, and the special legislation during World War I that initiated permanent federal
funding of vocational education in the secondary
schools. At the local and state levels, concern was
often intense, but still education was not seen as so
crucial to the well-being of society as to promote a
sense of large crisis, to command the sustained attention of public officials and the general public,
and to generate the dogged will and the special programs to correct its errors. After all, the raising of
the young would still be mainly in the hands of the
family, church, and community. Men could still
make it without extensive formal schooling; the
image of the self-made man on the frontier, in
industry, and in commerce still loomed large in the
American mind. If there was such a thing as an educational column, or even "educational news," in the
newspaper, it was back somewhere around the want
ads.

Not long after World War II, however, education
moved to the front page. The federal government

stepped in—and stayed in—first by subsidizing college education for veterans of World War II; then
(in the early 1950s) by federal court action against
racial segregation in the schools, a genuine fighting
issue that, in attacking established prejudice and
entrenched discrimination, tore at the souls of men
and the fabric of the community. It was the end of
innocence for American education. Finally, in the
latter half of the 1950s, as the country became anxious about keeping up with the Russians in science
and technology, academic excellence took over the
center of the stage as a concern of national spokesmen and federal agencies.

In the 1960s, the problem of the education of
blacks underwent a radical redefinition. The earlier
concern with the integration of blacks and whites,
so much focused at first on Southern schools, was
supplemented and often replaced by new views.
The first shift was to a belief that there should be
compensatory education for the "culturally deprived," an effort made to give special treatment to
those whose background put them at an educational
disadvantage. The emphasis shifted from integration to improvement and enrichment of the programs for poor blacks and poor whites in the schools
they already attended. The second shift, a few years
later, was to the view that the large urban school
districts needed to be decentralized and "community control" reestablished in order that black
parents and other lay groups could have a more effective influence on the education of their own children. Then, too, after 1964, higher education
emerged as a dramatic national problem, with stu-

dent discontent generating extensive public debate on reform of the bureaucratized university. Mass higher education proved to be treacherous ground, as seemingly irresistible demands for expansion, equality, and participation ran into traditional structures and a growing resistance to rising costs.

The 1970s and 1980s will surely see new public definitions of the basic problems. Certain tensions are always present: for example, between general and vocational education and between elite and populist conceptions. But the priorities among problems set by inherent and emerging tensions fluctuate in the minds of experts and laymen. The flux in definition, we should note, adds to the problems of those who work in the halls of education. An urban school administrator who took all the public debate of the last two decades seriously and struggled to meet the problems thus defined would surely have felt that the whole enterprise was unsteadied by the shifting winds of public opinion. In the late 1950s he would have struggled to initiate new programs for academically gifted students, only to find a few years later that he was being vilified for spending so much money on the elite. Then compensatory education, in its turn, became a subordinate matter as attention was focused on the battle over control and the decentralization of the bureaucracy.

Since modern societies are characterized by rapid change and confusion over ends and means, opinions will continue to vary and conflict, and they will change over time. But American society, only loosely moored by the anchors of tradition, seems

14

especially subject to changes of opinion on educational issues. Thus, part of the educational problem is the erratic course of its public definition.

As we look to the future, we can see that certain problems will persist operationally and will have high claims on public attention. Inequality of educational opportunity seems destined to remain the primary problem, both here and in other countries. It is followed closely in importance by the problem of quality education for all social strata and the problem of utilizing educational resources—money, personnel, technology—more effectively. We have said little about this latter problem, but as educational costs continue to rise, increased productivity in education will become more of an issue.

Beyond these three problems that will predictably draw public attention from time to time, there seem to be other issues that are equally important, whose time for public concern has not yet come. Among these issues are teacher morale, teacher training, and institutional overload. Through a long period of adding new activities and responsibilities, and assuming new burdens, the educational institution has probably taken on too much. It performs too many functions and is expected to fulfill too many expectations. We expect schools and colleges to solve grave national problems—social inequality, disenchanted youth, unemployables in the work force, breakdown of community, and the drive for scientific preeminence. Some of the burden of such expectations could be realistically shifted back to the institutions of residence, work, and politics and to new institutions yet to be developed. Here we have much to learn from the experience of other societies, carefully adapting to our own conditions what has proven successful under theirs. The overload of particular schools and colleges can also be reduced considerably by greater differentiation within education itself, especially at the elementary and secondary levels. The American public high school program is now apparently too homogeneous to meet the increasing variety of group demands and cultural tasks—a variety of needs that can be served only by a variety of institutions. Greater differentiation also has the notable advantage of permitting the smaller parts of the system to have a comprehensible simplicity and an engaging distinctiveness, while the whole is unavoidably characterized by a mind-boggling complexity and the coldness of a remote, massive structure. Basic structural reform, therefore, is necessary to relieve overload and promote diversity.

The following articles drawn from the *New York Times* reflect much of the best public thought about education in the last two decades. The categories within which they are grouped represent a mixture of the shifting public definitions of basic educational problems and the editor's sense of what remains basic or is rapidly becoming a fundamental issue. The first three parts focus on three problems: the search for excellence; the education of the urban poor; and the confrontation of the new adolescent with the educational bureaucracy. In Part Four, the articles discuss proposed reform of and in the public schools. The articles in the last part concentrate on the "crisis" in higher education, stating some of the problems of the changing nature of postsecondary education and some possible solutions in clarifying purposes and reestablishing identities in the institutional fabric of higher learning.

PART ONE

The two articles in this section, published between 1955 and 1960, state well the public interest in quality and excellence that at that time became the foremost concern. The first article, "Education for All Is Education for None" written by Douglas Bush in 1955, reflects a hard traditionalist approach. In unabashed old-fashioned terms, it wages battle against John Dewey and the attitudes and methods of teaching that supposedly dominated the schools under the philosophy of progressive education. The article argues for a stiffening of the curriculum in the elementary and secondary schools, particularly through a toughening of requirements and instruction in English and foreign languages. It is a stern argument for the traditional basics—a point of view that was about to become most persuasive and to help swing the educational pendulum back from progressivism. But that is not all. Professor Bush also trained his critical guns on mass higher education, fearing a great lowering of standards in the

The search for excellence

university. To hold and enhance its quality the American university should become more, rather than less, selective, with a diverting of average students from the university to the junior colleges.

Fifteen years later, we may note that this increased selectivity has indeed occurred in many states and regions of the country. Many private universities and private colleges have become academically and intellectually more selective. The state university, more important in numbers of students, has become a more selective institution in the public sector. The four-year state college occupies a middle ground in selectivity, and the two-year community college takes up the role of an open-door institution that absorbs the bulk of the students in the first year after high school. The traditionalist position has thus not been rendered hopeless by an ever larger degree of mass higher education, but rather is expressed structurally in parts of an educational division of labor. Those most concerned about the

highest possible standards and the protection of es-
oteric cultural activities in the mass society can still
find something to cheer about in the workings of the
American university.

In the second article, "Five Basic Problems of
Education," Fred M. Hechinger sums up the dominant viewpoint in attempting to define the problems of education at the end of the 1950s. He as-
signs first priority to the search for quality. How can
we raise standards for all, and especially for the top
2 percent, the creative ones whose trained talents
are necessary for "the country's progress" and for
"competitive coexistence in a cold war period"?
The proposed solutions at that time were cur-
ricular—e.g., reinstate the compulsory four years of
English for all high school students. In the context
of Sputnik, reform called for elimination of softness:
there should be more science and foreign languages; more tracking rather than less; earlier
rather than later selection, in order to identify and
nurture the gifted; and more homework and higher
standards for all. European systems were seen as
models of rigor against which the American school
seemed deficient in training the mind. The temper
of the time gave public resonance to the ideas of
those who had fumed for years about the softness of
progressive education and were determined to "reinstate" standards, rigor, and discipline.

We can note no mention of race or social class.
The concern over "cultural deprivation" and "inner
city schools," we now know, was waiting in the
wings, but it had not yet been admitted to the public stage. The overriding dominance of the concern

The Problems of
American Education

for academic quality, as traditionally understood, kept most discussion within traditional categories: How do we get the right courses back into the curriculum? How do we find superior teachers for the basic subjects? How do we find the money to pay for the pursuit of excellence in a system of mass education?

This concern was to be overwhelmed by other more pressing social demands in the attention given education in the 1960s, but it is a permanent concern in large and heterogeneous industrial societies. When education must serve so many and in so many different ways as it now does, overall quality will be problematic from one point of view or another. The amount and intensity of concern will rise and fall and will be given vigorous expression at one time and very little at another. But it is never far beneath the surface. A useful guide in the observation of educational affairs is to watch for the changing awareness and definition of "the problem of quality."

Education for all is education for none

DOUGLAS BUSH

In schools, colleges, and universities today, the results of the huge increase in the student body suggest a rather painful thought: the principle of education for all, however fine in theory, in practice ultimately leads to education for none. In other words, the ideal of education for all forces acceptance of the principle that the function of education is primarily social and political rather than purely intellectual; if school standards are geared to an almost invisibly low average there is not much real education available for anyone, even for the gifted.

To mention one of many examples, there has been an appalling growth of illiteracy at all levels, even in the graduate school. (Somehow stenographers are still literate, even if their college-bred employers are not.) At every commencement one wonders how many of the hordes of new bachelors of arts can speak and write their own language with elementary decency, or read it with understanding. After all, the polished mind is suspect, whether in a student, professor, or presidential candidate. And illiteracy, and contentment with illiteracy, are only symptoms of general shoddiness.

Obviously one main cause of this state of things has been the sheer pressure of numbers, along with a deplorable shrinkage in the number of qualified teachers. But the situation would not be so bad as it has been if the downward pressure of numbers had not been powerfully strengthened by misguided doctrine and practice. The training of teachers and the control of school curricula have been in the hands of colleges of education and their products, and these have operated on principles extracted from John Dewey's philosophy of barbarism.

(If that phrase seems unduly harsh, I may say that I have in mind Dewey's hostility to what he regarded as leisure-class studies; his anti-historical attitude, his desire—intensified in his followers—to immerse students in the contemporary and immediate; and his denial of a hierarchy of studies, his doctrine that all kinds of experience are equally or uniquely valuable; and it would not be irrelevant to add his notoriously inept writing.)

The lowest common denominator has been, not an evil, but an ideal. The substantial disciplines have been so denuded of content that multitudes of students, often taught by uneducated teachers, have been illiterate, uninformed, and thoroughly immature. There is no use in priding ourselves on the operation of the democratic principle if education loses much of its meaning in the process.

The Problems of
American Education

When we think, for instance, of education for citizenship, which has been the cry of modern pedagogy, we may think also of the volume and violence of popular support given to the anti-intellectual demagoguery of the last few years. Mass education tends to reflect mass civilization instead of opposing it. And even if education were everywhere working on the highest level, it would still face tremendous odds.

The great problem has been and will be, first, the preservation of minority culture against the many and insidious pressures of mass civilization and, secondly, the extension of that minority culture through wider and wider areas. The rising flood of students is very much like the barbarian invasions of the early Middle Ages, and then the process of education took a thousand years.

We hope for something less overwhelming and for a less protracted cure, but the principle is the same, and Greco-Roman-Christian culture not only survived but triumphed, and with enrichment also. If we think of our problem in the light of that one, we shall not be disheartened, but recognize both as phases of man's perennial growing pains.

Throughout history it has been a more or less small minority that has created and preserved what culture and enlightenment we have and, if adverse forces are always growing, that minority is always growing, too. In spite of the low standards that have commonly prevailed in public education during the last fifty years, I think the top layer of college students now are proportionately more numerous than

they were thirty years ago and are more generally
serious and critical.

There is a growing nucleus of fine minds, and
teachers are concerned with the enlargement of that
all-important group. At the same time, without re-
treating from that position, one does wonder what it
is in our educational process or in our culture at
large that so often causes a liberal education to end
on commencement day. Why do so many undergraduates become alumni? Why does starry-eyed
youth lapse into flabby, middle-aged vacuity, into
the Helen Hokinson wife and her husband?

I have no novel and dramatic remedy for the evils
that have shown themselves so clearly already and
will become more formidable still. But I might
mention a few things of varying importance which
do not seem utopian. Of course, I represent no one
but myself, and I cannot even say, like a member of
the House of Lords, that I enjoy the full confidence
of my constituents.

In the first place, I see no reason why the flood of
students should be allowed to pour into college,
why automatic graduation from school should qualify anyone for admission. We ought to recognize
and make people in general recognize that a desire
for economic or social advantage, or for merely four
years of idle diversion, is not enough.

Under such pressure as is coming, surely the state
universities have the strength to set up bars and
select their student body instead of admitting all
who choose to walk in the front door and then, with
much trouble and expense, trying to get rid of some
through the back door. Doubtless such procedure

would require a campaign of enlightenment and persuasion, but legislators always have an alert ear for the cry of economy, and the public must be convinced that higher education, or what passes for that, is neither a birthright nor a necessary badge of respectability and that useful and happy lives can be led without a college degree or even without membership in a fraternity or sorority.

As things are, we have an army of misfits, who lower educational standards and increase expense, and no branch of a university staff has grown more rapidly of late years than the psychiatric squad.

Secondly, many people have grounds for the belief that the multiplying junior colleges can and will drain off a large number of the young who, for various reasons, are unfitted for a really strenuous four-year course. Junior colleges, however, should not be recreational centers for the subnormal.

Thirdly, I think the need for formal education beyond high school would be much lessened and the quality of both secondary and higher education obviously raised if the colleges and universities, getting the public behind them, made a concerted and effectual demand that the schools do their proper work and do it better than a great many schools have been doing it.

Quite commonly, a distressing proportion of a college course now consists of high school work. For example, we have grown so accustomed to a battalion of instructors teaching elementary composition to freshmen that we take it as a normal part of college education, whereas, in fact, it is a monstrosity. Imagine a European university teaching

The Search for Excellence

28

the rudiments of expression! If high school graduates are illiterate, they have no business in college.
For a long time and for a variety of reasons we have
had slackness all along the line; somehow, some
time, strictness and discipline have got to begin.

Increased enrollments have almost inevitably led
to increased reliance upon large lecture courses.
There are administrators who assume that there is
no limit to the effectiveness of a lecture course except the size of the auditorium, and there are also
teachers who see positive virtues in lectures and
can themselves display them. Perhaps because I
never remember anything I hear in a lecture, I do
not share that faith. I favor classes small enough to
allow discussion, and that is expensive.

But there are possible economies that would be
highly desirable in themselves. We do not need to
maintain the naïve doctrine that there has to be a
course in anything in which anyone ever has been
or might be interested. Further, a good many catalogues list courses that can only be called fantastic,
and I don't think I am guilty of partisan prejudice if
I say that these are rarely found among the humanities. At any rate, if we had fewer and less specialized courses, and if we did not have our armies of
composition teachers, a considerable number of
man-hours would be released for smaller classes.

One thing that has suffered grievously and conspicuously in this last generation has been the study
of foreign languages. The usual reason given is
again the pressure of numbers, the numbers who
are not going beyond high school, but again a positive reason has been open or quiet hostility. Lan-

guages have been pretty well crowded out of the school curriculum, and of course there has been a corresponding decline in college study. Nothing has been commoner in recent decades than the applicant for admission to a graduate school who has had little or no acquaintance with any foreign language except possibly a year or two of Spanish.

Serious study of a foreign language means work, and a first principle of modern pedagogy has been the elimination of work. Thus, during the years in which we have all become conscious of one small world, and in which this country has become the leader of that world, educational theory and practice have retreated into cultural parochialism. There is no need to argue how necessary for the ordinary citizen is some knowledge of a foreign language and a foreign people.

In the last few years a good many parents have been aroused, and the Modern Language Association has been putting on a vigorous campaign, so that progress has been made; but there is a long way to go. It is encouraging that in some cities successful experiments have been conducted in the teaching of languages in elementary schools, where, for good psychological reasons, they ought to begin. I wish there were something encouraging to be said about the ancient languages, but we are concerned with actualities.

Finally, since I touched on the large number of young people who are in college and shouldn't be, I might mention those who are not in college and should be and who may be lost in the oncoming flood. Educators and others are more conscious than they once were of our failure to recognize and foster promising students who cannot afford college, and increasing efforts are being made in that direction, but we are still far behind England, for example, where bright students are picked out at the age of 10 or 11 and brought along on scholarships. If we spent on exceptional students a fraction of the time and money we have spent on nursing lame ducks, there would be a considerable change in the quality of education.

One last word on a different matter. Like everything else, the Ph.D. has been cheapened by quantitative pressure and it might be earnestly wished that it were not a union card for the teaching profession. There are plenty of young men and women who would be good teachers without such a degree, and the degree itself ought to mean something more than it does. Along with that may go another earnest wish, that both administrators and members of departments would abandon the principle of "publish or perish." Socrates would never have had a chance at an assistant professorship.

Five basic problems of education

FRED M. HECHINGER

Ever since the cold war moved into outer space, the American people have been concerned about education. No longer is the sky the limit; even the moon is only a whistle stop. And in this futuristic contest, the classrooms are the launching platforms.

Hardly a week passes without several television programs peeking behind the scenes of education. Not long ago, a broadcaster cornered a few high school students, and their deplorable ignorance set off a national storm of criticism. The Rockefeller report on education got top billing on the front pages of even small-town dailies. Rear Adm. Hyman G. Rickover, father of the atomic submarine, received a sympathetic public ear when he proclaimed that, if the money for education coud not be found in the federal budget, the defense appropriation should be cut.

President Eisenhower appointed a special "Com-

mittee on Education Beyond High School." The
Ford Foundation made the largest gift in the history
of private philanthropy for the increase of professors' salaries. James Bryant Conant, Harvard's
former president, has devoted the past two years to
an attempt to find out what is wrong with American
high school education. In fact, the "Conant Report,"
which is set for publication next Wednesday, has already stirred up more excitement than many government white papers.

Everybody is concerned about education; but
"education" is an elusive, amorphous thing. Before
it can be understood and improved, some of the
crucial problems must be singled out and defined.
As an observer of the educational scene, I have
visited classrooms, talked with teachers, listened to
parents, sat through speeches and conventions,
scanned the statistics and studied the reports.

Let me set down what seem the five most immediate problems; then let us see what the experts rec-
ommend.

THE PROBLEM
1. How can American standards of education be
raised, and what, especially, can be done to meet
the challenge of the exceptionally gifted child?

American democracy promises every child a full
elementary and secondary education, but the un-
answered question has always been how to do this
without surrendering to the lowest common denominator. Our educational *laissez-faire,* which permits

even able students to pick "elective" snap courses,
has allowed standards to slip.

The raising of educational standards for the great
mass of students would mean a spectacular improvement in the country's total reservoir of skills.
But what about the small number of exceptionally
gifted children—the top 2 percent? The talents of
these, if lost, are irreplaceable. In terms of the
country's progress and of competitive coexistence
in a cold war period, they may well hold the
key.

THE PROPOSED SOLUTIONS

There is almost unanimous agreement that the
search for quality in a system of quantity rates first
attention. To cope with the problem of a curriculum
which has been loaded down with an almost unlim-
ited variety of subjects from driver education to citizenship training, the Rockefeller report, entitled
"The Pursuit of Excellence," demands that "we
reach some agreement on priorities in subject-
matter." Educators are asked to make up their
minds which of the many elective courses are most
important.

The Conant report will go a step further. It will
clearly demand that all high school students complete four years of English, three to four years of
history and related social studies, one year of mathematics and one year of science. Students in the top
20 percent would take three additional years of
science, three more years of mathematics and at
least three years of one foreign language.

The Search for Excellence

For all students there must be improved guidance. Dr. Conant asks for one guidance counselor for every 250 to 300 high school students. And, in order to assure adequate programs and facilities, he asks for elimination, through consolidation, of all high schools with graduating classes of fewer than 100 students.

All proposals for the improvement of education demand a greater sense of continuity of subjects and a greater scope of understanding. Study of a foreign language for less than three years, says Dr. Conant, is like drilling for oil and then stopping before striking it. In the study of history, too, efforts are largely wasted unless there is a sense of the natural sequence of events.

For the 2 percent of gifted pupils, even more of a concession to the difference in human talent must be made. "A school system that insists on the same instruction for the talented, average and below average child," said Rear Admiral Rickover, "may prevent as many children from growing intellectually as would a system that excludes children because of the social, political or economic status of their parents. Neither system is democratic."

The experts agree. "Any educational system is, among other things, a great sorting-out process," says the Rockefeller report. But while the European sorting out is achieved almost entirely by impersonal examinations, the American experts call for a variety of tests, some scoring native talent, others the actual achievement of the student, with personal observation and guidance. Once the gifted students are recognized, the experts want them to be given advanced work, without separating them from their classmates.

Toward the end of high school, the extra work would be increased. Thus, juniors and seniors would be offered college-level instruction in some subjects, as they now are under the Advanced Placement Program sponsored by the College Entrance Examination Board. Another program for early admission to college, initiated by the Fund for the Advancement of Education and hailed by all the experts, has sent more than 1,000 gifted students to college during the past five years without completion of the last year or two of high school.

THE PROBLEM
2. How can we get better teachers?

There is no way to improve the quality of American education without an adequate supply of good teachers. Already a serious shortage of highly educated manpower exists. This shortage will become increasingly critical unless we find enough of what the Ford Foundation calls the "seed corn"—teachers who, through their superior efforts, help to raise new generations of educated brains.

Perhaps even worse, the standards set for the teachers are often pitifully low. For example, at a convention in Bowling Green, Ohio, recently, an education spokesman "demanded" that chemistry teachers be given at least thirty-two hours of college study in that subject. A Russian student in a college-preparatory high school, by comparison, gets more than 340 hours of chemistry before graduation.

The Search for Excellence

THE PROPOSED SOLUTIONS

"No educational system can be better than its teachers," warns the Rockefeller report. It estimates that the number of new teachers needed in the next decade is somewhere between one-third and one-half of all college graduates in that period. The present ratio of college graduates entering the teaching profession is only one out of every four or five. And yet, even today, the report warns, the problem of quality is critical. As of 1956, 33 percent of all elementary teachers did not hold an A.B. degree, while more than 21 percent of all public school teachers had less than four years of college.

Since the training of all teachers depends on the quality of the training of college teachers, there is special significance in a report by the National Education Association that "since 1953–54, holders of the doctor's degree among newly employed, full-time [college] teachers have decreased 25.2 percent." And the manpower pressures of the immediate future may make this situation even worse.

The Rockefeller report calls for an improvement in the courses and training procedures given teachers. "If the programs for the preparation of teachers are rigid, formalistic and shallow, they will drive away able minds as fast as they are recruited," it warns. "Unhappily, preparation for pre-college teaching has come all too close to that condition.

The report warns against the practice of handling teachers as "interchangeable units in an educational assembly line." At present, "the best teacher and the poorest in a school may teach the same grade and subject, use the same textbook, handle the same number of students, get paid the same salaries, and rise in salary at the same speed to the same ceiling." The ironic result is that school administration—and the end of active teaching—often becomes the only refuge for able teachers who want to advance their careers.

The problem of getting a sufficient number of teachers is primarily one of recruiting and of offering an attractive career. "But even with aggressive recruitment there appears to be little or no likelihood that we can bring into teaching at any level anything approaching the number of *qualified* and *gifted* teachers we need," says the Rockefeller report. "We must therefore utilize our superior teachers more effectively."

All the experts agree that, in the words of the Rockefeller report, "one way to make better use of the ablest teachers is to eliminate many of the petty tasks which occupy a teacher's time. Less highly trained classroom assistants may accomplish much in the lightening of this burden." The Fund for the Advancement of Education, putting this theory to the test in Bay City, Mich., found it successful, and it has spread from there to many communities across the country. A bonus, it was found, came when many of the aides, seeing teaching at its best, became so interested that they went back to college to get their teacher training.

Other experiments have been sparked by the success of the first one. The use of "teams" of teachers, made up of one "master teacher," one regular teacher, and one untrained assistant has made it possible to increase the class size for some subjects to three times a normal classroom quota, while, at other times, permitting one teacher to work with only eight to twelve pupils. The use of television has also made it possible to get more of the best teachers into contact with more students.

THE PROBLEM

3. Should we emphasize science as against the liberal arts?

However we respond to the challenge of sputnik or speculate about the importance of moon shoots, one fact is inescapable—science and technology are intimately linked with modern man's destiny.

Traditionally, there used to be a clear dividing line between the "liberal arts" and the sciences. The high school student who thought he had no interest in a career of science frequently was allowed to "get by" with a minimum of mathematics and science instruction. Reports about the Russian schools, which go to the opposite extreme of requiring a stiff dose of science and mathematics for all high school students, have intensified the problem of just how much science training should be required of every high school graduate.

THE PROPOSED SOLUTIONS

The experts agree on two fundamental points: (1) that, despite the panic headlines, science must not crowd out the humanities; (2) that it is vital for all students, not just the scientifically inclined, to have a thorough measure of basic mathematics and science.

The Problems of
American Education

On the first point, The President's Committee on Education Beyond High School says that the country "would be inexcusably blind if it failed to see that the challenge of the next twenty years will require leaders not only in science and engineering and in business and industry, but in government and politics, in foreign affairs and diplomacy, in education and civic affairs."

On the second point, Dr. I. I. Rabi, Nobel Prize physicist and chairman of the President's Science Advisory Committee, says: "We must teach science as an intellectual pursuit rather than as a body of tricks." And he adds: "As yet, if a man has no feeling for art he is considered narrow-minded, but if he has no feeling for science, he is considered quite normal. This is a fundamental weakness."

Probably the greatest waste of scientific talent stems from social clichés which discourage girls from studying science and mathematics as "unlady-like." Dr. Conant found that, even in the best high schools, fewer than half of the gifted girls elect four years of mathematics.

The experts agree that it is not a question of "either–or" between science and the liberal arts. The Rockefeller report warns as much against the narrowly trained scientist as against the educated man who is illiterate in science.

THE PROBLEM
4. Who should go to college?

Already more than 3,000,000 young Americans are enrolled in college—a total of one-third of the eligible age group. Is universal college the next step, following the universal high school? Some state universities have, in practice, accepted this principle; they consider a high school diploma an automatic admission ticket. Other college spokesmen warn against the danger of indiscriminate admission policies as an invitation to lowered standards. They are, however, more concerned that rising costs will price the colleges out of the market for many able students.

One fact is clear: even if the present policy of selection is continued, most colleges would have to double or triple in size by 1975 in order to accommodate the same percentage of students who go to college today.

No expert wants to restrict college admission, but all would like to see standards raised so that the restrictions could be built into the procedure of selection. They applaud current trends in that direction. They cite the announcement by the University of Illinois that by September 1960, its freshmen will no longer be nursed along in remedial English courses. They point with approval to more than a dozen colleges which have revived foreign language requirements for admission.

The problem is not so much whom to keep out of college, but rather how to make sure that those who should go to college do so.

The two roadblocks, the experts agree, are motivation and finances. To remove the first, they say that young people with talent will have to be shown more effectively that there is real value and excitement in higher education. To remove the second, they suggest more scholarships.

The president's committee called for ten times the present total amount of scholarship money, estimated at about $60,000,000. It wants about 200,000 "of the ablest and neediest high school graduates annually" to be assured of a college education by having the financial burden removed from them.

In addition, it calls for between 25,000 and 50,000 subsidized campus jobs so that another large group will be able to support itself with "work-study" programs. In order to build higher education firmly into the American way of life, the president's committee also suggests that the tax laws be revised so that students and their parents would be assured of credits or deductions.

All the experts agree that there should be a greater number of two-year colleges for those who are unwilling or unable to commit themselves to four years of higher education.

Finally, the Conant report will urgently demand another reform plan which would eliminate those students who feel that they are inadequately prepared to make a living when they leave high school, and who go to college for vocational training rather than for education. The Conant plan would expect the high schools to offer vocational training of highest caliber to these students.

Considering the importance of the problem of who should go to college, it is disappointing to find the experts vague and hedging in their replies. The reason is simple: they are torn between rational planning and the commitment to an ideal. The first calls for toughness in setting up restrictions so that the colleges and universities can be made into institutions of excellence; the second dreams about the removal of all limitations from a child's educational horizon. At present, the American genius for compromise is in search of a formula that will be democratic without destroying the standards of scholarship and education.

THE PROBLEM
5. How do you pay for all this?

If mass and class in education are to be combined, perhaps for the first time in history, then the cost will be high. What compounds the difficulty is the almost pathological fear of government control through government financing. Yet, from the problem of the loss of potentially able teachers to higher paying jobs to the fact that local spending is not even beginning to catch up with school construction needs, every sign points to an inescapable truth: the present sources of money are insufficient to pay for a first-class mass education system.

Many schools are overcrowded, understaffed, and ill-equipped. There is an estimated shortage of 142,000 classrooms and an "excess" of almost 2,000,000 pupils. And within ten years the high schools will have arrived at a point where they will face 50 to 70 percent more pupils than they can now accommodate.

The Problems of
American Education

THE PROPOSED SOLUTIONS

None of the experts has tackled the money problem with complete candor. The fear of an all-out fight over the principle of federal aid has led to a flood of cautious statements and even more cautious legislation. Yet between the lines the implication is clear: federal aid will have to be a permanent part of the picture.

What are the real needs? Our total expenditure for education, from elementary school through the universities, today is approximately $14 billion annually. This is 3.6 percent of the gross national product. The experts estimate that, in order to attain the goals of quality in a system of quantity, the nation will have to spend $30 billion annually ten years from now, with those $30 billion measured in terms of today's purchasing power. This would mean, according to the best economists' predictions, about 5 percent of the gross national product.

The Rockefeller report points out that local and state tax systems are "in some respects archaic." School expenditures are charged almost entirely to the revenue raised through property tax—and this is also the tax which meets with the most solidly organized and most vocal opposition. It is no coincidence that the rejection of school bond issues in New York State reached an all-time high last year— despite sputnik.

"It is this weakness in the state and local taxing systems more than anything else that gives rise to current proposals for increased Federal support of education," says the Rockefeller report. "For those

The Search for Excellence

who wish to resist or postpone the resort to Federal funds and at the same time not constrict education services, there seems to be only one alternative: a thorough, painful, politically courageous overhaul of state and local tax systems."

Almost certainly this is not going to happen, and definitely not in time to bolster a weakened edifice of education.

The only public acknowledgment of these unpleasant facts was made by the White House Conference on Education, late in 1955, which voted better than 2 to 1 in favor of federal aid to education, to be devoted specifically to school construction.

Congress omitted all federal aid to school construction, however, after the administration's federal aid proposals in 1958 completely dropped the demand for money for buildings.

Congress and the public had their eyes on scholarships, which they considered the chief ingredient of a "crash program" to compete with the Soviet Union. When it came to a vote and a series of compromises, the less than $1 billion aid bill offered mainly student loans (not scholarships); some graduate fellowships, plus special financial lures in the form of partly written-off loans to draw students into the teaching profession; and special funds for the improvement of guidance, language and science teaching, vocational education, and research. The largest single amount—$300,000,000—was earmarked to buy science equipment for school systems in the various states. The most critically needed items, funds for buildings and for teachers' salaries, were overlooked.

The Problems of American Education

Thus, the real federal aid problem as a key to the financing of the schools remains an issue, with the fear of federal control still the major roadblock to more sweeping appropriations. The Rockefeller report points out some safeguards that could be built into federal aid to prevent it from leading to federal control:

(1) Federal funds would be "one source of support among many."

(2) State, local, and private sources of funds "should continue to be the major factor in the support of education."

(3) Federal funds should be used only to balance the serious gaps in the total educational system, and should be given in such a manner as to encourage state and local governments to use their own resources."

Whatever the sources may be, the experts have no doubt whatsoever that, financially, we already face a real emergency. "It will not be enough to meet the problem grudgingly or with a little more money," says the Rockefeller report. "The nation's need for good education is immediate; and good education is expensive. That is the fact which the American people have never been quite prepared to face. At stake is nothing less than our national greatness and our aspirations for the dignity of the individual. If the public is not prepared for this, then responsible educators, business leaders, political leaders, unions and civic organizations must join in a national campaign to prepare them."

The Search for Excellence

PART TWO

The first article, "The Bunker Hill of Desegregation" by Donald Gross, serves to remind us how long the problem of racial integration in the schools has been with us and how tough and protracted the fight has been. The blacks who in Boston in *the 1830s* took up the fight to abolish separate schools for blacks fought a long, uphill battle even to achieve the first victory. They took the issue to the local school board and lost, and, moving into the courts, lost again. They then entered the political arena directly, gradually made some allies, and finally, after two decades of struggle, got a new state law passed that abolished separate schools. Similar efforts continued in other Northern cities, but changes followed at an exceedingly slow pace, with New York City not legally desegregating until thirty years after Massachusetts did. A child or an adult, then as well as now, could age a great deal while waiting for the legal abolition of separate schools.

The second article, "Integration: Third and Criti-

The black and the poor

cal Phase" by Wilma Dykeman and James Stokely, reviews the six years after the historic Supreme Court decision of 1954 that outlawed deliberate school segregation. It triggered a series of community confrontations in the border states and the South, as black parents attempted to enroll their children in formerly all-white schools and as school boards struggled between the new legal mandate and the angry reactions of many whites. These were the days during which "Little Rock" (Arkansas) became the symbolic center of racial tension in this country, a time for some state governors to take a defiant stand that won them reelection while insuring them a dubious place in history. At the end of the 1950s, national attention was still focused on the South, where only slow progress had been recorded. The issue was still defined as one of "school desegregation" and "school integration."

In the article by Dorothy Barclay, "Challenge to Education: The Poor," we enter a new era. Now (in

48

the early 1960s), she tells us, teachers and administrators are talking about the problem of educating "poor children," "the underprivileged," "the disadvantaged," "the culturally deprived." Two publications just out attested to the problem: Frank Riessman's book, *The Culturally Deprived Child* and a statement by the National Education Association entitled *Education and the Disadvantaged American*. Barclay offered some shocking figures: one out of three children in the large cities was in the category of deprived or disadvantaged, and the proportion was destined to rise to one out of two by 1970. She correctly forecasted bitter battles in the years ahead around this new central problem of the education of the urban poor. Gone was the primacy of the concern for excellence. Sputnik may have put Rear Admiral Rickover and other basic education critics in orbit around the American public school, but the public eye was being forced down from the stars to the earthy mass at the bottom of the educational ladder. Subdued also was the concern for school integration of the Little Rock era. Racial integration would persist in ideal and in practice, but it was about to be subordinated to a hard realization that improvement in the education of millions of black poor children would have to be wrought right where they were, in the ghetto schools.

In the last article, "For White and Black, Community Control Is the Issue" by Nathan Glazer, we enter yet another phase, one dominated by the cry of "community control." Many black groups had not only given up on school integration by the late 1960s but had also given up on the will and capacity of a centralized school bureaucracy to deliver the kind of education that they, as parents, wanted for their young. The concern became one of swinging the pendulum back from professional-bureaucratic control toward lay control. Glazer puts this black militant position in broad perspective, seeing it as part of a revolt underway against centralization and bureaucracy within many sectors of American life and in many other countries. He maintains that the fight for "community control" has been underway for at least fifteen to twenty years—essentially all of the 1950s and 1960s. The middle class picked it up first, with the search for influence and control very much a part of the flight to the smaller communities of the suburbs. Just imagine the pleasure of the ex-urbanite when he picks up the telephone to complain to city hall about a municipal service and actually gets a polite answer and quick action! Then, blacks and lower-class whites took up the issue. But unable to move to the suburbs and thus locked in where they are, they have demanded greater neighborhood control over schools (and other city services), primarily through a breaking up of the large district into a batch of quasi-autonomous smaller ones, each with its own board. As a rule, laymen have more influence in the small districts, professionals in the large. Glazer argues that community control is making headway and must, and will, succeed. Where it does, it will give lay groups more influence relative to that of the professionals who staff the schools.

The Black and the Poor

The Bunker Hill of desegregation

DONALD GROSS

The Negro honor students accepted their awards politely and thanked the mayor. For outstanding scholastic achievement they had been given copies of a modest little book entitled "The Life of Benjamin Franklin." However, the students were not overly enthusiastic. They were pupils at a segregated public school and knew that the prize students from the white schools not only had received shiny Franklin medals, but had been invited to a public dinner in their honor.

This happened in Boston—in 1829—and it set the stage for the first major attempt to desegregate the nation's schools. Boston, which put up a statue to honor the first American to die under Redcoat fire—a Negro—hardly seems the place to look for racial oppression. The North of a century ago, however, practiced formal discrimination very much like the South today.

But the Negro's voice was beginning to be heard. In Boston, it was the voice of a Negro by the name of William Nell. He was one of the Negro students awarded a copy of "The Life of Benjamin Franklin" at the Belnap School for colored children in 1829.

William Nell got to attend the dinner for the honor students that year—as part of the Negro dining-room help. He decided then, as he later recalled, "to hasten the day when the color of the skin would be no barrier to equal school rights."

As a Boston citizen and Negro civic leader, he launched a campaign, in the 1840s, to integrate Boston's schools. It was a campaign that eventually attracted national attention and set precedents, still followed today, wherever segregation is attacked or defended.

Nell had no Supreme Court decree to help him. He began his campaign quietly by visiting the colored people who had children in school. Wouldn't they prefer to have their youngsters go to a school closer to home? Wouldn't they like a school better equipped than the school for colored children? Didn't they agree that going to school with white children would help everybody understand that whites and blacks were *all* Americans, deserving equal opportunity? Wouldn't it give the Negro children better opportunities when they grew up?

The response was disheartening. Life was hard enough for free Negroes in white society. The jobs they got were shabby. The pay was low. They were quickly abused when they made mistakes. There was trouble enough without asking for more. Wil-

The Problems of
American Education

liam Nell told his friends to think it over. He would
be back.

He turned to the Abolitionist party, headed by
William Lloyd Garrison and Wendell Philips.
These leaders promised to assist him through publicity, by drafting petitions and by helping to get
signatures for them. The first petition, submitted to
the Boston School Committee, was flatly rejected.

The integrationists steeled themselves for a long
fight. But the continued intransigence of the School
Committee and the prodding of William Nell gradually aroused the Negro population. Meetings were
held. Pamphlets were printed. Pickets were sta-
tioned at one of the Negro schools to discourage
parents from sending their children to it.

Finally, in 1846, the Boston School Committee,
faced with mounting pressure, agreed to a formal investigation. The result, after a lengthy debate, was a
decision to retain separate schools for colored children. The majority report stated bluntly: "In our
opinion, the less the colored and the white people
become intermingled, the better it will be for both
races. Amalgamation is degradation."

Discouraging as this was, William Nell's forces
knew they had raised the issue to the level of public
discussion and concern. They had also stirred the
courage of certain Negro people who were willing
to stake their jobs and reputations as "peaceful citizens" on some form of militant action.

One such Negro was Benjamin Roberts, father of
Sarah Roberts. In April 1847, Sarah applied for admission to the primary school nearest her home but
was refused. She, like other Negro youngsters, was

requested to attend a segregated school much farther away than the white school near her home.

The following year, Roberts instructed his daughter to enter the near-by white primary school without permission. When she was rejected, he filed suit under a Massachusetts statute which provided that a child unlawfully excluded from public school instruction could recover damages from the city or town where the exclusion took place.

Legal action was pressed to the State Supreme Court where Charles Sumner, later to become Reconstruction leader in the United States Senate, pleaded the cause of Sarah Roberts and integrated schools in eloquent terms. Much of what he had to say was prophetic of the Supreme Court's historic decision of May 17, 1954, which was based on the premise that "separate but equal" school facilities do not provide equality.

"A separate school, though well endowed," Sumner argued, "would not secure that precise equality which they [the Negro children] would enjoy in the common schools. Segregation from the mass of citizens is of itself an inequality. It is a vestige of ancient intolerance against a despised people."

The State Supreme Court, however, handed down a decision adverse to Sumner and his client. This decision, too, was prophetic, for it served as a precedent for many of the segregation laws enacted by the South up to the present. It held that the prejudice that Sumner claimed was fostered by separate schools was "not created by law, and probably cannot be changed by law."

Boston's Negroes and their friends decided to change their tactics. They went outside Boston where communities with proportionately lower Negro populations had already integrated their schools. A campaign was started to lobby for a state law forbidding segregated schools.

Finally, in 1855, the legislature passed a bill to abolish separate schools for Negroes throughout the Commonwealth of Massachusetts. The bill was signed by the governor on April 28 of that year.

To make certain the changeover would go smoothly when it became effective the following September, William Nell spent much of his time during the summer months visiting school authorities throughout Boston, talking with Negro and white parents, calling meetings and writing pamphlets urging cooperation from both races.

When school opened Nell and a delegation of Negro mothers made the rounds of the city's schools "to see the laws of the old Bay State applied in good faith" and to iron out any difficulties that might develop. None did.

Thus ended the first struggle against public-school segregation. Efforts to do away with segregated schools in other Northern cities continued through the years of the Civil War and after. It was not easy. New York City's public schools were not legally desegregated until 1884.

But, wherever citizens acted to end segregated schooling in the large cities of the North, they had Boston as a precedent and a successful example.

Integration:
Third and critical phase

WILMA DYKEMAN *and* JAMES STOKELY

"The advance of school desegregation in the fall of 1960 marks the beginning of a new phase in the struggle to win in reality what was granted in law by the Supreme Court decision of 1954. The Deep South at last faces the demand that it comply with the law."

This statement was made last month [October 1960] by the Southern Regional Council, a biracial fact-finding agency with headquarters in Atlanta. The "new phase" erupted into violence thirteen days ago, when four Negro children entered the first grade classes of two previously all-white public schools in New Orleans.

In the words of one sardonic resident of that city, "all hell, most of the legislature and the lunatic fringe we have with us always broke loose." "The skirmishes are over. Now come the real show-downs," a Southern Negro leader said.

As the glaring spotlight of world and national attention is once more focused on ugly mob scenes in
a Southern metropolis, what is revealed about the
drama of desegregation?

I.

Desegregation in Southern public schools has
made progress. In May 1954, seventeen states and
the District of Columbia required racial separation
in the public schools. By September 1959, only five
of the deepest Deep South states still remained
completely segregated at the public-school level—
Georgia, Alabama, Mississippi, Louisiana, and
South Carolina.

In the other dozen states desegregation had pro-
ceeded with what might be called "deliberate
speed," to employ the term used by the Supreme
Court in 1955. The words have proved ambiguous
enough to give rise to considerable controversy.
Negro leaders, and particularly those of youth, have
grown restive at what they consider the excessive
deliberateness of the South, while many white
leaders insist that the speed demanded by protest
groups is unrealistic. "Token desegregation" has
become their most frequent point of contention.

Two phrases have marked the desegregation process up to this time. The first consisted of fairly
speedy and voluntary desegregation undertaken,
promptly after the Supreme Court decision, by the
border states and the District of Columbia. This was
accomplished in approximately two years. The second phase began in 1956, with the advance of de-

segregation into some of the eleven states of the Old Confederacy.

This experience was marked by federal court orders as the result of suits initiated by Negro parents compelling desegregation in certain specific communities of the Upper South. With the reopening of schools on an integrated basis in Little Rock and the collapse of massive resistance in Virginia this second development seemed to reach its climax.

One state in which factors of both the first and second stages of desegregation played a part, however, was North Carolina. Its plan of voluntary token desegregation is still in effect—and still under attack.

"Token desegregation," one report on the South has observed, "means the admission of just enough Negroes to predominantly white schools to get by the law; 'just enough' can be few, indeed. In Charlotte, to take the extreme case, three Negroes were in desegregated schools in 1957–58, four in 1958–59 and exactly one in 1959–60."

During the two phases, 768 of the 2,834 biracial school districts in the seventeen-state area and the District of Columbia have had some sort of desegregation. Reaction to the pace was voiced recently by an officer of the National Association for the Advancement of Colored People, Gloster B. Current. Speaking to a Southern audience, he declared:

"We deplore the fact that in the six years since the Supreme Court order desegregating schools only 6 percent of Negro children are in integrated schools."

The Problems of
American Education

The influential *Louisville Courier-Journal* said in September:

"Houston and New Orleans are under orders to desegregate this year. But the snail's pace at which integration is being achieved makes the bitterness of younger Negroes understandable and does nothing to persuade them that the rule of law is superior to the rule of demonstration."

There can be little doubt, indeed, that frustration over what has been called the policy of "calculated delay and minimal compliance" in desegregation of schools provided much of the impetus for the lunch counter sit-in movements throughout the South.

The conflict at New Orleans marks the beginning of a third phase in the school struggle. For the first time, a school system in one of the so-called hard-core states, is in process of desegregation. What happens there this year will determine in part what happens in years to come in the four other main resistance states, which legal ammunition they must abandon, which reserves they must recruit to manufacture, all in the hope of infinite delay.

Top segregation leaders in adjoining Mississippi conferred with Louisiana legislators the day after the four Negro children entered New Orleans schools. Governor Ross R. Barnett, on a tour of South America was not present, but the acting governor of Mississippi, Paul B. Johnson, said that he had initiated the conference, not because he was "trying to interfere in the affairs of another state," but because "it is our affair from the standpoint of state sovereignty and the affair of every other state in the Union."

II.

Desegregation of schools can be brought about by the courts of the United States; true *integration* of students can be achieved only by monumental and sustained efforts of goodwill and intelligence on the part of individuals involved. At this level there must be confession of greater failure. The failure is particularly noteworthy because it springs, in part, from lack of understanding, in the nation, in regions and communities, of this vast difference between desegregation and integration.

"I sit in class with them," a Clinton (Tenn.) High School white boy says of the Negroes in that once strife-ridden institution, "but that's all. We don't have anything to do with each other outside of listening to the teacher."

On the affirmative side, however, when Negroes were admitted this fall, after long litigation, to the high school in Burnsville, N.C., one Negro boy was put on the football team and reportedly became a hero when he scored the school's first touchdown.

"There has been acceptance of the Negro pupils at the intellectual level," a teacher at Norfolk, Va., told a reporter a few days ago.

"When a Negro was elected to the honor society from the sophomore class at one of our high schools here it wasn't even considered news enough to put in the local paper. However, when there are overtures to discussion of anything except the classroom subject matter I have seen cold rebuffs to Negroes by white students."

This teacher asserted that the violence at New Orleans had had its effect on integration in Norfolk,

The Problems of
American Education

resulting in some renewed tensions, as reflected in the slapping of a Negro girl by a white student.

Interaction between the Deep South's bitter defiance of integration and the Upper South's reluctant compliance has been noted by the Southern Regional Council. It comments:

"Perhaps the truth has been that desegregation cannot move more rapidly in the Upper South, cannot break from the courtroom and be assumed as a community responsibility, while the Deep South is uncompromising. When desegregation breaches the Deep South the myth of Southern ability to defy the law will have been fatally punctured; the consequence could be an emotional release in the Upper South that would enable desegregation to move without the lash of the law."

III.

Certain facts and elements will remain basic to the continuing desegregation struggle in the South. A fundamental truth is that the current upheavals are not so much manifestations of an inflexible status quo as representations of a democracy in process of painful growth.

Perhaps the fact should be clarified once more that the South is undergoing a triple revolution, industrial, urban, and social. And it is helpful to remember that blue denim may be exchanged for blue serge and a hundred mules buried in the boneyard more easily than old emotions can be exchanged for new logic, or one single prejudice buried.

As Ralph McGill, publisher of the *Atlanta Consti-*

tution, declared to a recent social-science forum in North Carolina: "The current strife at New Orleans points up another of the death struggles of a barrier between us and full and equal participation in the future of our country."

Growing awareness that this *is* a death struggle for an undemocratic way of life intensifies the fervor of its last-ditch adherents.

"The tighter the noose chokes the harder we kick," one Southern lawyer said recently, "at least for a little while. And for a while I think things may get worse down here before they get much better. The important point is, of course, that it's a long haul, but we're inching ahead. Personally, I've got damn little patience with those pundits who thought it would be done day before yesterday or that it will be finished day after tomorrow. All of us who are going to see this thing through in the South might as well fasten our seat belts, because there's rough weather ahead. Unless, of course, some miracle of national or Southern leadership occurs."

Unpleasant as the prospect is, then, there is little doubt in the minds of many concerned and observant Southerners that defiance and violence are elements that will be present in Southern school desegregation for some time to come.

A long-time, well-trained student of Southern sociology said a few days ago:

"New Orleans is another turn of the screw. There is a sort of grim logic about this whole Southern experience as it unfolds; a certain number of gambits has to be played. Little Rock used up some of them, Virginia others, and now Louisiana will dispose of a few more. I don't mean to sound cavalier about the violence. Actually, the whole thing is like a tragedy, with the end already written."

Pursuing this same train of thought, a number of liberal residents of New Orleans say among themselves that closing all the public schools in the state for a short period might be strong but effective therapy. No Southern state has yet carried out the ultimate threat, on a statewide basis, of abandoning public education.

"I would hate to see Louisiana do it because I think she can work out her own situation without resorting to such drastic measures," one observer says. "But, from the standpoint of the future of the South as a whole, it might be just as well to get it over with. It would certainly be good to have some of these things settled before they get to Alabama or Mississippi or Georgia."

Another Southerner has said: "Surely we don't think we can back into the age of sputniks with our public schools closed. But if we have to learn the hard way I guess now is as bad a time as any."

Another decisive element in the continuing school desegregation struggle is political leadership. When Southern political leaders continue to tell their people that a way will be found to circumvent desegregation orders of a federal court they are sowing the wind and when, in the inevitable course of events, that day is never forthcoming, and the law must be complied with, their cities and states reap the whirlwind in mob reaction.

One of the most perceptive newspaper editors in the South says: "A point we have not understood

The Black and the Poor

clearly enough in this whole Southern situation is that trouble is almost always kicked off at the legislative level if there are one or two tough, old leaders to give the Black Belt boys in every state some leadership."

"New Orleans, at this stage, discloses this in clearer terms than any place we've had so far, but there will be more to come as desegregation moves into the states where the Black Belt counties form more than a little pocket. Unless—and of course you can't ever stereotype this sort of thing—there is some state leadership shrewd enough and strong enough to be able to talk realism to the Legislatures and to the people."

The tensions of the South's industrial revolution supplanting an agrarian way of life are evident in these conflicts between state legislatures dominated by rural counties in thrall to the past and metropolitan centers in hock to the future. Dr. Albert Dent, president of New Orleans' Dillard University, pointed out the local conflict during a conversation:

"New Orleans has resisted state interference in its schools just as the state had resisted the Federal Government," he said. "And, now that the state has interposed itself between the parish [county] school and the Federal Government, we should get a clear-cut legal decision on interposition. Interposition was born in Virginia, but Virginia stopped short of putting it to a legal test. Louisiana has not stopped short. Maybe we can bury it forever here."

With Atlanta under court order to commence school desegregation in the fall of 1961, it is probable that this basic conflict between a progressive city and a defiant rural state legislature may again be joined. And the question arises: What will Atlanta—and the rest of the South—have learned from the experience of New Orleans?

IV.

A few lessons may already be drawn from Louisiana's struggle. One is that time granted between a desegregation order and the date set for actual integration of a specific school serves little purpose if it is not put to constructive use. The first suit in behalf of Negro children against the segregated school system of Orleans Parish was filed in September 1952. In February 1956, District Judge J. Skelly Wright ordered the Orleans Parish School Board to make arrangements for the admission of children on a nonracial basis. But eight years after the initial suit and four years after Judge Wright's order, as late as July 1960, the factual *Southern School News* reported:

"New Orleans generally had ignored the possibility of school integration until the last several weeks."

A second lesson is that the vacuum created by public apathy and divided or irresponsible leadership is an invitation to open violence. One Southerner who has followed events in Louisiana closely and spent much time in New Orleans during the past six months reports somewhat grimly:

"You get violence where it's asked for—and it has been here. However, there is a learning process going on in the South. Compared to Little Rock, the

The Black and the Poor

New Orleans mob has been made up mostly of teen-
agers and they have been less unruly. The police
started firm in New Orleans and continued that
way. This has been a major factor in the situation.
United States marshals, and not troops, have been
acting for the Federal Government. And constructive citizens' groups have been mobilizing sooner,
in the crisis, than they did in Little Rock.

"There are two areas in which leadership failure
was especially tragic, it seems to me. One involved
the hierarchy of the Roman Catholic Church and
the other the business community.

"Parochial schools in New Orleans enroll approximately 35 percent of all the city's school-age children and I believe they have it in their power to
exert real leadership. If they had stood with the
public schools and desegregated at the same time
they could have altered the course of events. But
they never made their intention or their timetable
on desegregation clear, and this helped keep the
whole situation in confusion.

"As for the business community, it seems that
they have to learn each time for themselves, after
the rioting starts, that this can be costly. Several
months ago a business leader from Little Rock came
to New Orleans to talk with some of the merchants
and industrialists about the potential for damage to
business that lay in this school situation. Many of
the businessmen wouldn't even discuss the subject
with him and the rest were very cool to the case he
was trying to make for preparation to avert crisis."

A third lesson is that when the issues are brought
into open discussion, and the costs of defiance are

clearly stated, many Southern citizens will rally to support desegregation, if the alternative is a shutdown of public education. During the late summer and early fall numerous New Orleans religious leaders and the Junior Chamber of Commerce, the Central Trades Council of the A.F.L.–C.I.O. and the Independent Women's Organization, among others, took public stands for open schools.

Two groups were organized: Save Our Schools, Inc., and the Committee on Public Education. The unfortunate point about these particular New Orleans groups is that they represent what has been called a "late-blooming public interest." The Louisiana Citizens Councils, Inc., was organized years ago and is a powerful and determined force working for segregation. Several groups advocating establishment of private schools have been functioning for some time in New Orleans.

Finally, a lesson of the first magnitude concerns the question of anticipating violence and defiance.

"Will we go through the Civil War Centennial years," one Southern historian asked recently, "experiencing a second occupation of New Orleans, a second battle of Atlanta, a second surrender of Columbia? When will we begin to live with the message of Appomattox—and, for that matter, the Constitution?"

It is often stated that since public schools are everybody's business they are nobody's business, and certainly this might be extended to include desegregation of public schools. The Supreme Court could render the 1954 desegregation decision, but it could not create an implementing agency. Nor was there executive or legislative implementation on a national scale.

An increasing number of concerned Southerners believe that the situation is suffering from too little understanding of the factors involved and too little planning for the future. They believe it is up to our national leadership to affirm the inevitability and justice of desegregation at all levels of public life and up to our Southern leadership to apprise their constituents in realistic terms of the cost of defiance.

The suggestion has been made that the new president might well consider establishing an agency to serve as a clearinghouse between the federal government and the states, communities, and Southern leaders dealing with the whole process of racial desegregation and integration.

Certainly, the deteriorated situation in New Orleans indicates that one-shot, short-term solutions to these periodic explosions actually solve very little. There is every reason to believe that as Southern school desegregation moves into its third phase, penetrating the Deep South, this is only one of many crises to come.

Challenge to education: The poor

DOROTHY BARCLAY

The real excitement at conferences of teachers
and school administrators these days centers on a
question that should concern parents as much as it
does schoolmen—how best to educate a group of
youngsters so touchily controversial that people
can't even agree on a term for them. Underprivileged? Disadvantaged? Educationally handicapped. Culturally deprived? Just plain "poor
children," maybe?

As of 1960, one out of three children in our fourteen largest cities were of this group. By 1970, it is
estimated, the proportion will have risen to one out
of two.

Until recently two extremes of thinking influenced all efforts made to solve the educational
problem these children present. Since many, for
reasons we will come to, seem unable to meet traditional academic standards, the solution—according

to one powerful teaching faction—was to throw the standards out, eliminate hard subjects, water down others, inject courses aimed at "life adjustment," and reduce expectations to the point where a youngster had to do little more than sit in classrooms for twelve years to gain a diploma.

At the other extreme, a second faction refused to admit that these children had any educational handicaps that lavishings of love and displays of "acceptance" couldn't cure. All else they needed, this group insisted, was more of what worked so well with many middle-class kids—sleek surroundings and up-to-date teachers, "permissive" in their attitudes and "modern" in their methods.

Steadily growing ratios of nonreaders in the upper grades, reports of serious disciplinary problems, high drop-out rates, and a rapidly increasing population of unemployable youths testify to the failure of both extremes.

Two publications released last month [May 1962] approached this problem forthrightly. One is *Education and the Disadvantaged American*, a statement by the National Education Association. The other is *The Culturally Deprived Child* by Dr. Frank Riessman, a visiting professor of psychiatry at Columbia University's College of Physicians and Surgeons.

The first presents a measured assessment of the problem and reviews the practical measures currently recommended to meet it—smaller classes, increased remedial services, expanded guidance and counseling staffs, closer school-community and school-home cooperation, "enrichment" programs, and the like. Dr. Riessman's book—although many of the practical approaches he suggests are similar— has a fresh and, to us, genuinely exciting point of view. It calls for a closer look not only at the schools themselves but at the child in question.

Such a look, he holds, would reveal that many of the so-called disadvantages or deprivations this child is held to suffer exist largely in the eyes of his beholders. His life is certainly not a path of roses but, Dr. Riessman holds, the difficulties he faces and the kind of efforts he, and his people, make to meet them often serve to build in him an awareness, a resilience, and a strength many middle-class children sadly lack.

Schools, he agrees, must recognize the very real handicaps that he suffers in attempting to meet standards and adjust to procedures developed in terms of what suits his middle-class age-mate. But—and this is the point of crucial importance—instead of concentrating solely on compensating his weaknesses, educators must, at the same time, find ways to capitalize on his strengths. This double approach will transform schooling from a mere patching-up process to a true educational procedure—broadening, meaningful, in the best interests of both the child and society.

Leaving out of consideration children from families so disturbed and disorganized as to require totally different services, the disadvantaged child differs from his middle-class age-mate, yes, but not so radically as comparison with this group would

The Black and the Poor

suggest. How, generally speaking, does the typical disadvantaged youngster differ and what can be done about it?

Preparation for learning: He starts school lacking the kinds of skill-building experiences most middle-class children have had almost from birth— play with a wide variety of increasingly complex toys, puzzles, games; close experiences with adults who talk to him, reason with him, read to him, tell him stories and listen to his; take him on excursions intended to broaden his knowledge of his surroundings; accept and encourage his curiosity.

Experimental efforts are underway to eliminate this handicap by giving these children the experiences they need in special public nursery school programs or to compensate for it later with concentrated efforts in kindergarten and special emphasis on reading instruction during the early grades. Older children, entering high-standard school systems for the first time, may require special transitional classes concentrating in a sort of "cram school" fashion on reading, effective study procedures, test-taking techniques, and similar bits of school "know-how" that the middle-class child— theoretically, at least—develops gradually over the years.

Attitudes toward adults: Often the deprived child lacks consistent relationships with adults who meet his physical needs predictably and direct and correct him with understanding. He may spend most of his time with—and gain most of his emotional support from—other children. When this is so, he lacks the feeling most middle-class children have that adults, in general, are helpful and worthy of trust. He pays attention to his classmates rather than to the teacher; his loyalties are to them; they are the ones whose interest and admiration he wishes to gain.

He needs as a teacher someone with a personality forceful enough to command his attention—part of the time at least—and imaginative and creative enough to be able to put his group loyalties to work in projects that will genuinely benefit each individual. He needs a continuing example of adult steadiness and consistency.

Attitudes toward authority: If physical punishment has been frequent or severe (a familiar situation in this group) the child may be overly fearful of authority, which will handicap his learning; or aggressive and provocative, a problem to himself and others. To the pugnacious child, authority is synonymous with strength. The permissive atmosphere in which an overly controlled child flowers is often, to the belligerent, an invitation to "start something."

This being so, the teacher must establish an atmosphere of firmness. To free the cowed child and control the aggressive one, clear-cut standards must be established with the teacher as the recognized authority. (Acknowledging the special difficulty individual students sometimes present to a teacher with a full class to consider, one educational group recently recommended a sort of "flying squad" of specialists to cope with young insurrectionists in real emergencies.)

Attitudes toward education: Polls indicate that many parents in the disadvantaged group value ed-

The Black and the Poor

ucation highly, but as a result of their limited life experiences—and the tremendous pressures on them simply to survive—their view of education is limited. It is unrealistic to expect their children avidly to embrace "learning for learning's sake" or to respond automatically to the "finest our culture can provide." Many individuals do but they are not typical. The majority have a thoroughly practical—and entirely understandable—"what's in it for me?" approach. (So, we believe, do most middle-class youngsters during their middle school years. However, since their parents support the school's approach these children come in time to understand and accept it.)

For the disadvantaged/deprived child to become genuinely convinced of the values of education per se, he must be exposed to teachers sufficiently convinced themselves to transmit their enthusiasm for learning. They must be able to lead these children from areas of their known interests to wider fields. Many need tangible motivations and rewards. "Intellectual challenges," effective with a few are too full of the threat of failure to work consistently with the majority. They respond with protective apathy.

Emotional needs: The child raised in a hurly-burly kind of way may strongly desire occasional expressions of physical warmth. But a teacher who genuinely understands his problems and encourages his efforts to meet them will do more to build the self-respect and confidence necessary for learning than one who swamps him in emotion.

Learning "style": Dr. Riessman, drawing on a wide variety of research, holds that there are certain

definite differences in the way the disadvan-
taged/deprived child learns. Such children by and
large, he says, are slower, more painstaking, more
"physical" in the ways they go about learning. But
this should not be interpreted—as it currently is—as
an indication of dullness. This dogged "style," in
fact, is frequently found in highly creative individuals, regardless of background.

This special learning style deserves respect and
intensive study. The current premium schools place
on speed of learning, production and response, rewards the glib and superficial student and seriously
handicaps the one who concentrates deeply,
"warms up" slowly, and moves with measured
tread. In the long run, however, the latter—permitted to work at his own pace—will often demonstrate
equal (at times, greater) total achievement.

We foresee in the months and years ahead some
bitter battles over "right" and workable ways of
meeting these differences. One thing is certain,
however. So long as they remain unmet not only all
our children but our entire society will be the
poorer.

For white and black, community control is the issue

NATHAN GLAZER

It may in the end turn out a tragedy that the issue of community control of schools was first raised on such a massive scale in New York City, where it inevitably became entangled in the escalating mutual distrust and dislike of Negroes and Jews, and in the increasingly fierce if ritualized conflicts that characterize labor-management relations between civil-service unions and government in New York City. We cannot wish away the reality that in New York City a public-school population with a majority of Negro and Puerto Rican children is now taught by a teaching staff with a majority of Jews; nor can we wish away the reality that New York City's teachers have followed in the path of transit workers, sanitation workers, and social-service workers in militantly fighting for the defense and expansion of their salaries and privileges.

But both these special factors will have conse-

quences far beyond the boundaries of New York
City because New York is also the capital of the
mass media and the seat and learning situation of
many intellectuals—and they are likely to draw,
indeed already have drawn, conclusions from the
terrible teachers' strike that will not apply and
should not apply to "community control" and
"parental participation" in general, and not even in
New York City.

The issue that has exploded in New York City—
and increasingly we can expect it to come up all
over the country—is one, we should be clear, of
"community control," and not really one of "decentralization," even if that is the way most people
refer to it. "Decentralization" means a pattern of organization in which decisions are made at the local
level rather than centrally—but these decisions can
be made by the agents of the central authority without the participation of the local community. "Community control" means a pattern of organization in
which the local community has power over decisions. You can have decentralization without community control (though if you have decentralization
the local community people will at least know
where to go to complain or put on pressure); you
cannot have community control without some substantial measure of decentralization. Nor does community control mean *total* community control.
Local officials can be removed by the state. If the
state will not act, and the suppression of rights is too
blatant, the federal government may intervene (Little Rock). Thus community control is never and
need not be total. Nor is it nor need it be a mandate

The Black and the Poor

for the teaching of race prejudice or the suppression
of rights—though it has been used for these and
other evil ends.

Many of us are beginning to forget that the fight
for community control, and for the restriction and
the breaking up of the powers of great bureaucracies, particularly where they affect the ordinary
day-to-day life of people, has been underway for
perhaps fifteen years, and that it is not a product of
the black revolution alone. Indeed, for fifteen or
twenty years, the middle class has shown a growing
discontent with the bureaucracies that control the
ordinary social services that affect citizens. It did
this long before it was forced to be concerned with
the problems of the urban black poor, and even in
countries where the issue of race did not intertwine
with and complicate all other problems.

Fifteen years ago we were in the middle of the
first burst of literature on the "suburbanization" of
American life. At that time, suburbanites were not
attacked for abandoning the central cities to their
difficult problems of increasing crime, rising welfare loads, intractable educational problems, and to
their prospect of racial violence—while to some extent some of these were problems even then, none
were anything like the major issues they have become since. At that time, if we recall, the suburbanites were criticized for depriving *themselves*
and their children of the rich urban experience—varied ethnic groups, income groups of different levels, cultural opportunities, more interesting politics and the like. And the suburbanites'
argument—where they had defenders, at any rate—

was that they were exchanging a situation in which they were the object of distant and indifferent bureaucratic forces to one in which they had direct access to and direct influence over government.

Thus I recall an article by Harry Gersh in *Commentary* describing his move from Brooklyn to Westchester—and reporting with wonder that when the garbage was not collected there was someone to *call,* and he could expect a response. Here was a middle-class citizen who nevertheless found he exchanged powerlessness in the city for some power in the suburbs. Robert Wood, in his book *Suburbia,* did present a criticism of the suburbanite for leaving the arena of major political decisions and did warn that if the middle-class population moved off to local municipalities of a narrower class and ethnic range, it would be more difficult to deal with the great problems of the society, and in particular those that became evident in central cities.

Yet to many the main effect of the book was to underline how much the suburbanite gained by living in a small community which, even if it was economically part of a larger metropolis, had a narrow range of citizens and problems. Here he gained direct access and some modicum of control. If he had a position on a public issue, his fellow citizens were likely to agree with him in larger numbers than in the city, because their interests were the same. And if he had a point of view on elementary education, on zoning, on snow removal, on library services, not only would he find that he could organize some of his neighbors who agreed with him, but also that it was possible to influence local officials to take account of that point of view; or if they did not, it was possible to replace them with his friends and neighbors. It was a heady sense of power for people long deprived of much capacity to influence government—and it was a powerful attraction to get out from under the swelling and impervious bureaucracies of the central city.

The middle class thus led the way to the discovery that the urban bureaucracies, made increasingly insensitive by the replacement of political bosses by municipal unions, could be got out from under—by moving. Let us recall, too, who were the first critics of public housing. They were the planners and the middle-class reformers, not the poor who lived in public housing, or those who spoke for them as their militant leaders. The critics were Lewis Mumford, Catherine Bauer Wurster, Elizabeth Wood, Paul and Percival Goodman.

These men and women in varying degrees knew the situation in public housing and spoke from experience as well as from a general theoretical opinion, but in attacking the massive public-housing projects that began to rise in New York City and elsewhere shortly after World War II, they combined esthetic with social criticism. They attacked the public-housing bureaucracies, in Washington and in New York City, which made it impossible, it appeared, to design more attractive and human-scaled projects. The middle class despaired of bureaucracy in housing first—not that of course it meant that much to the middle class, which in any case lived in other settings.

And we can make the same point about the critics

of urban renewal and urban expressways. The most
influential single book on urban renewal was perhaps Herbert Gans's *The Urban Villagers*, which
told with controlled objectivity and yet with passion
the story of the destruction, by urban renewal, of
the West End of Boston, and in particular of its
working-class, second-generation, Italian community. The West End was not Greenwich Village, but
it had an Italian community, cheap and small-scale
housing, a pleasant site near downtown, the urban
amenities of small stores and street life celebrated
by Jane Jacobs in *The Death and Life of Great
American Cities*. The West Ender, as Gans described him, was certainly attached to his community and his housing—but he was incapable of fighting for it, for he had no well-developed political
skills.

But a sociologist and intellectual like Herb Gans
was able to arouse other people—sociologists, intellectuals, and others—to the enormity of the crime
against the West End, and when in New York the
urban-renewal authorities tried to move into West
Village—a similar community, but with many more
intellectuals and writers—the community fought
back, bitterly. Jane Jacobs, Eric Wensberg, and
others were deeply involved in that fight, and it
took several years, in the early sixties, to finally
bring the project to a halt—almost.

I recall the bitterness felt by those involved in
that fight at the power and the imperviousness of
the urban-renewal authorities. These had full-time
staffs of publicity men, planners, lawyers, administrators, federal money—and plenty of time. The

local residents had, in this case, writing and political skills, but they fought part-time against the full-timers. And it was at that time that there first developed and became prominent among younger, radical planners such ideas as the one that the community, like the large central bureaucracy, deserves to have its own full-time staff, its planners and advocates so it will not have to exhaust its energies and its money in fighting a public bureaucracy—formally its "servant." The feelings of the middle-class people who fought urban renewal in the West Village, and who fought the plan for the Lower Manhattan Expressway—where again, they faced a full-time bureaucracy well supported by public funds—are to my mind very similar to the feelings now expressed by the poor and the black in many parts of our big cities. And we will not properly understand or respond to these latter feelings— if we are middle-class—unless we recall those earlier fights.

It was about the same time too—in 1961—that there was an explosion of anger against the Board of Education—and once again, it was not an explosion led by the poor and the slum dwellers. The Board of Education it turned out was incredibly incompetent in spending money to build new schools—schools needed by middle-class people moving to Queens and the Bronx, as well as by poor people living in older parts of the city. The Board of Education was replaced. A scandal—a minor scandal—helped, but the frustration of the middle classes of the City of New York at the imperviousness of the board and its agents to those who were technically its masters

The Problems of
American Education

was undoubtedly the chief politically combustible material fueling the outburst and the subsequent change in the procedures for selecting the board— changes that, alas, seemed to accomplish nothing in making the board and the school system more responsive to people's demands.

I recall vividly—10 years ago—the horror stories that then circulated. Graduates from good schools who wanted to teach in the public schools could not get information and forms from indifferent and ignorant clerks at headquarters; parents could not get information as to the zonal boundaries of various schools. Ideas for innovation—such as using parent aides in the schools, using the city's resources of writers and artists in the schools, even if not licensed—could not get a hearing. Parents were considered foreign persons in the school. They could not enter it without a permit. I recall I could not even take my 5-year-old daughter to her first class in a public school—because parents were not allowed in school. Quite mad explanations would be given—they might break a leg and the school would be responsible, etc.

The local community advisory boards for 25 new local school boards—a very meager and hardly successful attempt at some degree of decentralization and parent influence—were set up originally in 1961, not because of the pressure and urging of the poor and the black, who were then scarcely active in these matters, but at the demand of the middle classes. Martin Mayer's *The Schools*, in 1961, had a great deal of powerful material condemning the impervious bureaucracy of the New York City

The Black and the Poor

schools—and he spoke out of a concern for education that had at that time much less to do with the
black and poor as such than with a concern for education in general, which he felt was being thwarted
by an overcentralized bureaucracy, too remote from
any pressure that an aroused community and concerned parents could exert on it.

   In our involvement with the tragic details of what
happened in Ocean Hill-Brownsville, with the grim
reports of racist teaching in some of the community-
controlled schools, and with the reduction of the
rights and privileges built up by teachers in these
schools (many of whom have served loyally in situations which would probably not be tolerated for a
week by those who criticize them), we are in danger
of forgetting that the demand for community control
is based on far more than the experience of blacks
and the poor. I have indicated that the experience of
the middle classes of New York and other cities—
their opposition to practices of urban renewal and
highway construction in the central city, their frustration in their efforts to exercise some control over
the content and character of teaching and the management of the school system in New York City,
their unhappiness over city services that were not
responsive to their needs—has led to their own
style of community control: moving to towns where
they have more power, or into projects which have
their own police forces, or moving their children
out of public schools and into private schools. Many
of the children going to private schools in New York
City, we should recall, are children of poorer
middle-class and of working-class families. Those

The Problems of
American Education

attending parochial schools and Jewish day schools far outnumber the children going to fashionable private schools. Of course, the issue here is not "community control" in any simple sense, for it could be argued that the parents of children in religious schools have less control, and this in one sense is true. But what they do have is the power to select an environment in which their children are educated, even if in some cases it is a more rigid and authoritarian one than that of the public schools.

But if we are to get some idea of the full force of black demands in this connection, we must look outside New York City, and outside the country, to discover how powerfully all kinds of ethnic groups are demanding substantial autonomy and even independence. The same issues are rising everywhere—indeed many might say the same irrationalities. But if everyone is becoming irrational in the same way, one cannot help feeling that we are in the grip of a movement against bureaucracy and centralization—particularly where ethnic and racial divisions are involved—that in some way has to be taken into account. Thus, the association of this movement in the United States with the black and the poor (not all the black and the poor, of course) may conceal to many of us its real power and seriousness.

The catalogue of growing ethnic passions around the world is by now familiar. What is perhaps less familiar is the virulence with which these passions are being expressed and the degree to which they are now divorced from any objective facts of repression or inferiority. Thus, the Flemings of Belgium have long felt themselves to be dominated culturally, economically, and politically by the Walloons. In recent years, the French-speaking Walloon section of the country has been in economic decline, the Flemish part of the country has been economically rising. Politically it is now certainly dominant. But this has done nothing to reduce the sense of resentment of the Flemings. If anything, it seems to have increased it.

To the outsider, the demand that the partially French-speaking University of Louvain should no longer conduct any work in French—because it was situated in the Flemish part of the country!—seemed the height of irrationality. But it was fought for with violence, and the university is to be separated into two parts, with the French-speaking section reestablished at great cost beyond the linguistic frontier. If this can happen in Belgium, where Walloon domination of Flemings is scarcely to be compared to the historic oppression of blacks by whites in this country, is it possible to expect that we will not begin to see the division of universities or colleges in this country?

Quebec is engaged in a process which it seems must lead to equally unhappy results. Montreal is a city that lives in fear of separatist French violence. The English-speaking already fear laws that will restrict their right to educate their children in English. The desire for freedom, it seems, among those who have suffered from an inferior status cannot be assuaged merely by the full right to conduct whatever cultural activities they wish, or by full political power, or even by economic concessions designed to raise them to the level of the formerly dominant groups. It moves on inexorably to the demand, at least among some extremists, for the full "purification" of the territory, so that just as French is seen to defile Flemish territory, English is seen to defile French territory.

One of the most striking examples of ethnic separatism is now to be found in the French-speaking section of the dominantly German-speaking canton of Bern in Switzerland. Switzerland has long seemed to many of us a remarkable model of the largest degree of community control and participatory democracy imaginable. The central government is almost without power, the name of the president is hardly known to the citizens, and even the cantons into which that small country is divided yield most of their powers to the smaller communities which make them up. These are dominated by the direct voting of citizens on every conceivable issue—in many cases by the face-to-face town meeting, which has control over a much wider range of governmental activities than the vestigial town meetings of New England. Yet full citizenship in the most decentralized of all states, with the greatest degree of popular participation in government, does not satisfy some of the French-speaking citizens of the canton of Bern. There have been bombings and the demand to establish a separate republic.

The people of Wales and Scotland, who have been the beneficiaries for decades of special programs to build up the economies of declining parts

of Great Britain, also support at this point rapidly
growing separatist movements, which have also
engaged in some acts of violence. At present there
is some concern over whether the investment of the
Prince of Wales can be carried off without unpleasant incidents.

In all these cases—and in many more I could
refer to—we find not only the demand for cultural
opportunity, economic equality, political consideration in proportion to one's numbers in a unitary
state but what to me is the irrational demand that
the "foreigners," the "others," with whom one has
been associated in an integrated state for centuries,
be *removed*—a demand that, it is true, is held in
many cases by only a few extremists but one that
eventually becomes politically potent through the
silencing, via public opinion, of the moderates who
see no objection to the maintenance of a mixed society. Everywhere the liberal hope for mixed societies—mixed in ethnic and racial character—gives
way before a demand, now coming from the ostensi-
bly dominated rather than domineering groups, for
the clearing out of the dominators, so that the formerly inferior group can conduct its own life, without involvement with others. And, of course, we see
the same demand developing in black communities
in this country. Undoubtedly this, too, is at present
the demand of a minority. But the majority is con-
fused, passionless—and for the most part, silent.

If one were to make a complete catalogue of the
rising demand for participation, of the rising opposition to bureaucracies, even when these appear to be
reasonably competent, selected by rational and ob-

jective standards, and considerate, this article would shortly be out of hand. But there is one other functional area in which black separatist demands can be matched around the world, and in situations where racial and ethnic division is not an issue—the demand for participation in university government. This has now been raised in almost every country in the world, except Russia (where perhaps it has been raised but we know nothing about it), Israel, and Cuba. It has led to truly revolutionary changes. In France the universities have, for the first time since the age of Napoleon, changed their system of government to allow for elected bodies in which students will have substantial representation. There is no question that the ancient universities of Germany and Italy will undergo similar changes; the students have demonstrated that they can prevent them from operating and can even physically destroy them if they do not undergo these changes.

Thus, for a variety of reasons, we must separate the issues of community control and participation from the specific circumstances in which they have been raised in New York. These issues have been raised by the middle class as well as the poor, by whites as well as blacks, by groups that have not been oppressed—at least in recent times—as well as by groups that have been, in ethnically homogeneous societies as well as in ethnically heterogeneous ones. Clearly they reflect some worldwide movement of dissatisfaction with the modern state and its manner of operation. Even though this state is itself—in all the countries I have discussed—a democratic state, in which representatives directly

The Black and the Poor

elected by the people govern, through agents selected by the democratically elected representatives, it is considered by many as oppressive as if it were a dictatorship. Certainly the agencies of the modern state, in the view of many people, have escaped from popular control.

I think those who denounce the modern bureaucratic state exaggerate enormously the degree to which the agents of the state have escaped from popular control. I think they further engage in the worst kind of intellectual brainwashing when they fail to take seriously the differences between states in which there are popular elections and those in which there are not (or in which the popular elections simply approve the choices of the ruling party), states in which there are functioning civil rights from those in which there are not, states in which there is an independent judiciary from states in which there is not.

Nevertheless, one key issue has already been settled—in a formally and actually democratic state, disaffected groups, whether blacks, or the poor, or students, can act as if the state were a dictatorship, can gain wide sympathy for their position, and can maintain the kind of disruption that makes it impossible for many institutions important for the society to operate. Thus, universities can be brought to a standstill. High schools and now even elementary schools can be disrupted. The police of a democratic state can be cast in the role of oppressors—to the point where intelligent and educated people can justify the murder of the policemen of a democratic state. More or less the same thing can be done with other agencies of the state, whether highway construction agencies or urban renewal agencies, to the point indeed where they cannot operate.

Despite this, I think it is true that most people—in this country and in others—are more or less content with the operations of the bureaucracies of the democratic states: consider the votes in this country, or in France, or in Germany, or in Japan. I think it is true that most of the people who man the bureaucracies are men of good will, interested in doing as good a job as is commensurate with their training, their abilities, and their salaries. I think the process of selection for the bureaucracies is carried out in the democratic states with increasing concern for fairness and for merit, and that replacement of political selection and personal influence by objective tests (which probably in many cases measure nothing relevant to the job), is nevertheless an advance for justice and equity.

But all this does not seem to matter. While to most people the bureaucracies, whatever the frustrations they suffer from them, are seen as *theirs* (they are after all *related* to the teachers, policemen, civil servants, party officials, etc.), for many others, for increasingly dissident and violent minorities, the bureaucracies are seen as foreign, and when seen as foreign, everything becomes justified. Teachers can be spit upon, social workers can be physically attacked, policemen can be killed, the physical premises of government and educational institutions can be destroyed—and there will be an audience looking on, a good part of which will be sympathetic and encouraging.

The Black and the Poor

This is the situation we face in many of our cities
—as I have suggested, it is a situation we face in
a good part of the rest of the world too.

What courses lie open to us? If we believe—as I
do—that what we have is an overall democratic and
rational system, open to change, we will be tempted
to consider the repression of those who act irratio-
nally toward it. I think in most cases this will not
work. Particularly in settings in which respect for
the agents of authority is required, it is scarcely possible that this respect can be recreated and reawak-
ened through repression. The police do not, after
all, operate through force. Hannah Arendt has
argued effectively that the state is not based on violence, physical force, but on power, and when physical violence is necessary to maintain authority,
then it means power has been lost.

Now this has happened to the police in black
neighborhoods. They are very often torn between
the impossible choice of using violence, physical
violence, in making arrests to uphold the law, or of
simply abandoning any effort to uphold the law.
Power has been lost, violence is necessary now if
authority is to be maintained—but in a democratic
society the exercise of violence, to the degree necessary to reestablish authority, is scarcely to be considered. Thus we have the result: lawlessness prevails, tempered by occasional police violence, and
the chief victims are those who dwell in black
neighborhoods and the few whites who must work
there (storekeepers, the police, teachers, social
workers).

The same thing is happening in public schools in

The Problems of
American Education

black areas—the process is perhaps most advanced in New York, but is seen in many other cities too. The exercise of the teacher's authority, which once required only a severe look, a word, an admonishing touch, sending the student to the principal, now requires in more and more cases physical violence—we can call it restraint—direct forceful battling with rebellious students, sometimes by the teachers, sometimes by the police.

We can find the same thing in the welfare offices, and in other government offices, and even, shocking as it is to those of us raised in a setting in which libraries were to be approached in silence and books treated with care, in public libraries, which also now increasingly need guards if they are to operate—at the university level, as well as at the local level.

When authority is lost—and I think it has been lost in schools in black neighborhoods, by police in black neighborhoods, and by a good number of the officials who deal with black neighborhoods—the only way it can be restored is by a change in the actual distribution of political power. I myself am not convinced that big bureaucracies in democratic states, and even highly centralized ones, do not work—they work well enough when their authority is accepted. The centralized educational system of France seems to make all the people literate, and up until a few years ago seemed to select efficiently a higher civil service and other important groups of specialists to run the state. The highly centralized educational system of Japan seems to work even more efficiently if we consider such tests as learn-

The Black and the Poor

ing to read and write and do mathematics. And I would wonder really whether the educational system of New York City, which seemed to have such wide acceptance among the people of the city in the thirties, has changed for the worse since then—I doubt that it has become more bureaucratic, or less responsive to public pressure, since then. The police have become more professional, less violent, more honest, and other government activities too are more honest and more efficient. David Riesman has argued that the universities and colleges are much better than they were in the thirties.

So I do not rest my argument for basic changes on the ground of the growing inadequacy of these institutions; I would rest it on the fact that they cannot gain acceptance of their authority among substantial minorities who have the power to resist any possible good they can do. At that point, I think we have to consider new forms of organization, and it is on this basis that I look favorably on plans like the Bundy proposals for breaking up the school system of New York City, and the participation of parent-elected groups in the governing of the smaller districts.

I do not want to go into the details of appropriate systems of decentralization and of greater community control for various government functions. I think we should recognize that we already have a substantial measure of community control in the form of elected bodies for municipalities, states, and the federal government. We have some partially working models for an increased measure of community control that could be expanded. The

The Problems of
American Education

three demonstration districts in the school system of New York City are to my mind such partially working models.

Rhody McCoy seems to find it in his interest to insist that community control in New York City has been "destroyed" because the district was forced to take back the union teachers it tried to exclude. But no rational assessment can accept this judgement. Most of the teachers who have been accepted back formally will probably leave fairly soon—the power of the local board, the unit administrator and his staff, and the loyal teachers and students to make life unpleasant for them has already been demonstrated in a hundred ways. The demonstration unit still survives, with just about all the teachers it hired. It is getting more money, from foundations and from special programs for the educationally underprivileged. In other words, partial decentralization and community control in New York City is already a reality, and there will be more.

But leaving aside the special case of the demonstration school districts of New York City, we see other examples of decentralization and community control establishing themselves—even without benefit of overall schemes for revision of local government—along the lines of the Bundy proposal. Thus, the Community Action programs set up under the poverty programs are established now in more than 1,000 communities. Within defined poverty areas, there are often elections or some other process for getting a representative board. The boards have powers over a budget, over a planning process for various local programs, over some ongoing local programs. On occasion, their powers are expanded. For example, many of them now have some voice in allocating the substantial federal funds now spent for the education of the poor under Title I of the Elementary and Secondary Education Act. As a result of the Green Amendment, these Community Action agencies can now only continue if the appropriate local government agrees to their continuance to administer antipoverty programs. At the end of 1968, 883 of 913 reporting local governments elected to continue the existing Community Action agencies.

Thus the Community Action agencies, which were born in conflict, and have lived through intense conflict, have turned into really effective examples of decentralization and community control. In most communities, the locally elected power-holders, the mayors and councilmen—who of course also reflect community control, but at a higher level—have agreed that the bodies that represent poor areas for antipoverty programs should continue.

As Daniel P. Moynihan wrote at the conclusion of his *Maximum Feasible Misunderstanding,* ". . . community action . . . survived: a new institution of sorts had been added to the system of American local government." And the Republican administration has now accepted it. In the nature of things, when an institution survives, one finds things for it to do—or it finds things for itself to do. Those of us who believed that the conflicts over relatively small programs of no impact would become so fierce that communities would be torn apart with no gain have for the most part been proved wrong. While the conflicts were indeed fierce in many cities, in the end the local Community Action agencies have become established, have been accepted by local city government, have proved useful—at least useful enough so that the overwhelming majority of city governments are not prepared to abolish them.

With the rise of ever more extreme forms of black militancy, in addition, the leadership of the Community Action agencies, which seemed militant enough in 1964 and 1965, now turns out, within the political spectrum of poor black areas, to be generally somewhere in the middle. The agencies have provided a training ground for large numbers of local black community leaders, many of whom have become more militant, it is true, but many of whom are now on the first rungs of careers in electoral politics, and look forward to participating in the system as democratically elected representatives of citizens, rather than tearing it down.

The same process is now underway as we develop Model Cities agencies in many cities. These agencies will administer much larger funds, for a much greater range of city functions, than Community Action agencies. They must be set up with the approval of local elected bodies—which has somewhat muted the conflicts in their creation, for city governments now have less fear (than in the case of the Community Action agencies) that an alliance of radical federal officials and radical local people will set up a government in opposition to them.

These agencies have a difficult task, but one no more difficult than the Community Action agencies had. They must represent the people of a local area;

The Black and the Poor

they must develop a complex program with many
different parts (the legislation requires that their
programs have elements that try to improve housing, public safety, health, education, employment,
and a good deal more in the poor areas); they have
to get local approval of programs that often arouse
the suspicion of the city agencies in these various
fields; they must get coordinated funding of all
these programs from a variety of federal agencies,
etc.

Once again, to this observer at least, it appears
that in our penchant for attacking all problems simultaneously and in achieving a high level of participation we may have placed a burden on Model
Cities agencies that they may not be able to fulfill.
Yet, in some cases with which I am familiar, I am
impressed with the high level of many of those involved in developing Model Cities programs, and
with the political skill with which these varied obstacles are being overcome. And once again, we are
giving opportunity to new leaders, many black, who
are gaining valuable experience and valuable political skills, and who see their future as dependent on
their ability to deliver services to people, rather
than on their ability to arouse them to a destructive
rage.

Thus in a variety of ways, in various areas of government, a greater degree of decentralization and
community control is being established. Whether
we should try to formalize this process in the way
the Bundy proposals do or in a more elaborate effort
that breaks up city government into local subareas,
with elected boards and separate administrators, I

The Problems of
American Education

am not sure. But I am impressed by the fact that in the two cities overseas that are perhaps most comparable to New York in size, London and Tokyo, there is a system of borough (London) or ward (Tokyo) government. The boroughs or wards are smaller than our boroughs in New York—there are about 80 in both cities. They have an average population of about 300,000 each. They have elected councils or legislatures. They have control over elementary education, over health and welfare services, over some local housing programs, over libraries and recreational services. In Tokyo, at least, these wards generally have large, substantial headquarters, in which there are meeting rooms for citizens as well as government offices, and these headquarters are landmarks in a distinguished, contemporary architecture. The history of local government in England, Japan, and the United States, has very little in common, yet despite this there may be advantages to this way of organizing the government of a very large city that we should consider.

There are undoubtedly safeguards we will want to consider and build on as we move toward community control. In other countries the main limitation to community control is simple efficiency, and that is one limitation here. It will not be possible for local community governments of small scale to take effective measures to improve metropolitan transportation or to control air pollution, to run colleges (though some might—they do in London), or to manage the social security system. But in this country, we have other problems to contend with.

The Black and the Poor

Since one of the main reasons for this drive is to increase the number of black jobholders and civil servants and to increase the control of blacks over branches of government that affect them, we cannot really fully guarantee the rights to seniority and to specific jobs of all civil servants, as one could in other countries. We will have to expect some kind of turnover as community control becomes stronger—and we need measures that cushion this transition for those hurt by it unless we are ready to go through more New York teachers' strikes. The municipal unions will also have to realize that the principle of merit alone will have to be supplemented with the principle of representativeness— as it already is perhaps in many cities outside New York, which have found it possible to recruit far more black school teachers, principals, and administrators than New York has.

The argument is often made that the introduction of the principle of representativeness will mean that people recruited for public service will be less qualified or competent than those who are recruited on the principle of merit alone. A good deal depends on how we define "competence" or "qualification." If we define it only in terms of the tests that have been developed, this certainly is true. But the tests themselves are only one way to getting at competence and qualifications. Very often test-making begins to lead a life of its own, and tests are developed and used that are themselves rarely tested to find out if they really select better teachers or policemen or firemen. Other cities (for example, Philadelphia and Chicago) do seem to have much larger proportions of black principals and teachers—even taking into account their larger Negro populations—than New York does. Further, for many purposes we have to define race itself as a qualification. A Negro teacher or principal, all other things equal, will, we expect, have a better understanding of Negro pupils and parents, and will do a better job for that reason alone. We have to take this into account in making appointments.

One strong argument against a greater degree of community control for poor and black areas is that since the areas are poor, they will not be able to raise their own taxes on their own property tax base (as can suburban school districts and other governments), thus they will be dependent on the tax resources of the city, the state, and the federal government, and these will not be distributed to them in the measure required if these areas have a larger degree of independence. In other words, the argument is these areas need more money, not more local control, and more local control will mean less money.

I don't see the force of this argument. We have already accepted in this country—both in state aid formulas and in federal aid formulas—the principle that resources should be distributed on the basis of need, not on the basis of a real contribution to tax revenue. This principle is often used to give more money to rural areas and Southern states, but in the Elementary and Secondary Education Act, and in other acts, we now see money flowing to poor areas of cities on the basis of need. There are also various cases working their way up through the court sys-

tem that may lead to a greater measure of public
money going to poor areas.

Community control as such does not carry a major
threat to this process. What does is the possibility
that we will see the rise to power in the new small
governments of black militants who will teach race
hatred and an illusory and false view of history and
reality. This is real danger, and the fact is we cannot
fully protect ourselves against it. We must hope that
the good sense of black parents and citizens will on
the whole prevail, but we must realize it has not
been possible for the federal government to protect
Negroes from local and state governments in the
South that teach racial hatred and systematically
prevent blacks from gaining access to equal education, equal justice, equal participation in government. We must try to prevent the systematic oppression of minorities—it will be black minorities,
again—in Northern local government, as we try to
prevent this oppression in Southern local government. But in view of how long it has taken us to
make even the progress we have made in the South,
we cannot be very optimistic, and I think we must
expect that some of the governments that will be set
up in the Northern cities may well be oppressive,
corrupt, inefficient, and irrational. Budgetary controls in the hands of cities and states may prevent
the worst abuses, just as budgetary power in the
hands of the federal government has helped move
the South toward equal treatment.

In the end, I think the main redress of those who
do not like the new governments that are established is the redress that is always available in a

democracy—changing the government, whatever the degree of pressure or terror applied by it, or if that seems too hard, moving away. As long as these safeguards are available, we can move toward decentralization and local control.

PART THREE

This section presents a series of intriguing articles on the experience of young people in schools and colleges. The articles argue that in one way or another the young are different, or the institutions of schooling are different, from their counterparts in the recent past. Youngsters, particularly those of the middle class, are now subjected to a prolonged adolescence and are shaped by a subculture formed around this stage of life. The institutions, in their turn, have become larger, more complex, more specialized, and decidedly more bureaucratic. Our new adolescent must grow up in the new educational bureaucracy.

The first article, "The New Stage of American Man—Almost Endless Adolescence," by Bennett M. Berger, a sociologist, offers a fundamental—and still controversial—perspective on the position of youth in modern society. He believes that the young, excluded from adult responsibilities, have a marginal, ambiguous position in the general social

The adolescent meets the bureaucracy

structure. This position leaves them free of the restraints of institutional commitments while at the same time rendering them sensitive to moral inconsistencies, much as marginal men or outsiders have always been sensitive to the strains of the society they see through the glass. And we find that the main framework of their experience in "education" is founded in specific schools and colleges where they are concentrated in large numbers and adopt means of close communication; where they are exposed by instruction to the ideal aspects of culture, while in an important sense kept in storage until age brings them out the other end into work and marriage. What is new, then, is both that adolescence is a long, self-conscious stage *and* that it is located, in social and physical space, largely within the gates of educational bureaucracies.

Harvey Swados, the novelist, discusses this theme in a highly specific way in the second article, "The Joys and Terrors of Sending the Kids to College." He sees a wide generation gap between educated upper-middle-class parents and their sophisticated offspring in the context of mass higher education and a change in the meaning of a college education. The parents in their day saw college as a golden opportunity, much as lower-class parents still do today, but their "kids" do not share that view. Bored by high school, they enter college with new hope—only to be bored again and unsure about the value of so much preparation for what is supposed to lie out there in the postadolescence real world. We do not know how widespread this phenomenon is, other than that it still seems characteristic of a minority. But that minority numbers in the tens and even hundreds of thousands and, full of bright, sophisticated, and articulate youth, helps set the tone of present-day adolescence.

The next two articles in this section attend directly to the growing bureaucratization and professionalization of academic work. Martin Mayer, in "Close to Midnight for the New York Schools," holds up for view the shortcomings of centralized bureaucracy in large urban school systems. Focusing on New York City, the largest of the mammoth urban systems, his points bear also on Washington, D.C., St. Louis, Pittsburgh, and other large cities. The centralization of authority at district headquarters in such large systems, with their heterogeneous populations and clienteles, leaves principals and teachers little autonomy in adapting general policy to their own situation. As the system ages, rules and multiple levels of administration clog the channels of effective communication. As paperwork multiplies, a stage is reached that can only be called bureaucratic overload. Gradually, everyone begins to feel powerless and there is a loss of both teachers' confidence *and* public confidence. Then it is time for the pendulum of organization to swing toward decentralization. Particularly in a pluralistic society—the many neighborhoods and factions of the metropolis—decentralization gives various local groups, within and outside the system, a piece of the action.

The current argument against the bureaucratic defects of large-scale organization is applied to higher education in the article by Andrew Hacker. Mr. Hacker, in "The College Grad Has Been Short-Changed," describes succinctly the trend toward large institutions as part of mass higher education. He points to the consequences, by way of decreased student contact with professors and administrators and the growing sense of impersonality. This is bound to result in less loyalty, and campus factions are likely to become self-conscious interest groups—outcomes that have appeared more sharply since 1965 when Hacker was writing. This article also contains a wrong prediction—that students were already settling down after a few outbursts in 1964–65—which we can use as a caution in predicting the collective behavior of students. Whatever the causes and provocations, student behavior remains a highly unpredictable phenomenon, seemingly subject in high degree to quick swings in mood and sentiment, as well as to the calculus of logical diagnosis and rational plan of action.

The many criticisms of academic bureaucracy

bring back echoes of Thorstein Veblen, whose lonely classic in 1918, *The Higher Learning in America,* argued brilliantly that businessmen as trustees of universities were applying their ethics and their models of organization to campuses. His thesis has remained controversial in attributing the *source* of the bureaucratic model to the business-man-trustee. One can argue strongly that the main source has been internal, that various groups on campuses and particularly the administrators at the center have promoted bureaucratic forms as they have struggled with their own part of the problems of quantity and quality, freedom and order. But whatever the source, the phenomenon of bureau-cracy is strong and apparently has fundamental consequences for how teachers teach and how students learn. Much more serious thought and research needs to be given to this feature of modern education.

The new stage of american man—
Almost endless adolescence

BENNETT M. BERGER

When I was an undergraduate 20 years ago, I was
chairman of one of the radical student groups at my
college and an active official in the regional inter-
collegiate association of that group. I marched in my
share of picket lines, published an article attacking
my college president for anti-Semitism, was sung to
by the sirens of the local Communist party and
even, in a burst of creativity, wrote what in this age
of instant classics I suppose qualifies as a classic
militant's love song. I called it, "You and I and the
Mimeograph Machine" and dedicated it to all the
youthful romances born amidst the technology of
moral protest.

Later, when I got older and became a sociologist,
I resisted becoming a "political sociologist," by
which in this context I mean what a lot of the militants mean: a former activist who traded his credentials as a conscious moral and political agent in

exchange for the rewards of expertise about political behavior. Though the remarks about student militance which follow may be analytic, I yield nothing to the young in the way of moral credentials.

In trying to throw some sociological light on the nature and character of student unrest, I am not going to comfort the militants by saying that students protest because this is a racist, plastic society or because the curriculum is irrelevant or because the university has sold its soul to the military-industrial complex or because the university is a machine in which students are treated as raw material— when, indeed, their uptight teachers take time from their research to treat them as anything at all. On the other hand, I am not going to comfort their critics by saying that students rebel for kicks or because their upbringing was too permissive or because they are filled with a seething self-hatred or because they are symbolically murdering their fathers in a recurrent ritual melodrama of generational conflict.

What I will try to do is show how certain conditions generic to the direction of our present societal development have helped to bring about the present situation among youth and in the universities. I will also hazard a prediction as to the effects of these conditions during the next decade. An understanding of the problem will not make the solution any easier, for knowledge is not power, but it can at least arm us against panaceas.

The problem of student unrest is rooted in the prolongation of adolescence in industrialized countries. But it should be understood that "adolescence" is only minimally a biological category; there are only a very few years between the onset of puberty and the achievement of the growth and strength it takes to do a man's or woman's work. As we know, however, culture has a habit of violating nature. Protoadolescent behavior now begins even before puberty (which itself is occurring earlier) with the action—and the orientation—we call "preadolescent," while at the other end, technological, economic and social developments conspire to prolong the dependence of the young, to exclude them from many of the privileges and responsibilities of adult life, and therefore to *juvenilize* * them.

The casual evidence in support of this deep institutionalization of adolescence is diffuse and quite remarkable. It includes such spectacles as 6-foot, 200-pound "boys" who in another time and place might be founders of dynasties and world-conquerors (like Alexander of Macedon) cavorting on the fraternity house lawn hurling orange peels and bags of water at each other, while tolerant local police, who chucklingly approve, direct traffic around the battlefield. It includes the preservation of childlike cadence and intonation in voices otherwise physically mature. It includes the common—and growing—practice (even in official university documents) of opposing the word "student" to the

---

* "Juvenilize": a verb I have devised to describe a process through which "childish" behavior is induced or prolonged in persons who, in terms of their organic development, are capable of participating in adult affairs. If the process exists, there ought to be a verb to describe it.

**The Adolescent
Meets the Bureaucracy**

word "adult"—as if students were by definition not adults, even as the median age of university students rises with the increase of the graduate student population.

Adolescence, then, is not the relatively fleeting "transitional stage" of textbook and popular lore but a substantial segment of life which may last 15 or 20 years, and if the meaning of adolescence is extended only slightly, it can last longer than that. I have in mind the age-graded norms and restrictions in those professions which require long years of advanced training, and in which the system of sponsorship makes the advancement of one's career dependent upon being somebody's "boy" perhaps well on toward one's middle-age—a fact not uncharacteristic of university faculties.

Much of the discussion of "youth culture" in recent years reflects the prolongation of adolescence, since it is not surprising that a period of life which may last from age 12 to age 35 might develop its own cultural style, its own traditions, and its own sources of motivation, satisfaction—and dissatisfaction. There is thus an enormous stratum of persons caught in the tension between their experience of peak physical strength and sexual energy on the one hand, and their public definition as culturally "immature" on the other.

This tension is exacerbated by a contradictory tendency: while modern industrial conditions promote juvenilization and the prolongation of dependence, they also create an "older," more experienced youthful cohort. They have more and earlier

The Problems of
American Education

experience with sex and drugs; they are far better educated than their parents were; urban life sophisticates them more quickly; television brings into their homes worlds of experience that would otherwise remain alien to them. Young people, then, are faced not only with the ambiguity of the adolescent role itself and its prolongation but with forces and conditions that, at least in some ways, make for *earlier* maturity. The youthful population is a potentially explosive stratum because this society is ill-equipped to accommodate it within the status system.

Erik Erikson's well-known theory of the "psychosocial moratorium" of adolescence takes the facts of adolescent prolongation and transforms them into a triumph of civilization. By emphasizing the increased time provided for young persons to postpone commitments, to try on social roles and to play the game called "the search for identity," Erikson suggests that the moratorium on lasting adult responsibilities contributes to the development and elaboration of personal individuality. I have no wish to quarrel with Erikson's general thesis here; I have done so elsewhere. Instead, I want to emphasize a fact that is seemingly contradictory to Erikson's observations about the moratorium on adult commitments. Namely, there have actually been increasing and clearly documented pressures on young people for earlier and earlier occupational planning and choice. "Benjamin," ask that famous Graduate's parents repeatedly, "what are you going to *do*? " And the question is echoed by millions of

prosperous American parents who, despite their af-
fluence, cannot assure the future economic position
of their heirs.

Logically, of course, prolonged identity play and
early occupational choice cannot be encouraged at
the same time; the fact is, they are. And like other
ambiguous values (and most moral values are ambiguous, or can be made so), this pair permit different groups of youngsters to rationalize or justify
the kinds of adaptations that differing circumstances in fact constrain them to make. The public
attention generated by protesting youth in recent
years (hippies, the New Left, black militants) ob-
scures the fact that the majority of young people are
still apparently able to tolerate the tensions of prolonged adolescence, to adjust to the adolescent role
(primarily, student), to take some satisfaction from
the gains it provides in irresponsibility (i.e., "freedom") and to sail smoothly through high school into
college where they choose the majors, get the
grades and eventually the certifications for the occupations which they want, which want them, and
which higher education is equipped to provide
them—degrees in education, business, engineering,
dentistry, and so on.

For others, however, the search for identity
(quote, unquote) functions as a substitute for an occupational orientation; it gives them something
"serious" to do while coping with their problems of
sex, education, family, and career. In college most
of these people tend to major in the humanities or
social sciences (particularly sociology) where they
may take 10 years or more between the time they

enter as freshmen, drop out, return, graduate and go on to pursue graduate degrees or give up on them entirely. I will return to this matter, but for the moment I want to make two general points: (1) that the contradictions create understandable tensions in the young and feed their appetite to discover "hypocrisy" in their elders; (2) that this condition is largely beyond the control of the universities; it is generated by the exigencies of a "postindustrial" society which uses institutions of higher education as warehouses for the temporary storage of a population it knows not what else to do with.

The situation has become critical over the past 10 years because the enormous numbers of the young (even small percentages of which yield formidable numbers of troops for worthy causes) and their concentration (in schools and cities) have promoted easy communication and a sense of group solidarity among them. Numbers, concentration, and communication regarding common grievances have made increasingly viable, in almost precisely the way in which Karl Marx described the development of class consciousness among workers, the creation and maintenance of "deviant subcultures" of youth.

This youthful population is "available" for recruitment to moral causes because their marginal, ambiguous position in the social structure renders them sensitive to moral inconsistencies (note their talent for perceiving "hypocrisy"), because the major framework of their experience ("education") emphasizes "ideal" aspects of the culture and because their exclusion from adult responsibilities means that they are generally unrestrained by the

**The Adolescent
Meets the Bureaucracy**

institutional ties and commitments which normally function as a brake upon purely moral feeling; they also have the time for it.

The two great public issues of the decade (the Vietnam war and the rights of despised minorities) have been especially suited to enlist the militant predispositions of the young precisely because these issues are clearly moral issues. To take a strong "position" on these issues requires no great *expertise* or familiarity with arcane facts. And the moral fervor involved in taking such a position nicely reflects our traditional age-graded culture to the extent that it identifies virtue with "idealism," unspoiledness and innocence, precisely the qualities adults like to associate with the young.

It is almost as if the young, in the unconscious division of labor which occurs in all societies, were delegated the role of "moral organ" of society— what with all the grown-ups being too busy running the bureaucracies of the world (with their inevitable compromises, deals, gives and takes) to concern themselves with "ideals." This even makes a sort of good structural sense because the unanchored character of the young (that is, their relative unfetteredness to family, community, and career) fits them to perform their "ideal" functions—in the same sense and for the same reason that Plato denied normal family life to his philosopher-kings and the Roman Catholic Church denies it to their priests.

It is the combination of moral sensitivity and alienation that accounts both for the extreme juvenophile postures of moral critics like Edgar Frieden-

berg, Paul Goodman, and John Seeley (which sometimes reach the belief that the young are simply
better people than the old or middle-aged, and
hence even a belief in juvenocracy) and the fear of
and hostility toward militant youth by writers epi-
tomized by Lewis Feuer in his new book on student
movements. In the latter view, the idealism of the
young becomes corrupt, violent, terroristic, and destructive precisely because, alienated, detached
from institutions, youth are not "responsible"—that
is, not accountable for the consequences of their
moral zealotry upon the groups and organizations
affected by it.

So one is tempted to say that society may just
have to accept youth's irresponsibility if it values
their moral contributions. But evidence suggests
that adult society is in general sympathetic neither
to their moral proddings nor toward granting the
young any greater responsibility in public affairs.
Research by English sociologist Frank Musgrove
clearly documents that adults are unwilling to grant
real responsibilities any earlier to the young, and
there is good reason to believe the same is true in
the United States, as is suggested by the repeated
failures of the movement to lower the voting age to
18. And as for the "idealism" of youth, when it goes
beyond the innocent virtues of praising honesty,
being loyal, true, and brave and helping old ladies
across the street, to serious moral involvements promoting their own group interests ("student power")
or those of the domestic or "third world" dispos-
sessed, the shine of their "idealism" is likely to tar-
nish rather quickly.

The Adolescent
Meets the Bureaucracy

Moreover, the moral activism of youth *is* sometimes vulnerable to attack on several counts. The "morality" of a political action, for example, is weakened when it has a self-congratulatory character (and the tendency to produce a holier-than-thou vanity in the actor). It also loses something when it does not involve substantial risk of personal interests or freedom (as it unambiguously *does* with the young only in the case of draft resisters). In the end, along with the society's prolongation of adolescence and encouragement of "the search for identity," continuing praise of the young for their "idealism" (except when it becomes serious) and continuing appeals to them to behave "responsibly"—in the face of repeated refusal to grant them real responsibilities (except in war)—are understandable as parts of the cultural armory supporting the process of juvenilization.

Colleges, universities, and their environs are the places apparently designated by society as the primary locations where this armory is to be expended. It is clear that the schools, particularly institutions of higher learning, are increasingly being asked by society to perform a kind of holding operation for it. The major propaganda campaign to encourage students not to drop out of high school is significant less for the jobs which staying that last year or two in high school will qualify one for than it is for the reduced pressure it creates on labor markets unable to absorb unskilled 16- and 17-year-olds. The military institutions, through the draft, help store (and train) much of the working-class young, and the colleges and universities prepare many of the heirs of the middle classes for careers in business, the professions, and the semiprofessions. But higher education also gets the lion's share of the identity seekers: those sensitive children of the affluent, less interested in preparing themselves for occupations which the universities are competent to prepare them for than in transcending or trading in the stigmata of their bourgeois backgrounds (work ethic, money-grubbing, status-seeking) for a more "meaningful" life.

It is these students who are heavily represented among the student activists and among whom the cry for "relevance" is heard most insistently. Does it seem odd that this cry should be coming from those students who are least interested in the curricula whose relevance is palpable, at least with respect to occupations? Not if one observes that many of these students are, in a sense, classically "intellectuals"—that is, oriented toward statuses or positions for which the universities (as well as other major institutions) have seldom been able to competently provide certification.

The statuses such students want are those to which one appoints oneself or which one drifts into: artist, critic, writer, intellectual, journalist, revolutionist, philosopher. And these statuses have been undermined for two generations or more by technical and bureaucratic élites whose training has become increasingly specialized and "scientific." In this context the cry for relevance is a protest against technical, value-neutral education whose product (salable skills or the posture of uncommitment) contributes nothing to the search by these students for "identity" and "meaningful experience."

Adding final insult to the injury of the threatened replacement of traditional humanistic intellectuals by technical élites is the ironic transformation of some of their traditional curricula (social sciences particularly) into instruments useful to the "power structure" or "the establishment" in pursuing its own ends. It makes no sense to call a curriculum "irrelevant" and then to turn right around and accuse its chief practitioners of "selling out"; the powerful do not squander their money so easily. The ironic point, then, is not that these curricula are "irrelevant" but that they are far *too* relevant to the support of interests to which the Left is opposed.

The villains here are the methodological orthodoxies of the social sciences: their commitment to objectivity, detachment and the "separation" between facts and values. In the view of radical students, these orthodoxies rationalize the official diffidence of social scientists regarding the social consequences of their research, a diffidence which (conveniently—and profitably—for social scientists, goes the argument) promotes the interests of the established and the powerful. This is far from the whole truth, of course. There is plenty of research, supported by establishments, whose results offer the establishment little comfort. But like other "nonpartisan" or value-neutral practices and procedures, the methodological orthodoxies of the social sciences do tend in general to support established interests, simply because the powerful, in command of greater resources and facilities, are better able to make use of "facts" than the weak, and because avoidance of ideological controversy tends to perpetuate the inequities of the status quo.

But the demands for a more activist and "committed" social science and for social scientists to function as advocates for oppressed and subordinated groups may not be the best way of correcting the inequities. A thorough *doctrinal* politicization of social science in the university is likely to mean the total loss of whatever little insulation remains against the ideological controversies rending the larger society; and the probable result would be that the university, instead of being more liberal than the society as a whole, would more accurately reflect the still-burgeoning reactionary mood of the country.

For students who tend to be "around" a university for a long time—the 10-year period mentioned earlier is not uncommon—the university tends to become a kind of "home territory," the place where they really live. They experience the university less as an élite training institution than as a political community in which "members" have a kind of quasi-"citizenship" which, if one believes in democratic process, means a right to a legitimate political voice in its government.*

This conception of the university is quite discrepant with the conception held by most faculty

* Much remains to be clarified about the nature of "membership" in academic communities. So much cant has gone down in the name of "community" that I often feel about this word much like that Nazi who has gone down in history as having said, "When I hear the word 'culture,' I reach for my revolver."

**The Adolescent
Meets the Bureaucracy**

members and administrators. To most faculty members the university is the élite training institution to which students who are both willing and able come to absorb intellectual disciplines— "ologies"—taught by skilled and certified professionals whose competences are defined by and limited to those certifications. But which way one sees the university—as a political community or as an élite training institution—is not purely a matter of ideological preference.

The fact seems to be that where training and certification and performance in politically neutral skills are clearest, the more conservative view is virtually unchallenged. This is true not only for dentistry and mathematics but for athletics, too. Presumably many militant blacks are not for any kind of a quota system with respect to varsity teams, and presumably football players in the huddle do not demand a voice in the decisions that shape their lives. But where what one's education confers upon one is a smattering of "high culture" or "civilized manners" or the detached sensibility and ethics of a science whose benefits, like other wealth, are not equitably distributed—in short, where the main result of liberal education is *Weltanschauung*—it indeed has "political" consequences.

These consequences were not controversial so long as the culture of the university was fairly homogeneous and so long as the "aliens" it admitted were eager to absorb that culture. They have become controversial in recent years because the democratization of higher education has revealed the "class" character of academic culture and because

The Problems of
American Education

of the appearance on the campus of students who do not share and/or do not aspire to that culture. These newcomers have arrived in sufficiently large numbers to mount a serious challenge to the hegemony of traditional academic culture.

Despite their many differences, the new militant "ethnic" students and their supporters among "white radicals," "street people," hippies, and other young people on the left have in common their antiacademicism, which is the campus version of the antiestablishment outlook. This is true notwithstanding the fact that the academy has been the most liberal sector of establishment thought and the most sympathetic to at least some of the aspirations of dissident students. Partly, of course, their hostility to the academy is rooted in the fact that the university is where they're at, the institutional location in which they have to work through their prolonged adolescence and the problems associated with it. But beyond this, there is real conflict between the traditional criteria of academic performance and what dissident students demand from academic life.

Research suggests that most of the white radical students have grown up in a milieu where "intellectual" matters were discussed, where books were probably present in their homes, where middle-class manners and style were their birthright, and where, therefore, they learned how to "talk"—that is, where they developed the sort of verbal facility enabling them to do well enough in high school and to seem like promising "college material" if only because they look and sound much like college students have always looked and sounded. With the ascendence of the view that everybody has a right to a higher education (along with the fact that there's no place else to send well-born adolescents), most of them wind up in colleges and universities.

Some of them, despite their verbal facility, are not really bright; many others, despite their ability to get good college grades, strongly resist "conforming" to many of the requirements for professional certification which they demean as mere "socialization." Confronted by academic demands for rigor in their thinking, for sufficient discipline to master a systematic body of knowledge, for evidence that they can maintain a line of logical thinking beyond one of two propositions, and bring evidence systematically to bear upon a problem, many of them are found seriously wanting—some because they are not bright enough, others because they think it a point of honor to resist the intellectual demands made on them.

When their numbers are large enough to enable them to turn to each other for mutual support, it is not surprising that they should collectively turn against the system of criteria which derogates them and, in a manner not unanalogous to the "reaction formation" of slum delinquents who develop a subculture in opposition to middle-class school norms which judge them inadequate, develop an antiacademic viewpoint which defines abstraction, logical order, detachment, objectivity, and systematic thinking as the cognitive armory of a repressive society, productive of alienation, personal rigidity, and truncated capacity for feeling.

Preoccupied as most of these students are with

"identity problems" and moral protest, it is again not surprising that many of them should be less interested in the mastery of academic disciplines, even if they have the ability, than in pursuing what they are likely to call "gut-issues" or nitty-gritty. The kinds of problems they apparently are interested in studying can be inferred from the examination of almost any "Free University" brochure, and what these add up to is a sort of extension division for the underground: practical, topical "rap sessions" on Vietnam, civil rights, encounter groups, pottery, psychedelics, macrobiotics, Eastern religion, rock music, and so on.

In the conflict with the established interests of science and scholarship in the university, radical students do win significant victories. New courses do get approved; experimental curricula do get tried out; students do get appointed to important committees; greater weight is attached to teaching in the appointment and promotion of faculty members. But large numbers of these radical students, exhausted by conflict and depressed by negative criticism, drop out of school. In dropping out, however, they do not immediately disappear into the labor market. They tend to remain in the university community, employed occasionally or part time in dead-end jobs, living in furnished rooms or communal houses near the university, and most important for my purposes here, still participating in the marginal student culture which they know so well.

Their participation in this culture is made possible to some extent by the fact that their youth protects them from the degrading consequences of

being poor and having no regular or "approved" status in the community. Part of the age-grading system which postpones adulthood is the temporary protection of the young against the stigmata which, for older people, are normally attached to poverty. But over time, this group of "nonstudents" can be regarded as downward mobile, and thereby hangs an interesting prospect.

The United States has no major tradition of large-scale downward mobility. The only major image of intergenerational decline is associated with decadent aristocratic families in ruined Southern mansions. Given the general tendency for downwardly mobile groups to resent the system which derogates them, and given the fact that the channels of upward mobility today are largely through higher education, the hostility to the university of these radical, middle-class "nonstudents" is probably maintained even after they leave it. The irony is that in dropping out, the hippie and New Left children of the middle classes provide opportunity for the upward mobility of the new black and other ambitious "disadvantaged" students.

The blacks and other ethnic militants are presently using higher education in a manner different from that in which their predecessors from the lower class used it. For earlier ethnics, the university served as a channel of mobility for *individuals* from the talented poor; today, it is sought as a means of collective mobility. There are two aspects to this movement. There is the emphasis on ethnic studies programs designed to provide the members of the respective ethnic groups with a sense of pride in

their history and culture, and there are the demands
that the university play a more active role in ame-
liorating suffering in the ghettos, not merely
through programs of research which exploit the cooperation of ghetto residents without helping them
measurably, but by taking the university off the
campus, bringing it to them, in their terms, on their
turf, for their own purposes.

In the struggle to achieve the ends of the militants, black and white, the traditional university is
very vulnerable because the militants have great le-
verage. Just as the blacks can conceivably turn the
urban core into a guerrilla battleground, militant
students can bring the universities to the proverbial
grinding halt. Continual rallies, classroom disruptions, picket lines, building seizures, student intim-
idation, and general paranoia (to say nothing of the
almost continual meetings by faculty and administration committees to cope with the crises and the
continual corridor and coffee room gossip by knots
of faculty members) can bring the teaching and
other academic functions of the university to a virtual standstill.

This prospect raises seriously for the first time the
question of whether the traditional university, as
we know it, is an expendable institution. And another question, as well: Is it possible that a decision
has been made somewhere that it is better to risk
the destruction of the university by confining the
unrest to the campus than to allow it to spill over
into more critical institutions? Pickets, sit-ins,
building seizures and nonnegotiable demands are
one thing on the campuses. Imagine them at C.B.S.

**The Adolescent
Meets the Bureaucracy**

on Madison Avenue: no TV until S.D.S. gets equal time; at the Stock Exchange: the ticker tape does not roll until corporation X gets rid of its South African holdings; at the headquarters of the Bank of America: no depositors get through the doors until interest-free loans are made to renovate the ghettos. There would be machine guns in the streets in no time at all!

In 1969, despite the tear gas and the National Guard, it is still hard to imagine tanks and machine guns used against student radicals so long as their militance is confined to the campus. Because if they do close the universities down, exactly who would miss them? The most practical functions the university performs and its activities which are most directly relevant to the national economy (engineering, science, law, medicine, etc.) could be transferred to the private sector. The beginnings of such a transfer are apparent already in the educational functions carried on by private foundations, institutes, and industrial corporations.

And if the departments of English and history and political science and sociology and art and so on closed tight shut tomorrow, who would miss them? Aside from the implication of some social science departments in the military-industrial complex, the studies in humanities and social science departments are civilized luxuries with very few sources of government or business support. The student radicals have little sympathy for them and there is probably even less sympathy for them among the students' severest critics. These days, even conservative legislators, in the same breath that they denounce student militance, will quickly add, "Of course, this doesn't mean that there isn't plenty wrong with the university; there is." And if the student revolution can be bought off by substituting Bob Dylan for Dylan Thomas, McLuhan for Freud, Marcuse for Plato, rock for Bach, black culture for Greek culture, rap sessions for formal examinations, how many will care? Who needs high culture anyway? For the radicals it's an instrument of class oppression, and their oppressors, at least in America, have never been too keen on it anyway, except as a tax dodge.

Short of machine guns in the streets and outright revolution, what one can expect to see over the next decade in academic life is greater adaptation by the university to the new kinds of students it must serve and to the new publics whose anticipated support or hostility it must take into account in its planning. By the new students I mean ghetto youth, middle-class white radicals, and the identity seekers. By the new publics I mean those millions of citizens whose taxes support the great state universities but who never thought of the university as "theirs" until its politicization encouraged ambitious politicians to call this fact to their attention. Having once been reminded (by Governor Reagan and others), the voters are not likely to forget it soon.

If it comes about, this adaptation is likely to occur in a manner not dissimilar to that in which the major political parties have adapted to third-party movements in the larger political community: by isolating the *most* radical through the adoption of some of their programs and demands, while at the same

The Adolescent
Meets the Bureaucracy

130

time adopting severe and punitive policies toward
the more intransigent and violence-prone who are
still unsatisfied.

For ghetto youth, then, there will be more ethnic
studies programs and compensatory admissions and
grading policies and practices and more energetic
recruiting of ethnic students and faculty. But there
will be less indecision or tolerance in the handling
of sit-ins, seizures, and other disruptions. For the
radicals (ethnic as well as middle-class white), there
will be greater emphasis on programs granting academic credit for extension-type activities such as tutoring of ghetto children, neighborhood seminars
on consumer savvy, and community organization.
For the identity seekers there will be more encounter groups, more classes emphasizing
"openness and honesty" in dialogue, more experiments with less structured curricula and residential
communities, more "retreats," more student-ini-
tiated courses on subjects which engage their sense
of "relevance" to their interests, from sex to drugs to
rock. For all, there will be further loosening of the
in loco parentis restrictions which hardly anybody
in the university believes in anymore, and a little
more student power (at least influence) on faculty
and administrative committees. All this, combined
with a more effective public-relations campaign explaining the mission of the university and its problems in coping with the consequences of prolonged
adolescence, may just bring about a semblance of
peace on the campus. But without peace in Vietnam, it will be an uneasy peace at best.

There will be opposition. Academic conservatives will see in these new programs the prospect of the dilution or outright abandonment of traditional standards of scholarship. The legitimization of ethnicity, the amelioration of suffering by the poor, and the search for identity by the young may all be noble endeavors, they will say, but the major functions of the university are the creation and transmission of systematic bodies of abstract knowledge. Political conservatives will see in these programs harbingers of social changes which they oppose. Militant students imply more leaders and troops for restive ghettos; "the search for identity" and the self-exploratory activities the phrase suggests are redolent of the "liberalism," "permissiveness," and self-indulgence offensive to the traditional Protestant ethic which "made this country great."

Yet academic conservatives might well be reminded that the university is facing radically transformed constituencies, that academic disciplines which are well institutionalized and "traditional" today were themselves academically born in the blood of earlier periods of such transformations and that they were initially opposed by still more "traditional" fields. Political conservatives might well be reminded that student unrest was not invented by outside agitators, that its source is in social conditions conservatives affirm, and that it is not repressible short of military measures. The alternatives to the adaptable university involves blood on the quad and an expendable university.

The joys and terrors of sending the kids to college

HARVEY SWADOS

We live in a time in which irony, once the prerogative of poets and professors, has become the daily fare of ordinary middle-class folks. Saving up to buy a better car, they find themselves contributing to pollution and congestion. With the car in the garage, the husband moonlights and the wife goes back to work in order to be able to send the kids off to college in style—only to discover that to the children this culmination of their parents' working lives is hardly worthy of all that anxious sweat. For the children it is seen all too often not as a deliverance but rather as one more barrier to deliverance.

For both generations, hope is mixed with fear. No matter how tough the talk, the children are no less romantic than any earlier group of students who said good-by to their parents and went off to college. At the same time, they are probably more fearful (though they may repress it) than earlier generations of American students. The war drags on, the draft drags on—and now there is not even the certainty that a decent job will be waiting for the girl who majors in English or the boy who majors in physics. How do they explain this to their parents— to say nothing of their perception that if indeed all the old preliminaries won't lead to all the old payoffs, then the preliminaries themselves may be as pathetically out of date as everything else that they have left behind?

The parents may be sophisticated enough to discuss objectively this transitional period (or revolutionary era, if that language is better) between one kind of education and another. But they still find it hard to cope with the concept of college not as an opportunity but a disappointment, not as a magic pathway to professional or marital success but a staging area for hostile, aggressive demonstrations of contempt for the old, married, the professional.

In both generations, it seems to me, the disappointment—what a poor summation of all those tears, shouts, threats, curses, recriminations!— stems from an overvaluing of the idea of a university. With every passing semester the middle-class idea of a university bears less and less relation to reality. The working-class idea of college education as a passport from poverty to professionalism, or more modestly to a better life than that lived by service-station fathers and dressmaker mothers, is more in keeping with current reality to families involved for the first time with the college experience.

But euphoria about the network of mass higher-education institutions now coming into being cannot in itself overshadow, much less overcome, the agonizing uncertainty, the rankling shame, of frightened college-educated parents, or of their children in collision with the traditional liberal-arts colleges and the great state universities. It does not follow that the solid (and supposedly stolid) majority ought to be urged to take pity on those a rung or two higher on the ladder—all of us are swaying more or less precariously on that same ladder.

To be sure, those who make manifest their disappointment, in some cases their despair, are only a small fraction of the masses of students one sees quietly going about their business. It does not follow that they are utterly unrepresentative, as flash disorders on a dozen campuses should have proved to us. On a more personal level, the college writing courses I have been teaching for a number of years have attracted only a tiny percentage—a fringe group, one might say—of the student body. Yet certain themes have appeared in their apprentice stories so consistently that I have to think of them as expressing attitudes not confined to would-be writers, but widespread among middle-class American youth in general.

One of those themes, often in the context of an athletic event, or a hunting/fishing trip, has been the discovery of the vulnerability or fallibility of the writer's father (suddenly it is seen that he is not heroic but cowardly, not cool but hotheaded, not masterful but uncertain). Stories of this kind were submitted to me with such predictable regularity over the years, by students on both coasts as well as in midland America, that I had to think of them as stating—whether badly or well—a national response in ritualistic form to the passage from childhood to adulthood.

It is curious and interesting that in the last year or two I have found such tales being supplemented, if not supplanted, by stories which portray the professor rather than the parent as a sorry figure—a beard tugger, a nose picker, a pompous strutting poseur who loves himself for what he does without ever realizing that he does it badly.

We need hardly interpret these efforts to mean that all college students hate or despise their teachers. But their appearance does justify the suspicion that there is a certain relation between one disillusionment and another on the part of those at least attempting to articulate their reactions on paper.

If we are to make anything of the depth of the disillusionment, we have to examine the question of overvaluation of the university. From every direction high-school students are bombarded with advice and warnings about "getting accepted by a good school," or just "getting into college." Principals, teachers, guidance counselors all gang up on the adolescent, using the distant, undefined dream place as a combination carrot and stick with which to keep him in line during the difficult secondary-school years.

At home, the pressures are even greater. Fathers and mothers who, like all veterans, tend to glamorize those hazy days between childhood chores and adult obligations, can hardly be casual about whether or not their own offspring are going to be accepted at a college that will open doors—to profitable friendships and associations, to matrimony, or to yet further schooling at professional institutions. No matter how they try to underplay it, they can hardly help but communicate their own anxiety to their children.

Step one: "Why not apply to Siwash, what can you lose?"

Step two: "We can take a drive out there if you want, O.K.?"

Step three: "I know it's a drag, filling out those forms, but there are certain things in this world that you just have to do if. . . ."

If what? "If I want my freedom," the high-school senior has to say to himself. At this stage of the game, freedom means escape from a stifling collection of obstacles: the single building in which he has moved for years from one cube to another by the numbers and by the bells; the home in which he cannot experiment freely, smoking this or drinking that as adults do, or even enter and exit without producing a lie by way of explanation; and the parents who smother him with love and anxiety—or distrust and anxiety—at precisely the point in time when his whole being craves liberation.

Given all that, it is truly remarkable that so few college freshmen, shocked at discovering how narrow is the gap between that hideously boring and impatience-making high-school senior year and that routinized and get-it-over-with college freshman year, toss the whole thing aside. One has to suspect that many more would if it were not for twin forces of fear and guilt. Rebellious as most middle-class youths are at that age, their sense of obligation and their gratitude for parental sacrifice simply outweigh rebelliousness.

To the parents sitting at home and worrying, it is inconceivable that their child, having gained the promised land, can be so quickly disillusioned.

Step one: "Give it a chance!"

Step two: "Where else do you think it will be any better?"

Step three: "For God's sake, what do you want?"

Caught between wanting and fearing, between eagerness for the student to stay on and do the right thing (make the dean's list, meet nice boys) and fear lest in staying on he do the wrong thing (make bombs, marry a black), only the most tight-lipped parents can keep from adding an all but unbearable burden of guilt to the undergraduate's confusions. So they socialize with family and friends, hiding the tears and presenting smiling faces to those who ask after the absent child.

Step one: "Believe it or not, he's still at school. But he's switched his major from physics to pottery."

Step two: "He's going with a lovely black girl, but I'm afraid her parents disapprove."

Step three: "The school was just too impersonal. He's gone to Istanbul to find himself."

It is really not funny, not any of it. Neither parent nor student can be any more than dimly aware of the other's anguish. For the student, what he finds at the university is simply not different enough from what he had shuffled through at home and in high

**The Adolescent
Meets the Bureaucracy**

school. Surrounded on all sides by appeals and as-
surances of instant gratification (Freedom Now,
Peace Now, Fly Now, Buy Now), he discovers at the
university one more set of barriers and postpone-
ments all too like those he had supposedly graduated from back in the living room and the school
homeroom. He has to "get through" the freshman
year, the way he somehow "got through" the senior
year, in order to be able to sample the courses he
had hoped to taste from the tempting smorgasbord
of the catalogue. He has to be able to "get through"
the upper-class years in order to earn the forms to
fill out for graduate school. And then.

How can the parent, terrified lest his best-loved
founder on the ugly reefs of shiftlessness, dope, violence, present the calmly reassuring receptivity
which will encourage confidences and consulta-
tions on the part of his offspring? On all sides the
horror stories multiply: The friend who has to enlist
the aid of a psychiatrist to reclaim his flipped-out
son from a psycho ward; the relative who has to post
bond for his boy, busted not for using but for pushing; the neighbor who has to suffer his daughter's
stuck-out tongue when he comes upon her copulat-
ing on the greasy garage floor with a motorcyclist
who has been forbidden inside the house.

The hatred of such parents for their children, the
boundless and endless depths of the humiliation,
can only be guessed at. And no one can measure the
expense of spirit for those who grit their teeth and
hang on, swearing to themselves that they will not
play the recrimination game but will keep the door
open for the kids. Nor can anyone calculate who

hates the kids more—the outraged grand jurors of middle America who would hold college students responsible for everything that is happening, up to and including their own accidental deaths, or the liberal parents who regard their children as rotten betrayers of a trust.

Step one: "I don't give a damn if he never shows his face in my house again."

Step two: "I told my wife, if she sends that bastard one more dime, we're through."

Step three: "I'm not going to ruin my life because he's ruined his."

Is there any way out? Advice to tortured students and tormented parents from the kindly and well-meaning, no matter how learned or how gentle will seldom suffice. Nor will the testimony of the lucky ones—those who did not have to hunt for themselves in Eilat or Katmandu, but found themselves early in biochemistry, music, math, or law—explain or simplify for those less lucky. The wise parents would seem to be those who admit that *they* have been lucky—and vice versa.

Even as the young grow more sophisticated and the old more naïve, the emotional problems of both would seem to persist. The agony, one suspects, will go on until there is general recognition on all sides that education must be not a series of rituals but a process. This may sound excessively abstract and unhelpful; we have to spell it out in more precise terms.

No malign enemy lurks at the college gates, waiting to pounce on the unsullied young as they present themselves for processing. The bogies of

The Adolescent
Meets the Bureaucracy

corrupting companions (those "others" always responsible for introducing one's kids to drugs, sex, kooky politics) and upsetting ideas (contempt for culture, compassion for criminals but not for parents, aversion to mental discipline) do not suddenly materialize from nowhere on college campuses. They have been there all along, throughout high school and even junior high, and the sooner parents who have been too harried or too frightened to concede this face up to it, the better equipped they will be to cope with the bizarre misbehavior of the college generation.

What is shocking for the freshman is not the sudden contact with all those strange stimulants. It is rather the discovery that the liberation from education as ritual into education as process is simply not taking place; once more it is to be postponed, pushed off. Despite everything that has been done to them, despite everything that they have been exposed to, from the White House to the homeroom to the TV room, most students are idealistic when they begin college. But how much hypocrisy can they be expected to endure?

"We never even thought of dropping out when we went to college." Perfectly true. But those fortunate enough to have attended college 20 or 30 years ago were part of an elite that, rebellious or not, accepted certain notions about college education which no longer seem useful or valid. The life of the mind, the commitment to a world not bounded by moneygrubbing, and illuminated by art—these things were inextricably linked in our conscious-

The Problems of
American Education

ness with a college education and a continuing faith in ideas and the power of learning.

When I came home from college and accompanied my father on his endless general practitioner's rounds, I took it for granted that on Friday afternoons his call included a visit to the seminar where he tried to keep up with new developments in his field. And that, during a period when older men were still looked upon as repositories of accumulated wisdom, hardly in need of instruction from younger men.

Parents really ought to acknowledge to themselves and to their children that education is not something that is done to you for eight years, then four, then four more, followed by graduate or professional school, the name plate, and the long, slow decline. The very acknowledgment could be a first step toward destroying that great, ugly reef of hypocrisy on which mutual love and trust seem to founder.

If they do not make such acknowledgment, it is going to be made for them in any case by the inexorable working of our peculiar economic order. The market is now glutted in various fields with Ph.D.'s who cannot compete with young (and cheaper) M.A.'s. The Ph.D., which used to be the next best thing to an M.D., is now an absolute hindrance to success or even to making a living in particular areas and has to be supplemented by ongoing retraining and reeducation in order that the holder not be stranded like a beached whale, hugely overspecialized for an inhospitable environment.

**The Adolescent
Meets the Bureaucracy**

142

How many middle-class parents are now talking
about education with their children in these terms?
How many are anticipating the inevitable questions
and recriminations either by confessing that they
themselves stopped learning at the age of 22 and are
therefore suffering from a trained incapacity to
adapt to change, or by explaining that they are indeed making a personal effort to become reinvolved
with education on an indefinitely continuing basis?

How many are now ready to concede practically
that it makes no sense to demand of their children
what they themselves recognize intellectually as
obsolescent, the 8-4-4-professional-school lockstep?
How many discuss learning with them not as something one buys for protection against recession or
catastrophe, like life insurance, but as an integral
part of the life of everyone resisting stagnation?

Just about the best classes in which I have ever
been privileged to participate as a teacher have
been those seminars in which there was a mix not
only of sex and race but of age as well. In schools
with such diverse educational philosophies as
Sarah Lawrence, San Francisco State, and Columbia, I have learned from students who were 15 years
my junior and 15 years my senior, and they in turn
have learned from one another, in an atmosphere
free of rancor and recrimination. I cannot remember
taunts from the young or sneers from the old in any
of these situations; what I recall instead is the
heightened eagerness of the young to explain themselves and their perceptions to their elders, and the
relaxed calm of the older people when they spoke
from experience to those whom they did not feel

obliged to lecture or to hector. I have no way of proving it, but I do have a strong hunch that, after engaging at school in dialogues that were often peppery and pointed but never uncivil, the great majority of those seminar participants were far less ready to revert to confrontation language at home.

This is not to say that a simple solution to the problem of mutual mistrust lies readily at hand in some form of highbrow togetherness, or academically sponsored sensitivity sessions. But surely we are entitled to suspect that steps toward breaking down the compartmentalization of school and home, and ending the daily more meaningless distinction between "education" and "life," will serve to ameliorate the anguish now being suffered by both generations. The undergraduate who listens to the voice of a 45-year-old fellow student formulating a classroom comment (whether in marine biology, family structure, or Greek drama) will be less likely to insist on abandoning his quest of "the piece of paper" when he is three or six or nine credits short of what the older person physically demonstrates is valuable. And he will be pressed to explain why that abandonment in favor of producing leather belts or braided vests or handmade candles is not merely harmless or even "touching," but an acceptable application of his abilities when so many problems cry out for resolution by well-trained minds.

The same should hold true for the father who responds to his daughter's announcement that she does not wish to take stupefyingly boring education courses just because they are practical by warning her, "I've got too much invested in you in terms of time and money and worry to let you go ahead and do what you want to do!"

The girl who reported just that threat to me the other day added sadly, "It'll be all right; my parents are intelligent people and I love them but I do wish we didn't have to go through all this misery."

So do we all. And the final irony may be that solutions may be provided, not directly but as a by-product to the social necessity of sending obsolescent aerospace engineers and "defense" technicians back to school. Students who discover that they cannot count on eternally affluent parents to support basically self-indulgent life-styles, parents who discover that certificates of being educated are not equivalent to stock certificates or annuities, will be forced to confront each other's counterclaims more realistically.

While it has been true that the middle class is the pattern setter, we may discover in the years immediately ahead that the pressures of the underlying population for higher education (parallel to earlier pressures for decent wages, hours, and working conditions) may once again force the middle class to reevaluate its own patterns of behavior, within the family unit and also in the larger social context. The response to those pressures in our urban centers and industrial states, in the form of proliferating open-admission colleges of every conceivable sort, is already altering the expectations of middle-class people. Wives and mothers anxious for liberation (or at least larger horizons), ex-college students looking for less hysterically demanding learning situations than those prevalent in highly competitive schools, engineers and technicians phased out by the shift in national priorities—all are finding their way to the burgeoning neighborhood, storefront, municipal, and state colleges.

Even the junior academics, so recently discontented students themselves, are beginning to view these new schools not merely as rungs on the ladder leading to traditional intellectual strongholds but as exciting (if terrifyingly confusing and at times disheartening) centers of democratic experimentalism. Despite their lack of marching bands, sorority houses, halls of ivy, sedate research professors, and great libraries, that is where people are heading, and that can be where not only liberal-arts colleges and state universities may find new sources of life but where parents and children may start to find each other again.

Close to midnight
for the New York schools

MARTIN MAYER

Up close, meeting with individual teachers and
school principals and looking in on classes, an observer can feel a degree of optimism about the future of the New York City schools. The human resources of the city are unrivaled anywhere in the
world. The very turbulence of New York, its varieties of culture in swirling diffusion, its bright incen-
tives to ambition, keep the schools from the leaden
repetitiousness that is death to education. In every
building, there are at least a few teachers and a few
more children whose performance is so unexpected,
so intelligently original, that the heart sings
with hope. In the ethos of the institution, too, there
is a tradition of success, for these are the schools
that took the children of illiterate immigrants and
made them the leaders of a city. And the financial
support is nothing less than magnificent. No other
sizable city in America spends as much as 70 per-

cent of what New York City spends per pupil, and, despite all the propaganda to the contrary, only a few suburbs spend more.

Once the observer leaves the individual school, however, the situation looks quite hopeless. As the State Education Department documented in a report issued three years ago (but never printed, though the city had promised to do so), the average level of accomplishment of New York City pupils has dropped substantially below that of the state as a whole. The fine corps of older teachers who arrived in the Depression years are nearing retirement age, and the better young teachers flee to the suburbs or leave teaching—nobody knows how many, because the system has never gathered together in one place its information on teacher turnover.

Public confidence in the school system is fearfully low and dropping: White children are leaving the city public schools at a rate of 40,000 a year (and the Allen Report, in a little-noticed passage, predicted by percentages a rate of 60,000 a year in the near future). Of the leaders of the school system itself—the nine-member Board of Education and the 20-odd deputy and associate superintendents—only a handful have children who attend or ever did attend a New York public school. Even worse, the Negro middle class has almost entirely disappeared. Of the Negro leaders of the integration drive, the Wilkinses and Clarks, the Farmers and Joneses and Rustins, the Youngs and Galamisons, not one has or has had a child in a New York public school. Superintendent Calvin Gross put his children in the public schools—but he was an outsider, and the insiders destroyed him.

Worst of all is the narrow bitterness that permeates an enterprise which rests, after all, on the belief in a promising future for the community's youth. The tradition of success is almost gone—in increasing numbers, teachers and principals live with the expectation of failure and weave a safety net of excuses. A junior-high principal gestured at an assembly of 900 Negro and Puerto Rican children and said, "We just have to accept the fact that half of these children will never hold a job in their lives."

All change is resisted because it implies a criticism of the present—and feared, because it will be made without consulting the teachers who will have to live with the results. The hope for leadership has been disappointed so often that people have turned in upon themselves, learned to live with meaningless and fantastically detailed rule books, lost any sense of the possibilities outside the narrow structure of the hierarchy of jobs.

To the outside world—and to many of its best teachers—the system turns a face of vanity, arrogance, self-absorption. Max Rubin once said that his worst moment as president of the Board of Education came when he told a group at school headquarters that the nation was being searched to find the best possible man to be New York's superintendent—and the headquarters staff booed him.

Yet there were literally tens of thousands of teachers and administrators in the New York schools who knew better than any outsider the need for change, and who waited for Gross with fanatical impatience. The real tragedy of Gross's collapse is not that of the man himself—though his dismissal was managed with maximum cruelty—but that of the many who warmly welcomed his arrival and watched in despair as he isolated himself from their warmth, refusing direct contact with anyone but the cold conspirators of the senior bureaucracy.

Symbolically, he ordered the superintendent's directives to the staff issued not over his name, as had been his predecessors' custom, but over that of his executive deputy. He had no information except headquarters information; and when the members of the Board decided to restore their old prerogative of employing personal assistants who could feed them other information, he made it a matter of professional pride that the Board should have no information except what he fed them—and, of course, what they read in the newspapers.

Among Gross's last acts was a memo to the Board replying to a complaint relayed by a local school-board chairman from a group of school principals who were miserable and furious about the newest revision of the sixth-grade reading test, which requires children to work with a confusing answer sheet ill-matched to the question page. Gross wrote that Dr. Joseph O. Loretan, formerly head of the junior high schools and now deputy superintendent in charge of curriculum, thought the test "represents the best and latest findings of research . . . nor is the answer sheet ill-matched to the question sheet"—which meant, to anyone who has seen the test, that Gross never looked at it. Neither, in all likelihood, did Dr. Loretan; the question was

The Adolescent
Meets the Bureaucracy

doubtless referred through channels to Dr. J. Wayne Wrightstone, head of the school system's test division, and one of the authors of the test in question.

But the Board itself had forced Gross to seek his support from his staff when it publicly and foolishly repudiated the reasonable if not brilliant "integration plan" the new superintendent submitted in December 1963. By plunging into the integration question as though it were merely a problem to be solved, the Board also made it impossible for anyone to say publicly what everyone close to the situation knew was true—that relatively little could, in fact, be done in terms of meaningful and useful integration for the majority of the city's Negro and Puerto Rican children.

Since then, discussion of the schools has been dominated by the unrealities of "policy" in a matter that should be and indeed is a secondary issue for both school people and parents—secondary not for lack of intrinsic importance, but by comparison with the basic meaning of ethnic difference in the New York schools. This central fact, which everyone knows but nobody seems to wish to discuss, is that by the age of 12 the average Negro or Puerto Rican child in the New York schools is more than two full years behind the average mainland white child in academic accomplishment. Though they constitute nearly half the population of the public schools, Negroes and Puerto Ricans account for only 3 percent of the students at the city's special-entrance college-preparatory high schools.

Given the present gap between mainland white

The Problems of
American Education

and "minority" children, large-scale integration in the *work* of the school is almost impossible and very likely undesirable. Indeed, it is difficult to fathom the thought processes of people who insist that there will be gains in the racial attitudes of white or the self-image of Negroes from daily experiences which visibly proclaim that dark-skinned children are "dumber" than pale-skinned children.

None of this defends segregation, which is evil in itself; nor does it defend the existence of segregated *white* schools, each of which represents a missed opportunity to experiment with education for Negro and Puerto Rican children in an atmosphere of higher expectation. It does mean, however, that normal parents of any color need not be racist to refuse to send their children into classes where the tone is set by the low expectations of the schools have derived from their experiences with "minority groups." Integration, in other words, is not a beautiful plant which flowers automatically in the sun of goodwill; the ground must be prepared, and very carefully prepared, first.

Unfortunately, integration is not at the moment what the real fuss is about. What agonizes the "minority group" parent and sends her onto a picket line is not a longing to see her child mix with white children but the fear that the unemployed and unemployable young bum on the corner looked 10 years ago just the way her child looks today. And the fear is justified—the road most Negro and Puerto Rican children are traveling in the New York schools leads only to unskilled manual labor or the gutter.

**The Adolescent
Meets the Bureaucracy**

Not long ago, many of us felt that a large share of
the Negro failure in the schools was itself the product of segregation; but almost nobody whose opinion is worth considering believes it today. Personally, I think that open enrollment did make
some positive difference in the accomplishment of
the Negro children who rode the buses—but I can't
prove it and neither can anyone else. The New York
system swims in research, useless statistics, and excessive documentation (copies of the Feinberg
Oath, disavowing Communism, must be held in the
files until the teacher's 80th birthday, etc.), but the
schools never kept for these children the kind of
records that would make strong assertions possible.

Giving open enrollment its maximum value, however, there can be no comparison between the results of this experiment and the apparent results of
the special programs introduced in quantity in all-
Negro schools in Washington, D.C., Chicago, St.
Louis, and Pittsburgh. Here there were significant
changes in educational philosophy or in the internal
structure of the school—"basic education" in Washington, ungraded classrooms and heavy doses of psychological pressure in Chicago and St. Louis, team
teaching in Pittsburgh.

I sympathize with the New York superintendents
who feel that the results achieved in these cities are
now more apparent than real. But in human events
appearances have an odd way of becoming real—
and, surely, apparent results are better than no results. In the face of devastating failure, major
changes must be better than the sort of surface tin-
kering which is all New York has done or plans to

do. Such administrative changes as the Allen plan, calling for 3- or 4-year "middle schools" between the primary schools and 4-year high schools are just new frames for the pictures, and the New York schools have shown an infinite capacity for putting the ugly old pictures into bright new frames.

Like the former Chinese gentry, New York school administrators are ranked in a rigid hierarchy of status, achieved through the passage of Confucian examinations which fail to measure either the intellectual or temperamental qualities needed for the jobs. We would almost certainly do better with tests of general intelligence and aptitude developed by an outside testing service. Such tests could be planned so nobody could coach for them (now a great waste of time for teachers and a great source of revenue for administrators), and could be given routinely to qualify teachers for promotions recommended by their colleagues and superiors (both should be required). By and large, today's top leadership is not well educated itself; its central beliefs deal not with education, but with schools.

Among the more instructive experiences from acquaintance with the New York schools is the occasional bull-session of old-timers, talking about the men who were superintendents when they first became teachers. I sat in on one of these shortly after the death of Deputy Superintendent Frederick Pertsch, and one phrase kept coming up in the conversation: "He was a scholar."

Let no one doubt the importance of quality in leadership, even in a city as big as New York. In a single year, Deputy Superintendent Eugene Hult,

The Adolescent
Meets the Bureaucracy

154

who took no exams, completely changed the tone
(and thus began to improve efficiency) of a construction division that had looked like a mare's nest.
Because there are no scholars, nobody has changed
the tone of the divisions of instruction, curriculum
and personnel, and as a result the schools are forever dealing with the set problems of the last generation, employing an unbelievably dogmatic and
doctrinaire approach to education.

Last year, for example, a new reading series by
Catharine Stern was tried out in individual classes
in several Harlem schools. Its success was remarkable—I saw very ordinary Negro children in crowded
classes reading at the end of the first grade with a
fluency rarely found in second grade in the city's
better neighborhoods. The district superintendent
and his reading supervisor, both of whom had
started off quite suspicious of the Stern textbooks,
requested permission to extend the use of the series
through the district—and permission was denied,
because Mrs. Stern's "structural" approach was
considered "artificial" in its insistence on linguistic
consistency and its introduction of words by groups
of identical phonetic structure (lend-bend-send,
etc.). Indeed, after its wholly satisfactory tryout the
series was denied admission to the New York City
"approved list" of textbooks, an almost totally unse-
lected collection of the conventional dregs of the
textbook industry.

The same "reading experts" have refused to approve the use of the Initial Teaching Alphabet
("ita") system, despite positive reports from some of
the best-controlled "research" that has been done

**The Problems of
American Education**

in education in recent times. Developed in Britain, thoroughly tested in Bethlehem, Pa., and adopted by a number of New York private schools, "ita" uses an expanded and redesigned alphabet to introduce the sounds of English on the printed page.

Personally, I don't like "ita" either, but it would never occur to me that a personal dislike for something was a reason to forbid teachers to try it. One sometimes wonders what superintendents (including Calvin Gross) really mean when they use the word "profession."

Because all changes must be trimmed to fit the existing system, efforts to reduce segregation or improve instruction in slum neighborhoods have often worsened the situation. A year ago, for example, with a burst of publicity, New York announced the abandonment of the group-I.Q. test, on the grounds that it was culture-biased and discriminated against Negroes. But the reading test that was substituted slots children almost exactly where they were in the abandoned I.Q. test—and what difference there is works against Negroes.

At the same time, because placement would now be by "objective" achievement rather than by I.Q., the elementary division sent out a circular urging that children be most strictly grouped according to their performance level. The real result of the acclaimed abandonment of the I.Q. test, then, is that Negro children in 1964–65 are more likely to be in the bottom classes of "integrated schools" than they were in 1963–64.

Seven or eight years ago, a study revealed that slum schools were heavy with substitute teachers;

and the administration forever seeking publicized justice, announced that in the future the proportion of regularly licensed and substitute teachers would have to be equal in all schools throughout the system. But this new rule could not be permitted to touch the old rule under which teachers transfer out to posts in other schools according to their seniority. "Regular" teachers are not necessarily experienced teachers—a senior at a New York City college can acquire a regular license on graduation. So the new rule in effect compelled the system to assign into the most difficult schools the brand new products of the colleges. And today the average teacher in Harlem or Bedford-Stuyvesant has less than two years' experience.

It is now proposed to remedy this tragedy by forcing experienced teachers in relatively comfortable posts to move into the slum schools—a procedure which would destroy the *esprit de corps* of the better schools (the only strength the system has), substituting the unspeakably low morale of the system as a whole.

Quite apart from the fact that this measure could be enforced only after a six-week strike had shut all the schools and broken the union, it is hard to see what advantage slum children would in fact receive from daily contact with embittered teachers who would quit instantly except that their heavy investment in the pension plan keeps them tied to the New York Board of Education.

Of all the proposals to bring more experienced teachers to ghetto classrooms, only one commands universal assent: voluntary rotation. There are a fair

number of teachers in the better neighborhood
schools who would be willing to take a year or two
in the slums, provided they could return at the end
of that period to more cheerful surroundings.

On the East Side last year, my local district proposed such a plan, but city headquarters ruled that
the union contract requires any vacant teaching
post in the city to be put up in a kind of auction, and
awarded automatically to the teacher with the highest seniority among those who request it. And a
teacher who voluntarily rotated out to a slum school
would by definition leave her old post vacant.

At least two of the three negotiators who put
together the union contract did not believe that
there is any such provision in it, and the inexperi-
enced observer might wonder why the school system would prefer a war over involuntary transfer to
approval of a voluntary plan. For anyone who has
lived with the New York schools, however, the answer is easy: mechanical transfer by directive cen-
tralizes all personnel decisions at headquarters,
while a voluntary rotation plan would permit initiative from the field. And the goal of the New York administrative apparatus (set up, to be fair, at a time
when the city had been scandalized by neighborhood corruption) is to assure maximum control
from the center.

Centralization is not necessarily evil in itself.
When there is general agreement on what should be
done, central authority may be the most efficient way
to put the work in motion. But education is not
usually like that; more often, it is like the Irish saying about the priest knowing his parish better than

The Adolescent
Meets the Bureaucracy

the Pope does. And in the matters that have been
destroying the morale of the New York schools, the
plain fact is that *nobody* really knows what should
be done.

The two currently fashionable solutions are brute
money and prekindergarten programs, and both are
certainly worth trying. What has made them fashionable, however, is their congruence with the existing system more than their intrinsic promise. The
More Effective Schools program, by providing class
sizes of 12 to 20 and four teachers for every three
classes, nearly doubled expenditures in the 10 elementary schools involved this year; but it was also
an administrative weapon for further centralization:
a separate headquarters staff was established to supervise just these schools. Average class size has already been reduced by five or six pupils in the New
York slum schools over the last six years, to exactly
no effect; and St. Louis with class sizes of 35 to 40
has accomplished more than New York with class
sizes of 25 to 30.

Teachers could and probably should be paid
more, though salaries are no longer a scandal. Despite universal belief to the contrary, the question is
not crucial in the budget—salaries for classroom
teachers take up less than 40 percent of what New
York spends on its schools, and every classroom
teacher could get a raise of $1,000 for a third of what
the Board of Education requested in additional
money this year, without provision for salary increases. (Unfortunately, state law does not permit
the city to increase teacher salaries without increasing administrators' salaries even more.) And new

school buildings should certainly be built, especially in the slums, though the rate of building, in Harlem particularly, is rather impressively high— and some of the newest buildings are the worst ratholes, while some of the old ones are better schools than most.

Prekindergarten is such an attractive idea from all approaches that one hates to speak slightingly of it. But the fact is that Negro and Puerto Rican white children start only slightly behind mainland white children, and drop back seriously between the third and fifth grades; Dr. Martin Deutsch whose prekindergarten program is by far the most highly developed in the country has already found that children from this laboratory nursery quickly begin to lose the qualities that made them promising when they are immersed in the routine New York public school.

It must also be observed that insistence on the necessity for prekindergarten work exonerates the schools from responsibility for the failure of those children who do not receive such special help—a category which includes all the Negro and Puerto Rican children now in classrooms, and the great majority of those who will enter in the next few years.

"Your problem," a very high school official said last spring to someone not quite so highly placed, "is that you think it's a minute to midnight. Relax; it's after midnight."

From this point of view, of course, there is no "crisis" in New York schools; the decline will be fairly precipitous but no one will be able to mark a place where the system fell over the cliff and be-

The Adolescent
Meets the Bureaucracy

came a custodial institution for the children who have no future.

Still, expert opinion to the contrary, there may yet be time—provided the school system is prepared to recognize it has no assets other than the people working in the schools, both teachers and children; and that the future of the system as a whole rests not upon policy decisions taken at the center but on tens of thousands of individual decisions taken in the field.

The human energy of the city has not been touched. It lies wasting in the school buildings, waiting for the leader who can release it from the closed circuit of the system, who will accept the gamble of chaos rather than the neat order of certain failure. The very idea of "superintendency" must go, and what survives as a central office must be honestly a source of help for, rather than control over, the people on the job.

Some highly impressive work has been done in the New York City schools in the last decade—the "individualized reading program" in elementary school; parts of the do-it-yourself "SP" (for "special program") which freed teachers to design their own courses for bright junior-high children; original blends of innovation in math and science in the special-entrance high schools; the "related technology" programs in the best one-trade vocational high schools, which tied math and science instruction to shop work (and were then crippled by an administrative decision that such material should be taught by the shop teachers themselves rather than by the science teachers.)

The Problems of American Education

All this work has been the result of throwing
teachers on their own, every man for himself, *sauve
qui peut*. It is a gamble; the quality of these programs varies hugely from classroom to classroom—
but over the long run in education it is the best that
counts; and there is no accident about the fact that
New York got the best when it liberated schools and
teachers from the suffocating discipline of central
control.

Acting Superintendent Bernard Donovan, for all
his widely recognized capability, is scarcely the
man to make such a revolution. We now have the
odd situation where a Board's policy commitment to
decentralization is to be carried out by the man who
in a public speech last year said that New York
could not have different schools doing different
things because parents would wonder why their
children weren't doing the same thing as other children; where a commitment to a 5-3-4 pattern of
schooling is to be implemented by the chairman of
the staff committee that recommended retention of
the 6-3-3 system; where a commitment to enhanc-
ing the status and opportunities of the people in the
field is to be met by a leader who has made his entire career on the staff rather than in the line.

Dr. Donovan was, of course "acting superintendent" throughout the regency of Dr. Gross; and
it is unthinkable that the man who actually ran the
schools during these last two years of rapid decline
should now be confirmed as the legal authority. But
a lot of what happens in New York is unthinkable.

All this is written from Switzerland, which is far
away—only a little closer than school headquarters

to the realities of life in the New York schools. From this distance, the situation looks almost as hopeless as it looks from 110 Livingston Street. Fortunately, my children have kept in touch with their classes at P.S. 158, Manhattan, to which they will return next year. Letters from these classes keep in my mind the images of the very mixed bag of lively and attractive children with whom they go to school, the able, persistent, and warm teachers who work with them. Against the realities of these classes, the vapors of superintendents and Boards of Education seem trivial indeed.

There are still literally thousands of such classes where the middle-class aspirations of the school meet an ambitious community confident in its children, where deficiencies in program can be made up by vitality, continuity, the shared sense of the school as an institution leading to, and thus part of, the larger world. But there are fewer such classes every year.

The American tradition of the common school rests on the willingness of parents who have a choice to send their children to the public school. They do so because they believe the public schools adequate to what they regard as the needs of their children; when they lost faith in the serviceability of public education, they sent their children to private schools or to suburban schools, once described by U.S. Commissioner of Education Francis Kepple as "private school systems run on public funds."

And, though ministers and rabbis whose own children go or have gone to private schools are now making the matter a moral issue, the parents who

**The Problems of
American Education**

withdraw their children from the city public schools are not to be criticized for it. There is nothing admirable or truly humanitarian about people who are prepared deliberately and consciously to sacrifice their children for the sake of their political principles.

Anyway, there aren't enough of these vicarious martyrs to make a difference. If the New York schools are to be saved, they must be made attractive, which cannot be done by publicity campaigns, by shutting up Milton Galamison, even by spending additional hundreds of millions of dollars (after all, the vocational schools which attract so few capable children cost half again as much per child as Bronx Science does).

Confidence can be regained only locally, by soliciting the help of the parent community instead of (as now) rebuking it, by developing educational programs more significant, more coherent, and intrinsically more interesting than what New York now offers between Grade 4 and Grade 9, by encouraging leadership from teachers, not just from those officially licensed to lead.

Literally dozens of new approaches could be tried, all at once, in groups of schools. Teaching teams—several teachers jointly responsible for several classes—could be given complete responsibility for instruction, free from all central-office dictates, and could be beefed up with additional members who would work as the team decided, not according to central personnel policy. (There is no intrinsic reason why team leaders could not be, as a wing of the union proposes, elected by the team

164

rather than appointed, or why future principals
should not be recruited from among successful team
leaders).

"Nongraded" groupings of children of different
ages in the one room, could be formed to individ-
ualize instruction, as in Milwaukee and St. Louis
and Chicago. To get smaller classes for intensive
reading work, attendance hours could be staggered,
half of each class at school from 8:20 A.M. to 2:30
P.M., the other half from 9:30 to 3:30, as in the Los
Angeles suburbs. (This stretching of the day would
also give a justification for higher pay in slum areas.)

Universities could be given substantial responsibility for dozens of officially experimental schools
(money to pay for such ventures is in the new Federal Education Act). Large-scale employment of
neighborhood people to work under professional
guidance could keep schools open all day and all
night, and with the help of civil-rights groups might
develop some of that "each-one-teach-one" feeling
which is absolutely required if the schools are to be
effective in the most depressed neighborhoods.

All this should be tried on the initiative of the
schools and the districts—and would be tried, if the
school system had a quality of leadership that gave
its people reason to hope rather than reason to fear.

And it must be done today; tomorrow will be too
late. The projections of what is now happening to
the schools are already a stench in the nostrils of the
city. Let no one underestimate what is required:
desperate situations demand desperate measures.
We must have changes not only in structure, but in
personnel. We must have an entirely new leader-

ship cadre which can inspire those in the schools and learn from them what the true priorities are—not only in form but in substance; massive rather than isolated experiments in ways of teaching children whom the old ways have failed—not only in matter but in spirit. We must have a willingness to face defeat and to try again rather than whine about money or inaccurate newspaper reporting or the impossibility of the job.

There is, of course, a great tradition which argues that changes of this order are always and forever the only way to be saved.

The college grad has been short-changed

ANDREW HACKER

Hardly a commencement or baccalaureate address this week will not contain at least one allusion, however veiled, to the fact that this was the Year of the Demonstration. If some campus protests have been political while others have exemplified educational discontents, it remains to say that students at schools as widely contrasted as Berkeley, St. John's, and Yale have rallied, marched, signed, and sat in displays of vehemence and in numbers not equaled in this generation.

A major reason for these stirrings is that not a few American undergraduates have become convinced that they are being short-changed. Feeling cheated on the educational end, especially at the larger institutions, they are ripe for any demonstration against authority in general and campus officialdom in particular. Nevertheless, it must be recorded that the protests over the quality of higher education are foredoomed to failure. They are outcries against conditions which will become even further entrenched in the years to come.

What is distressing is that so many students, faculty members, and observers of the educational scene still think that serious reforms are possible. For this reason the facts of modern university life deserve to be catalogued, if only because so many of us will have to live with them.

In the first place, colleges and universities will become larger, and consequently more bureaucratic and impersonal. Within a generation, only a minor fraction of the student population will be attending small, independent colleges. Already 6 out of every 10 students are in institutions having enrollments of over 5,000, whereas a dozen years ago, less than half were in schools of that size.

The reason for this is not that small colleges are going out of business—hardly any do—but that most of them are becoming larger. This is especially the case with publicly supported institutions. Whereas every state used to have its network of normal and A.&M. schools, these are now being transformed into universities with no ceilings foreseen for their enrollments. What was once a teachers' college in Carbondale is now Southern Illinois University, with over 17,000 students. Plans are being made to expand New York's old normal schools—like Brockport, Fredonia, Geneseo, New Paltz, Oneonta, Potsdam—so they can absorb the tens of thousands of students in search of a college education. And except for a handful of Amhersts and Swarthmores, virtually all of the small private colleges are anxious to raise their enrollments, sometimes for financial reasons but also for purposes of prestige.

It is easy to give publicity to projects and experiments intended to counter this trend. About 10 years ago, for example, California declared that it would make its Riverside campus the "Amherst" of the system, with an enrollment limited to about 1,000 liberal arts majors. As of now, Riverside has grown to some 3,000 and its plans are to have as many as 14,000 students on the campus by 1980, many of them working for advanced degrees. So much for the "Amherst" idea.

Now we are hearing about the new Santa Cruz campus, this time to be the "Oxford" of the Coast, having a series of small colleges, each with its own professors giving tutorials, on a prominence above the Pacific. It is impossible to see how such an educational luxury can survive, especially in a state with so many teen-agers knocking on college doors. The Santa Cruz plan, like Riverside's before it, is expensive in fact and undemocratic in theory. These are two powerful strikes against intimate education, public or private.

Larger enrollments mean larger classes. In a small school, only 15 students would elect medieval history and a professor would be assigned to teach them. In a large place, 150 sign up for such a course—and the professor lectures to them en masse. (Why not have 10 professors, each teaching a class of 15? The answer, apart from the fact that no department has 10 medievalists, is that such an arrangement is outrageously expensive. That is why colleges are expanding their enrollments to begin with.) One result is that students will come to know fewer and fewer professors on a personal basis. But if they will have less to do with the faculty, they are destined for many more encounters with the administration.

On every campus, students find they must spend more and more time dealing with an expanding bureaucracy. Regular visits must be paid to administrative purlieus to fill in forms in triplicate, to be photographed in duplicate (face and lungs), to appeal, to petition, to ask permission. They must not fold, multilate, staple, or spindle the I.B.M. cards representing their studenthood; they must secure prior approval for all manner of social, political, and domestic arrangements if they are to ensure that their existence does not violate the rules contained in the thick handbooks of codes and regulations. (One might ask if this is not the case in every sphere of modern organized life. The answer is that a university is supposed to be a realm of scholars, a community of ideas and hence to be spared such encumbrances.)

The ranks of the administrators have been expanding much faster than those of the teaching faculty and this trend will doubtless continue. I have yet to learn of a single college or university where the growth rate of its administrative corps is less than that of the professoriat. Educational administrators, like their counterparts elsewhere, are adept at discovering new services they can perform, new committees they can create, new reports they can write.

They have an advantage over the professors in

this respect, for they possess both the will and the skill for arrogating new powers and functions to themselves. And they have, after all, a sweet reasonableness on their side. Would anyone care to suggest that a college could operate without registrars, controllers, deans of men, housemothers, public-relations emissaries, guidance counselors, activities advisers, residence managers, proctors, pastors, research coordinators, placement officers, clinic technicians, and development directors?

Every day these officials find new ways to intrude their presence into student life. It may well be that undergraduates are looked after better than ever before: They are ministered with food and housing, counseling and recreation, medicine and religion, career guidance and financial assistance. Yet if undergraduates are driven into the arms of the burgeoning bureaucracies this is partly because the professors are so seldom at home.

Much has been written and said about the retreat from the classroom, about the increasing unwillingness of professors to teach or otherwise to meet with students. No elaboration is needed here, except to say that the charges are true. This is the age of the foundation grant, of prolonged academic travel, of frequent leaves. It is also the era of conferences, workshops, and symposia that draw professors (all expenses paid) away from the campus, frequently in the middle of classes. The mere murmuring of the sacred incantation "research" is sufficient excuse to bow out of introductory courses, to confine one's offerings to graduate seminars, to depart for another institution where more grandiose projects will be more generously underwritten.

But the focus here is on the future of higher education and it is relevant to consider the rising generation of professors. These young men are being suitably indoctrinated even while in graduate school. For one thing, they learn the dominant fashions in their disciplines and commit themselves intellectually (if that is the word) to the going trends. This is especially necessary for the less talented (in other words the majority) for the rising tide of fashion offers the safest haven for mediocre minds.

Just a few months ago I was lecturing at a liberal arts college, a small upstate institution, with a strong teaching tradition. I was told by several department chairmen of their great difficulties in attracting new faculty members. The men they interviewed, most of them in their middle 20's, all wanted to be assured about research funds, abbreviated teaching schedules, grants, leaves, and the other prerequisites they are coming to expect. Even undergraduate colleges are being forced to match these demands if they are to recruit for their faculty—and what amounts to a part-time faculty at that.

Most of the new professors like to think of themselves primarily as scholars, and this attitude is held even by those incapable of making more than a quite minimal contribution to human knowledge. This being the case, who is going to do the teaching? This question would be a pressing one even if the every-man-a-researcher fetish did not exist.

The Adolescent
Meets the Bureaucracy

Assuming that one professor is needed for every 10 students, for every million undergraduates we add to our college rolls—and we are currently adding a million every three years—100,000 more teachers will be needed. Yet fewer than 15,000 Ph.D.'s are produced annually in this country—and not all of these go into teaching. And of those who do, not all are exactly excited over the prospect of spending their careers in the classroom.

At the same time, there is no indication that reputable colleges or universities are willing to sign up, on a permanent basis, people with lesser degrees. The chasm between the M.A. and the Ph.D. is a yawning one. After all, kindergarten teachers have M.A.'s. The notion that each college will establish a separate "teaching faculty," unencumbered by the publish-or-perish test, is illusory. The Ph.D. standard has been set, and nowadays even independent undergraduate schools find themselves going through the motions of expecting research and publication from their faculty.

The result will be larger classes, more machine-graded examinations and more televised instruction. (The "solution" of less classroom work and more "independent" study is another delusion; it takes a professor far more time to supervise and evaluate the independent work of students than it does to teach them in groups.) It is fruitless to discuss the wisdom of developments such as electronic education. They are going to come, like it or not, and whatever is inevitable ceases to be a worthwhile issue for discussion. If three million new places are going to be created for students over the coming decade, the 300,000 new professors who will be needed to teach them are nowhere in sight. And those who are recruited will spend less time in actual teaching than ever before.

Does all this really trouble most of today's and tomorrow's students? I suspect that it does not. When all is said and done, the vast majority of American undergraduates are not greatly concerned with the quality of the education they are receiving. The millions of teen-agers filling up our colleges and universities are there for career purposes. They know, better than their parents, that a degree is absolutely necessary for financial and social success; and they are willing to spend four not-too-arduous years to become properly accredited. Most undergraduates have enrolled for eminently practical majors—business and engineering for the boys and education for the girls. Those doing liberal arts subjects are the minority, and very few of these have any illusions that they are engaged in learning for its own sake.

Most of today's students are not intellectuals, nor are they capable of becoming so. They do not object to large, anonymous classes. They have no ideas of their own to put forward and they want to be told what they have to know. Eight out of 10 students discover that they have nothing to say at such times as they do meet with a real professor at close range. Hence their preference for fraternities and sororities, activities and athletics, and the nonacademic chit-chat with guidance counselors, activity directors, and religious advisers.

Once we admit that most young Americans have

The Adolescent
Meets the Bureaucracy

no genuine interest in or talent for the intellectual life, the problem of quality in education begins to recede. It may even cease to be a problem.

Certainly, this year's protesters and demonstrators were not representative of their classmates, and it is instructive how quickly their ranks have tended to dwindle away after the first flamboyant outbursts. So long as a school will give an undergraduate his passport into the upper-middle-class without demanding more than he can give with 15 weekly hours of studying, few are going to complain.

Perhaps the root of the trouble lies in the tendency to compare American colleges of today with those of earlier generations or with their European counterparts. At the turn of the century, only 4 percent of the 18-to-21 age group was enrolled in colleges and universities, and even in Europe today only about 10 percent are in institutions of higher learning.

The United States, in contrast, has committed itself to higher education for almost half of those of college age and the proportion may well rise to 70 percent. If the consequence is mass production, this is bound to happen when a nation tries to give the best of everything to everyone.

The only possible way to reintroduce quality into higher education would be to deny college places of any sort to three out of four who are now applying. But a democracy cannot tell its citizens—who are, after all, articulate taxpayers and awakened voters— that their children will have to make do with lesser credentials. An aristocratic posture makes sense only when the masses admit to their inferior status and defer to their betters.

When, as in America, the majority is affluent and self-confident, people come to feel entitled to all manner of things that were once the exclusive privileges of a minority. Admission to a college, with the opportunities it opens for ascending careers, can no longer be confined to a small fraction of the population. Having chosen to be a democracy we must accept its consequences.

Colleges and universities as constituted at present have too many contented constituents for them to change their ways. Most of the students, at least half of the professors and all of the educational administrators are faring better than ever before and are experiencing opportunities that only a favored few knew in earlier days. The dissenting members of the academic community are setting themselves against the combined forces of democracy in education and technology in learning. Like many rebels they are nostalgic for a society they never knew and a world they can never know.

PART FOUR

Both the increasing clamor about the defects of American public education and the growing sense of crisis have promoted a wide range of suggested solutions, experiments, and efforts to reform. One type of suggested solution tackles reform at the broad level of redistributing teachers or students, or both, among various schools and school districts. In these proposed reforms, we face such questions as: Should we increase the freedom of parents and students to choose schools? Will greater competition among schools make them more effective, or is a planned distribution and coordination the best way? What are the gains and the losses of increasing lay control to the detriment of professional control? An earlier article by Nathan Glazer, in Part Two, on the drive for greater "community control," depicts a major way to change the broad structure of American elementary and secondary education: decentralize the large urban district either by breaking it up into a number of small districts or by greatly

Reform in the public schools

shifting authority from the top and middle levels of the system to the lower units.

A second type of reform concentrates on changing what goes on in the classroom and centers particularly on the relation of the teacher to a group of students. Here there are many subtle questions of learning and teaching, extending from the psychological investigation of the individual students' processes of learning to a sociological sensitivity to the environment of the classroom and the social context of the individual learner.

We begin with "Slum Children Must Make Up for Lost Time," an article by Maya Pines on how best to help ghetto children. This article takes us squarely into the middle of a controversy over teaching methods in compensatory education. One approach, permissive in nature, favors reaching the personality of the child essentially through affective, trusting relations with teachers that will raise his self-esteem and school motivation; the intellectual or academic part of "catching up" will then supposedly follow. The opposing approach favors tough intellectual drill—pound the appropriate information into the slum child in the preschool and kindergarten years, so that he enters the competition of the elementary years with an intellectual grasp equal, by and large, to that of the child from an advantaged background; motivation and self-esteem will then follow. Pines favors the drill approach, feeling that it is appropriate for children of lower-class background, while the permissive approach has been appropriate mainly for the middle class.

Whichever side we favor, it is necessary to perceive how the social background of the young affects the teacher-student relationship. The home has a "hidden" curriculum, since it too instructs the child and does so before he enters school. We need to know more about these hidden curricula. Different backgrounds, possessing different latent curricula, set the problem of schools and teachers using different techniques with different social groups, rather than uniform methods for all. This necessity opens up the perplexing issue of reaching toward greater equality of educational opportunity by treating different students differently instead of treating them all the same. Finally, the psychological evidence found thus far to support the harsh-drill approach for slum children indicates that an authoritarian relationship between teacher and pupil may have its place in a democratic society. It may be the more effective teaching style for students in a certain age bracket from a certain social background.

The Problems of
American Education

The evidence is not clear, but at least the possibility must be entertained. In any event, we can be skeptical of methods that claim universality across ages and backgrounds. What will be best, or even minimally effective, will vary with the social context of the learner and the learning process.

The article in this set, "Let the Child Teach Himself," is a review by Ronald and Beatrice Gross of the much-admired Montessori method of teaching and learning. As the authors point out, a variety of styles of instruction are found in practice under the Montessori label. There is always the need to adapt the method as it is stated in textbook and theory to the local context, to the way the children are prepared for schooling by family and neighborhood. The authors also usefully point out that the Montessori method involves not only a theory of early childhood—how the very young sense the world—but also theories of the learning environment and of the role of the teacher. The environment is prepared by placing various physical objects, teaching materials, in locations around the room that will help cause the child to interact with them, in ways that subtly develop the ability to see, feel, and discriminate—and hence prepare him to read, write, and compute. The teaching role is recast toward indirect influence: the teacher must diagnose each child's current interests and level of understanding, decide on the most fruitful line of development, and then guide the student to the appropriate prepared materials. The child may "teach himself," in the jargon of the method, but only in the sense that he interacts with prepared teaching materials that have been placed in his way and through which he is sequentially guided. In short, the classroom as a learning environment is still very much there—and so is the teacher. Such reform is clearly sociological, asking the teachers to shake off the dictates of their traditional roles and to become instead planners of new environments.

One of the sweet ironies of human reform is the frequent need to "reinvent the wheel"—or at least swing back toward practices that reformers of an early day were glad to leave behind. In higher education, the most important efforts in structural reform have attempted to break up or replace the mass campus with a cluster of smaller quasi-autonomous residential units, much in the style long modeled to the world by Oxford and Cambridge Universities. On the American scene, these efforts are attempts to regain the size, climate, and supposed virtues of the small liberal arts college. Radical reform here is in many ways a return to the past. So, too, in reform efforts in elementary and secondary education, the direction is often toward relationships and practices found in schools of the past. This point is made exceedingly well in the last article, "A Daring Educational Experiment—The One-Room Schoolhouse," in which Winthrop Griffith discusses a one-room schoolhouse in Montana that is among the last survivors of a once-flourishing institution. Here, emphatically but by necessity, we find the values and practices of the informal, ungraded classroom. The school consists of one teacher and seventeen children, aged six to fourteen and spread across ten levels of instruction—all bunched in one room. The instruction is highly individualized and personal; the teacher moves about the room, zigging and zagging intellectually as the seven-year-old's math question is replaced by the problem of the twelve-year-old in another subject. The teacher also uses the young to teach the young, the older ones in effect acting as informal teacher aides—a radical technique in urban schools. The situation is hardly utopian: the equipment is old-fashioned, no specialists are available for problems that exceed the teacher's grasp, the oldest children need greater challenges, and eight years of education for each child are bound up in the ability of just one teacher. But the gains sought in modern reforms that emphasize informal teaching are strongly present in these remnants of the past—including as impressive benefits a tolerance of one another's differences and a caring and grace in helping the other person. Frustration is relatively low; motivation is relatively high, partly because the school can offer much more than the home. If motivation is at the heart of learning, an old one-room school peopled by eager children can probably hold its own with the large and expensive suburban school plagued with disenchantment and boredom. At least there are some lessons to be learned.

Slum children must make up for lost time

MAYA PINES

"Five or 10 years from now, when the kids who've been through Head Start are found still at the bottom of the academic heap, the racists and know-nothings will have a field day," warned the young psychologist, adding bitterly: "The only methods that work with these children are just not being used."

His despair is shared this fall by thousands of teachers and administrators as they realize that the new generation of slum children who entered school this year is just as unfamiliar with letters and numbers, just as vague about the structure of the English language, as that which came before it.

The children of poverty know far less than middle-class children when they entered the first grade. Since they also learn less from class, they fall farther behind with every year in school—which injures them emotionally as well as academically.

Eventually many of them stop trying, drop out, and join the vast pool of functional illiterates who cannot find jobs.

Class-induced differences become fairly evident soon after birth. At about 18 months, "disadvantaged" children start trailing middle-class toddlers in tests of language development and general intelligence. The differences are very clear at 3 years, and downright obvious by the age of 4.

Yet most existing preschool projects which aim to prepare poor children for school, such as Head Start, insist on modeling their programs on those of conventional middle-class nursery schools. "Because these children have the same needs and the same range of personality as all children, a child development center should have the same aims for their preschool experience in the center as it would for children in any school anywhere," declares Head Start's "Guide to a Daily Program." It lists the first three aims as follows: to help children "learn to work and play independently, at ease about being away from home, and able to accept help and direction from adults"; "learn to live effectively with other children, and to value one's own rights and the rights of others," and to "develop self-identity and a view of themselves as having competence and worth."

A decade ago, Margaret Mead had warned against "such fiascoes as the application of nursery-school techniques—designed to free the overneat children of middle-class urban homes by letting them mess around with finger paints—to the deprived children from the disorderly, patternless homes of migrant workers." What these children really needed, she said, were "the satisfying routines of the old kindergarten—itself an institution invented to deal with deprived children and which, when imported into middle-class education, had proved too mechanical and too routinized."

Even more important than the issue of permissiveness vs. routine, however, is the issue of whether preschool projects should actively try to develop young children's intellects.

Middle-class nursery schools operate on the theory that they can directly influence only the child's emotional and social development—not his mental growth. They assume that if they build up a shy child's confidence, or redirect an angry one's aggression, the child's intellectual development will take care of itself, following a sort of built-in timetable. Therefore they concentrate on teaching children to "get along with others" and "adjust to the group."

Deliberate teaching of mathematical or language skills is frowned upon in these schools. The largest period of time is reserved for "free play" with blocks, paints, trucks, and dolls, which is supposed to exercise children's imagination as well as their ability to think. The rest of the two- or three- hour day is spent at cutting and pasting, singing, story-telling, toileting, juice, and outdoor activities.

The best preparation for tomorrow is to live fully today, declares an article in *Childhood Education*, a journal of the Association for Childhood Education International. Thus, children are expected to learn from experiences that involve all aspects of life:

186

their emotions, their relations to other children, their fantasies, their field trips. They are supposed to learn number concepts by playing with building blocks. Reading readiness is expected to come from recognizing their first names over their coat hooks. At best, these theories produce a special atmosphere of joy and well-being, from which the children come home all aglow, as after a good party.

Academically, it matters little whether or not middle-class children attend these conventional nursery schools and kindergartens, according to a new group of psychologists interested in children's intellectual development. Either way, middle-class children tend to do well in the first grades of school because they have learned enough that is relevant at home.

The poor cannot afford such luxuries, however. What they have not learned at home, by the age of 4, they must learn elsewhere, and quickly. They must make up for lost time, unlearn old habits—which is much harder than learning new ones—and also keep up with the progress being made by others who do not have such problems.

Since the early nineteen-sixties, a fierce, though largely undeclared, war has been raging between the early childhood Establishment—people trained in traditional early childhood education or child development—and the innovators, who emphasize cognitive, or intellectual, growth.

The Establishment would like to postpone all instruction in skills such as reading, perhaps to the age of 7. It is very indignant about what Drs. Frances Ilg and Louise Ames of the Gesell Institute of Child Development called "the vultures of experimental education poaching on this tender territory, forcing advanced curricula. . . ." "We must continue to be vigilant in order to preserve childhood for children," declares Dell C. Kjer, president of the Association for Childhood Education International.

The innovators include sociologists, linguists, mathematicians, philosophers, and computer specialists, as well as psychologists of the stature of J. McV. Hunt of the University of Illinois, Jerome Bruner of Harvard, and Benjamin S. Bloom of the University of Chicago. They are concerned primarily with how young children learn to think and how best to help them. They believe that it is most important to stimulate children intellectually before the age of 4, and worry about specific ways to compensate for poor children's intellectual deficits.

So far, most preschool projects for poor children have been dominated by the Establishment group. Head Start centers are purely local operations, free to operate any program they choose; yet despite their varied auspices, nearly all of them end up with some version of the middle-class nursery school, which does not emphasize cognitive learning. The preschool classes spawned by Title I of the Elementary and Secondary Education Act in poverty areas also copy the middle-class model. So do the programs in the nation's pitifully few daycare centers.

Nearly all of these programs have failed to produce major improvements in children's readiness for school. Head Start can justly pride itself on its

Reform in the Public Schools

medical, dental, and social-work components: Its screening procedures have saved hundreds of youngsters from such conditions as worms, poor hearing, or bad eyesight. It has also involved many poor parents in school activities for the first time, and predisposed children favorably toward school. But like the other programs mentioned, it has generally neglected what the innovators believe to be a key factor for poor children: their preparation for academic learning. Past the age of 4, it seems, trips to the zoo or a chance to play with blocks can have very little effect on slum children's ability to think, read, write, or even speak.

One of the glowing exceptions, last summer, was a Head Start program in Canton, Ohio, based on the intensive remedial classes devised by Prof. Carl Bereiter and Sigfried Engelmann of the University of Illinois.

No other method provokes so much anger in the early childhood Establishment. It also alarms some of the innovators. While other experimenters have kept at least some trimmings of the middle-class model, Bereiter and Engelmann have turned completely away from it. Their brisk, two-hour schedule allows virtually no time for free play. Instead of having a central, motherly teacher for the whole class, the children are split into small groups that move from subject to subject, each with a different instructor. Instead of spending most of their time on nonverbal activities which hardly change from semester to semester, the children and teachers talk, shout, chant in full sentences—following a very specific plan.

"These are blocks," says the teacher to a group of 4-year-olds in the language-training class, holding up some blocks. "Say it all together now. Real loud: 'These are *blocks.*' Now listen carefully. Are *these* blocks? Yes, these are blocks. What are these?" "Blocks," replies a child. "Give me the whole sentence," admonishes the teacher. "These are blocks," says the child. Switching to a large ball, the teacher continues: "This ball is *big.* Say it all together: 'This ball is *big.*' "

In the arithmetic class, a teacher faces 5-year-olds who started the program a year before and asks: "Are you ready for tough stuff?" Then he writes on the blackboard: "$\Delta - 8 = 3$." He reads it aloud: "Triangle minus eight equals three." Undismayed, the children shout, with occasional prodding: "Triangle and eight are not the same size, because you're not ending up with zero. So triangle is bigger than eight. It's three bigger than eight. What's three bigger than eight? What's *one* bigger than eight? Nine! What's *two* bigger than eight? Ten! What's *three* bigger than eight? Eleven! So [triumphantly] *triangle* is eleven!"

In a sense, the program teaches English as a second language, using drills that resemble older students' foreign-language pattern drills. It teaches math as a second language. "With young kids, you have no option—you can't *tell* them what the rules are," explains Bereiter, "so you can either drill with things that all follow the same rule, as we do, or leave it to chance. Our goal is to speed up the learning."

The children spend about 20 minutes a day on

language, 20 minutes on math, and 20 minutes on reading. These drills take up half of the two-hour program. The rest consists of juice and cookies, drawing, singing, and outdoor activities. In Bereiter's opinion, the children's single biggest achievement is that they learn to speak in sentences, and can thus "unpack" meaning from statements. Though they could use language to get along socially before they started, he says, they could not use it to express ideas.

There is no substitute for true competence, he believes. These classes do wonders for the children's self-image because the children know they are really succeeding at something that appears very tough.

The first group of children in the program had been picked because their older brothers or sisters could barely keep up with the lowest track in their neighborhood's nearly all-Negro elementary school, or had repeatedly failed in school. After two years of training, these extremely disadvantaged 5-year-olds scored at mid-second-grade level in arithmetic and mid-first-grade level in reading and spelling on the Wide-Range Achievement Test. Several were far too advanced for even the top track in their neighborhood school. Instead, they broke the color line in a white school, where they are performing as well as children whose parents have university degrees.

When the Canton Superintendent of Schools, George P. Young, heard about this method, he decided to try it out on eight summer Head Start classes and compare their progress with that of eight other classes which would have a conventional curriculum. Though the results of this six-week experiment have not yet been fully analyzed, the 120 children who had the Bereiter-Engelmann program obviously progressed so much more rapidly than the others that "there is no doubting the significance of the program," says Mr. Young.

The children, who were 4 and 5 years old, were given Head Start's preschool inventory test and a basic-concept inventory test, both at the beginning and at the end of the project. The testers did not know which group each child had been in. On one test, the children in the new program showed almost twice as much gain as those who had undergone the conventional program; on the other test, they showed fully twice as much gain.

"It's been a very exciting, very productive experience," says Mr. Young, who extended the program to the regular school year this fall. As far as he knows, this is the first time that a school system has adopted this method for wide use in its kindergartens.

To date, Head Start is still largely a summer program for youngsters who will enter school the following fall. Since nearly half the children in the nation still do not have kindergartens to go to—especially in poor neighborhoods—this means that the bulk of Head Start children are 5 and 6 years old, way past the age at which they could benefit from preventive programs.

Remedial programs often require some pressure.

But this is not at all what most of the innovators
want, although it may prove necessary if one starts
as late as the age of 4 or 5.

The innovators would like to revolutionize education starting in the crib. They would like to
"hook" children on learning. They would like to
give each child a chance to enjoy intellectual challenges at just the right level for him—always a little
beyond what he has already stored in his brain. A
good match produces so much intrinsic motivation
and pleasure, says Professor Hunt, that learning
becomes a sport, as engrossing to children as base-
ball.

Some of the innovators would send battalions of
tutors into poor children's homes, like visiting
nurses, to provide appropriate toys and talk to babies, developing their intelligence. Others would
set up Children's Houses on every crowded city
block, with educational programs geared to toddlers. In well-baby clinics and pediatricians' offices
they would provide regular check-ups on intellectual development for every young child.

Slum children of 2½ or 3 would take part in specific learning sequences, perhaps based on the
famous Montessori educational toys. They would
play with letters and numbers, learn to count and
hear the differences between similar letters and
sounds. By the age of 4, they would begin learning
to read and write. By the time they entered school at
6, they would be a joy to their first-grade teachers.

Professor Hunt believes that if we dare go ahead
and really improve learning conditions for children
during their earliest years, we can probably raise

the average level of the nation's intelligence. He points out that physically, at least, Japanese children of this generation tower above their parents, thanks to a better diet during their earliest years. Future generations of Americans could well grow up to be much cleverer than we are, thanks to a better intellectual diet for each child.

A given infant may grow up to have an I.Q. of 80 with a poor environment, or 120 with a good environment, declares Dr. Samuel A. Kirk, an authority on retarded children. Only the outer limits of man's intelligence are fixed by heredity. But as a child grows older, more and more effort is required to produce a given amount of change in his intelligence—if such change can be produced at all. And the longer one waits, the greater the emotional cost of the change.

A meticulous researcher, Professor Bloom pored over 1,000 different studies of growth, each of which followed up certain youngsters and measured them at various points in their development. He concluded that the environment's impact on any human trait is greatest during the trait's period of most rapid growth. For example, a prolonged starvation diet would not affect the height of an 18-year-old, but it could severely retard the growth of a 1-year-old baby. Professor Bloom points out that by the age of 6, when a child normally enters school, two-thirds of his intelligence has been formed.

The most rapid growth of intelligence takes place before the age of 4. This is the crucial period, the cognitive psychologists believe. What a child learns then largely determines his future achieve-

ment—and if he is poor, it may provide his only
chance to escape from the slums.

A popular subject for study now is the "hidden
curriculum" in various kinds of homes. The curriculum in the middle-class home, it turns out, leads directly to the skills that are required for success in
school. It is transmitted primarily through language.
Middle-class parents read bedtime stories. They answer questions about labels, street signs, prices.
They use complex forms of speech which encourage their children to see the consequences of their
actions. By the time such children enter the first
grade, they are on the verge of reading (some have
already taught themselves), and they have developed pretty efficient ways of dealing with symbols.
Middle-class families take all of this for granted; so
do schoolteachers, who are largely middle-class
themselves.

The children of poverty, by contrast, learn that
the best way to stay out of trouble is to keep quiet.
In their homes, curiosity is often rewarded by a
whipping. The speech they hear consists of brief
commands or phrases; it does not encourage
thought. With transistor radios going constantly,
they learn not to pay attention to words, but to tune
things out.

For such children, school is a totally alien environment. They cannot please their teachers; they
cannot begin to cope with what is expected of them.
Only a few youngsters succeed in overcoming such
odds. The rest—even those from loving and stable
homes—fall by the wayside, repeating grade after

The Problems of
American Education

grade, while their teachers wait for them to become "ready" to learn.

Conventional nursery schools and kindergartens, with their long periods of "free play," may aggravate these children's distractibility, some psychologists believe. On the other hand, Bereiter's and Engelmann's are not the only ways to mobilize children's thoughts. One of the best antidotes to inability to concentrate is the Montessori method, which has shown a peculiar power to "fix" young children's attention, especially when started early enough.

Montessori's greatest achievement, half a century ago, was her extraordinary success with children from the slums. In a section of Rome where nobody dared go about unarmed at night, she showed how youngsters who had previously run wild while their parents were out at work could learn to read, write, count, and develop what she called "the power of spontaneous reasoning."

They learned all this freely—but in a carefully "prepared environment." Montessori believed that "things are the best teachers." She invented the richest array of educational toys seen to this day— hundreds of simple puzzles and games, each leading from the sensory to the symbolic, each preparing the child for a higher level of understanding.

Unlike the building blocks which form the staple of conventional nursery schools, her equipment is not meant to be used in fantasy play. The child in a Montessori class selects any toy he wishes, but then he is expected to use it in the way it was designed, so as to learn what Montessori planned for him to learn. If he picks the famous sandpaper letters, for example, he traces them with his finger until the movement of forming each letter becomes permanently engraved in his memory; in most cases, after a few months of such practice he begins to write with extraordinary ease. A child who selects colored counting rods of graduated lengths must order them into a staircase; this teaches him to compare lengths, and to classify, and also introduces elements of the decimal system.

Montessori's equipment always allowed the child to work at his own pace and required a minimum of help from the teacher—usually just a demonstration, at the beginning, of how the materials were to be used. It was largely self-correcting. Furthermore, the children were trained from the beginning to replace each item after using it, and not to disturb other children. Thus each child could choose from such varieties that 40 youngsters in the same class might well be occupied with 40 different tasks.

Professor Hunt points out that Montessori was one of the few educators to find practical answers to what she called the crucial "problem of the match." Given anything too complex, novel, or incongruous, children will withdraw, often angrily, or ignore it; anything too familiar or simple, and they will become bored. Montessori solved this problem by letting each child select sequences at his own level.

In recent years, the Montessori techniques have been revived in the U.S.—but largely for middle-class children, who need them least. Only a section of the new projects for disadvantaged children have made use of them, though an occasional Montessori toy is found in many schools.

The Montessori revival has been a sort of consumers' rebellion on the part of middle-class parents against the conventional nursery schools. These parents wanted their young children to learn more, and to become rugged individualists, rather than be overly adjusted to the group. So they began to import Montessori teachers from abroad and run their own private Montessori schools; they could easily afford it.

The poor, of course, have no choice in the matter. They depend on the early-childhood Establishment, which hates Montessori on the ground that her method neglects children's emotional development. Furthermore, there is a serious shortage of trained Montessori teachers. As a result, very few poor children have been exposed to the Montessori method here.

However, when 10 disadvantaged Negro children were enrolled in a Montessori school in Chicago recently, their I.Q.'s rose by 17 points in three months—a strong indication that they would do well in elementary school, since the I.Q. test is the best available indicator of future success in school.

Several other preschool programs which deliberately promote intellectual development have given signs of unusual success with poor children. In Greeley, Colorado, for example, extremely poor Mexican-Americans attend a new nursery school which combines Montessori techniques, other methods devised at New York's Institute for Developmental Studies, and the use of an electric typewriter which the child is free to explore while an attendant makes the sound of every letter that is struck. The children come in at the ages of 3 and 4, speaking almost no Spanish or English. By the age of 5, they are nearly on a par with middle-class children in reading readiness, and about a quarter of them can type words or stories based on their own conversation. The regular kindergarten teachers who have had graduates of this school judge them to be doing exceptionally well.

According to Dr. Glen Nimnicht, who started the school in 1964, the children who enter at 3 make far more progress than those who enter at 4. "It's not a simple addition of one year's progress plus another," he explains. "They do better because there is less difference between poor children and middle-class kids at the age of 3."

In Washington, D.C., tutors go into the homes of 30 Negro babies in one of the city's worst slums to stimulate them intellectually and encourage them to talk. This Infant Education Research Project begins when the babies are 15 months old. Every weekday from then on, the tutor comes to spend a full hour alone with each child. They play guessing games, sorting games, counting games; they look at pictures, read stories, blow bubbles—and all the time the tutor keeps up a conversation with the baby, explaining what they are doing and labeling everything around them.

One year after the tutoring began, the toddlers in the program scored between 10 and 15 points higher on the Stanford-Binet I.Q. test than did carefully matched controls. The tutoring will continue until each child turns 3, says Dr. Earl Schaefer, who started the program. At the age of 3 the children will be retested and, he hopes, placed in a nursery school.

For "high-risk" babies, the revolutionary Children's Center in Syracuse, N.Y., offers a program of deliberate intellectual stimulation plus tender loving care, beginning at the age of 6 months. It is revolutionary because other daycare centers take no children under 3, and often tend to neglect intellectual growth.

A typical "high-risk" baby in the Syracuse project will have older brothers who are in special classes for the mentally retarded, or who have already dropped out of school. He would almost certainly follow in their tracks without extra help. Instead, his I.Q. rises with every year in the center, until it reaches well above the national norm of 100.

These are still isolated, scattered experiments. But the cognitive psychologists find them extremely significant. Each represents a workable method of breaking the cycle of failure which awaits millions of poor children.

There are signs that some of the leaders of the early-childhood Establishment remain opposed to the new methods. As a result, the innovators now fear that the high hopes aroused by such projects as Head Start may boomerang, to discredit all preschool programs. Early learning, they say, is the most effective way to rescue poor children from the slums—and they would sorely like to give it a real chance.

Reform in the Public Schools

Let the child teach himself

RONALD *and* BEATRICE GROSS

The year was 1906. In the basement of a housing project in the slums of Rome a ragged, unruly gang of children filed into a sparsely furnished room that was their new nursery school. Suspiciously, they looked over the teacher.

She was Maria Montessori, the first woman to receive a medical degree from an Italian University and a person of great gusto, intelligence, and determination. But in addition to having a remarkable character, she had devised a remarkable educational method. Within a few months Montessori's pupils were transformed into an attentive, friendly, neatly dressed class of model students. And they were learning—learning more quickly than the middle-class offspring of educated parents who attended conventional schools.

Today the educational theories Montessori used in her *Casa dei Bambini* are enjoying a phenomenal resurgence throughout the United States. Her books, long out of print, are being republished. Many educators are convinced that Montessori techniques and insights can correct some basic flaws in American primary schools. Parents in New York, Chicago, Washington, D.C., Los Angeles, Houston, St. Louis, Philadelphia, and a score of other cities—eager for their preschool tots to learn reading, writing, and arithmetic—have organized more than 100 Montessori schools in the past six years. Not since the nineteen-twenties, when private schools spearheaded progressive education, has a teaching method evoked such enthusiasm among the public.

The Montessori revival is part of a wave of reform sweeping American education, based partly on the fear that existing schools and teaching methods do not develop the full intellectual ability of pupils. Substantiating such doubts, recent demonstrations by educators and psychologists have shown that children of 3, 4, and 5 need and thrive on a solid academic diet. Then, too, Montessorians make persuasive claims to teach children more, and at younger ages, by converting the children's own intellectual steam into "real learning." Particularly relevant for American children is Montessori's success with the kind of child we call "culturally deprived"—the big-city slum youngster who is a major target of [former] President Johnson's antipoverty program.

The Montessori method is based on several distinctive concepts. Though in practice Montessori schools differ widely in applying the doctrine—a flexibility that sometimes pained the authoritarian *dottoressa*—all Montessorians share a common philosophy based on three primary principles. The theories concern early childhood, the learning environment, and the role of the teacher.

Montessori believed that from birth to the age of 6 the child has an "absorbent mind" that endows him with a great capacity for disciplined work and a voracious appetite for learning. She held that the years from 3 to 6 are a particularly "sensitive" period, during which children can benefit enormously from serious knowledge.

Montessori believed that from birth to the age of 6 these sensitive periods, the child's mind will develop from within. Quite naturally, the child provides his own stimulus to achievement. Adult pressure, or imitation of adult behavior, is frowned on; so are group activities. Instead, the child chooses his own tasks, works at his own pace, and progresses individually in ungraded classes that span a three-year range. The result, according to Montessori enthusiasts, is independent, self-reliant children who are eager to tackle work.

Related to this awesome view of child development is observance of Montessori's second canon—the "prepared environment." On the theory that "things are the best teachers," the Montessori teacher provides special teaching materials that subtly develop the child's ability to see, feel, and discriminate between shapes, sounds, textures. Later, the child will use materials and perform exercises that prepare him for reading, writing, and computation.

The Problems of
American Education

A youngster of 2½ or 3, for example, will execute "practical life" tasks, such as learning to tie his shoe laces, scrub a table, and open the door for the teacher. He may sort buttons with his eyes blindfolded, or trace sandpaper letters with his fingers. Delighted with learning to do these jobs correctly, the child will practice them for hours. Thus does he learn to master simple requirements and follow directions—critically important abilities, as psychologists have discovered, to the growth of general intelligence.

The sandpaper letters, for example, help train the muscles of the hand for writing. He then learns the phonetic sounds of each letter, progresses to composing short words with a movable alphabet, and soon may make up whole sentences. From that point, it is a short step to the child's demand for story books that he can read to himself.

In the strictly utilitarian atmosphere of the Montessori classroom, there are none of the usual toy animals, dolls, trucks, or dress-up costumes. Children in "pure" Montessori schools are virtually restricted to materials she devised, which are intended to suppress fantasy and imaginative play. Children should not make believe, Montessori proclaimed; to encourage them along such lines is to encourage defects of character.

With didactic materials carrying the burden of instruction, the Montessori teacher operates discreetly in the background, which constitutes the third basic aspect of the method.

The Montessori teacher's principal task is not "teaching" but diagnosing each child's interests,

204

level of understanding, and most fruitful line of development. Then she guides the child to those materials and experiences that will build on his interests and needs. Because the children work without
constant supervision, Montessori classes may run to
40 or more, with several assistants to the teacher.

"A man is not what he is because of the teachers
he has had, but because of what he has done," said
Montessori. She insisted that at most the teacher
should "artfully intervene" to insure that the child
is successful and productive.

No educational theory, of course, can guarantee
that the intervention will be artful. That sensitive
skill depends on the person, not the precepts. Yet
when the Montessori teacher is both professionally
well trained and personally sympathetic to children
(a combination that is no more common among
Montessorians than among conventional teachers),
the results are impressive and exciting.

About one-fourth of the children in a typical Montessori class read before they are 6. Even more
students can add and subtract large sets of numbers.
Thomas Laughlin, a former screen actor who
founded the Sophia School in Santa Monica, claims
that his 5-year-olds are beginning to learn algebra.
Before they enter first grade, he says, "they are pars-
ing sentences, composing music, and speaking
French. By the time they're 12 they can have accomplished everything the 18-year-old ac-
complishes in a conventional American high school,
and many will have completed the equivalent of
two years of college."

This is the dazzling—perhaps somewhat exaggerated—image of Montessori which has attracted so many middle-class and upper-class parents. But academic achievement by Montessori pupils is less uniform and automatic than Laughlin suggests, because most Montessorians are not that interested in "speeding up" the educational process. A visit to a Montessori classroom reveals what and how the children actually learn.

At St. Paul the Apostle's School on West 60th Street in Manhattan, 17 children ranging from 3 to 4½ years old are working on individual mats or at tables. The room is quiet and purposely spartan. Softly but firmly, the atmosphere says: Learn.

Robert, 4, is intently pushing long, brown blocks along the floor and clacking them together. The teacher, Miss Elizabeth Stock, lays the blocks carefully down in order of size, placing her hands on both sides of the formation to align the sides. Once the blocks are properly arranged, she takes the thinnest one and, sliding it carefully and quietly, "walks up the stairs." Then she takes the formation apart piece by piece and leaves the boy to do it himself. What is Robert learning? By discriminating size, weight, and thickness, and doing things in a prescribed pattern, he is learning skills basic to arithmetic.

Betty, 3, goes through a repeating ritual. She places a pink towel near her small table, then neatly puts soap, a basin, a pitcher and a brush on the towel. Carefully, she pours from the pitcher into the bowl, soaps the brush, shakes it off, and with large, rounded movements scrubs the already clean table. When she has covered the table with soapy scrub marks, she dips the sponge, squeezes it dry, and methodically wipes the soap off, first vertically, then horizontally. Nearby a boy polishes his shoes, his work spread out on a piece of white paper so he can tell when he's getting the polish on the wrong target.

"The children are free to move about and choose what they'll work on," Miss Stock explains. "But they must adhere to certain rules. The children are expected to use each object as it was designed to be used; if they don't, I ask them to put it away and they must finish a self-chosen task before setting themselves another." As she spoke, a girl who had been cutting paper was sweeping the scraps into a dustpan.

Walking around the room, we notice that some children have changed their materials. A child who was fingering a sandpaper letter is trying to solve a three-dimensional puzzle. The boy who was polishing his shoes is now matching up small color tablets.

Sometimes the teacher calls several children together for a demonstration of a new device, but the general emphasis is on individual learning rather than group activities. "After I demonstrate the proper use of each piece of apparatus," says Miss Stock, "the children can tell for themselves if they're doing it right. These objects make the child want to correct his mistakes. So you see, Montessori is not really a method of teaching, but a method of facilitating learning."

Each day the students silently practice sitting, getting up, moving chairs, closing the door. The room at the end of the day is as neat as when it began.

In contrast to the rigorous climate of St. Paul's, the "prepared environment" of the Whitby School in Greenwich, Conn., is more relaxed. The classroom is bright and cheerfully decorated. Children sprawl on the floor, gather in groups at tables, or walk around the room at their pleasure.

This school is an Americanized version of the European doctrine. It stresses the dottoressa's techniques, but eclectically borrows from native experience. Thus, three young girls listen intently to a recording of Peter Rabbit, while at the other end of the room two boys meticulously count beads. They attach tabs after every ninth bead, soon mastering multiples of nine through 270.

Is all this Montessori? "No," replies the teacher, Miss Lesley Ann Bruce, "only the cumulative, independent work with the special materials constitutes 'the method.' But we believe that the other activities are consonant with Montessori's broad strategy—to engage the child early in his own learning."

In a Washington, D.C., Montessori class of 35 children and two teachers, a girl of 5½ dismantles a huge, wooden puzzle map of the Eastern Hemisphere. Accurately, she attaches tiny tabs to the separate countries and sounds out the names of each: "Ceylon, Syria. . . ."

Next to her another girl, 4, lays out 10 words ending with "it" on her mat, using red and blue cardboard letters. A boy of 5 runs his finger over triangular insets, then fits them into their proper places on a wooden board as he softly murmurs "isosceles, equilateral. . . ." On another mat, a 5-year-old serenely sorts out cylinders by holding each one next to his ear and discovering a subtly different sound.

"This is Montessori at its purest," the teacher, Sibyl Devereux, explains. "All over the world children in Montessori classrooms are doing pretty much what you see here. Our method is designed as an aid to life, and life and people are essentially the same all over the world."

Miss Devereux teaches at the D.C. Society for Crippled Children. Most of her pupils are mongoloid, brain-damaged, or physically handicapped.

Maria Montessori died in 1952, having lived to see her theories take root and thrive in Western Europe (especially Holland), India, and elsewhere. In the United States, where she lectured widely and drew capacity crowds, about 100 Montessori schools flourished by 1915. A few years later, however, the movement was dead.

The chief reason for the doctrine's demise was opposition by John Dewey's disciples, principally William Heard Kilpatrick of Columbia University's Teachers College. Kilpatrick, in print and in person, declared that whatever was good in Montessori theory was contained in Dewey's thought. What was original he criticized as excessively rigid and psychologically obsolete.

Similar controversy surrounds the current revival of Montessori methods, which has inspired among American educators the full range of reaction from enthusiasm to enmity.

**The Problems of
American Education**

One of the most enthusiastic is J. McV. Hunt, professor of psychology at the University of Illinois and one of the nation's leading experts on the development of intelligence and learning capacity. Pointing out that the progressive educators of 1915 condemned Montessori because her psychological theories seemed fifty years behind the times, Hunt argues that she may have been just about that far ahead of her time.

According to Hunt, modern research corroborates the existence of Montessori's "sensitive periods" for certain kinds of learning; if development is not cultivated, children will have great difficulty later. Intelligence, as Montessori insisted, is not fixed, nor does it develop in a predetermined pattern. Early stimulation is all-important, and the senses play a more prominent part in intellectual growth than has been assumed.

Evidence from many sources over the past decade—how children learn, careful observations of their everyday behavior—has revealed the inadequacies of old notions of motivation, based on reward and punishment. Recent findings demonstrate that human beings are born with the desire to know, the urge to explore, and the need to master their environment. In short, to achieve.

Related to these specific liberating ideas about human motivation are discoveries about human intelligence generally. No longer do scientists and educators concur, as they did for so long, in the stultifying concept of fixed intelligence and predetermined development. On the contrary, says Hunt, creating an interesting, challenging environment for the child, especially during the early years, leads to a "substantially faster rate of intellectual development and a substantially higher adult level of intellectual capacity."

Moreover, adds Hunt, since the optimum rate of growth would mean "genuine pleasure in intellectual activity, promoting development properly need imply nothing like the grim urgency which has been associated with 'pushing' children." In other words, children should be free to learn at their own pace, but each individual's rate of learning is largely dependent on the richness and complexity of his environment.

A number of teaching innovations illustrate this approach: ungraded schools, programed learning, and teaching machines, Cuisinaire Rods for teaching mathematics, and curricula based on the "discovery" method of learning. They are all strikingly similar to Montessori's basic strategy.

However, most American educators and child psychologists argue that the best elements of Montessori have become standard practice in United States nursery schools. At the same time, they say, American educational theory has raced far ahead of the dottoressa's ideas in encouraging flexibility, freedom, and individuality. In fact, the critics see much in Montessori methods that is potentially harmful to children.

Their major objection is Montessori's concentration on intellectual work in the classroom, to the virtual exclusion of the child's imagination. Children need dramatic make-believe play, the critics declare. It compels them to explain what they are pretending, to communicate their thoughts. As for the anger, jealousy, and fear that a child may express in such play-acting, most teachers believe that such emotions should not be bottled up, but expressed in an understanding environment.

Rather than the impassive neutrality of Montessori teachers, American teachers are, of course, more actively didactic. They are also more openly sympathetic, creating a bond of intimacy that brightens the school environment.

Nor do the opponents of Montessori concede that American nursery schools neglect the student's intellectual development. A good nursery school is stocked with the materials that develop the sensory skills Montessori emphasized. It provides instruction in subjects that range from science and woodworking to counting and reading. A visit to a construction site or a garbage disposal plant is not a waste of time, American educators argue. Such field trips, they explain, deepen the child's understanding of his community and of himself.

As with many other doctrines that take their inspiration from a single source, the Montessori movement has had its schisms. What may be called the "reform wing" in the United States is led by Nancy McCormick Rambusch, who founded the Whitby School in Connecticut in 1958 and the American Montessori Society. Occupying a middleground between all-out opponents of the Montessori method and its purist followers, Mrs. Rambusch advocates "an American approach to Montessori."

She admits that some current interpretations of the method are restrictive, out-of-date, and unsuited to American children. She believes that special materials, used alone, are "anemic" by present-day standards and that American children are too permissively reared at home to adapt to the regimen of the orthodox Montessori classroom. Much has been learned in the past 50 years, she says, which must supplement Montessori methods.

"But the essential insights of Montessori are just as valid today in America as they were in Rome half a century ago," Mrs. Rambusch insists. "First and foremost, Montessori recognized that the early years, from 2 to 6, are critically important for the child's future education. Some psychologists maintain that half of all the growth in intelligence takes place before the age of 4—and the next 30 percent between 4 and 8. Children need intellectual challenge in these years if they're to achieve their maximum development.

"Secondly," Mrs. Rambusch points out, "Montessori tells us that the only really important thing in education is to teach the student to want to learn and how to learn—and that the motivation for learning must come from within the child. Most American teachers still haven't learned that lesson, with the result that our schools still lean heavily on grades, tests, external pressures and rote learning. Even in the early grades most teachers spend most of the time maintaining discipline and suppressing noise and movement.

"But Montessori demonstrated conclusively that the most efficient and effective education takes place when the teacher stops trying to make the children attend to her *teaching*, and devotes herself instead to helping them *learn*, by themselves, through artfully contrived experiences, exercises, and materials. Our teaching machines, for example, are belated recognition of the importance of the *tools* of learning."

Even more belated, perhaps, is the growing awareness that the educational problems Maria Montessori faced in the slums of Rome are the problems that, on a vastly enlarged scale, confront us today in trying to teach disadvantaged children.

Nancy Rambusch has turned her energy to working with Negro and Puerto Rican children at the New York Foundling Hospital and to training other teachers to do the same kind of job in an integrated public-school program in Mount Vernon. Many other educators also believe that Montessori's system for building self-confidence and developing the senses by means of stimulating materials is the first step in educating youngsters from culturally barren backgrounds.

Indeed, the conviction that this task is possible, and worthy of the best efforts of our best teachers, may turn out to be Maria Montessori's greatest contribution to education. Her *Casa dei Bambini* in Rome was a social institution designed to redeem the lives of children who seemed doomed. That its mission succeeded remains Montessori's triumph—and our inspiration.

A daring educational experiment— The one-room schoolhouse

WINTHROP GRIFFITH

It's an unlikely place to find educational excellence. The town of Monarch is dying. Most of its frame buildings are empty and leaning toward ruin. Fifty years ago, the 4,000 people in the area were thriving from the wealth and wages of nearby silver mines. Today, Monarch's population is eight. Another 100 people live in the pine-shaded canyon which curves along with the Belt River for eight miles south of town. Many of them are poor, surviving with welfare payments on small ranches inherited from their fathers. The men with jobs have to drive a 104-mile round trip each day to and from Great Falls, the nearest city.

The Monarch School is brightly painted and stands in cheerful dignity on a bluff overlooking the town, but its equipment is meager. There are one classroom and one teacher for 17 children, ranging in age from 6 to 14 and from the first grade through

the eighth. The school has no microscope or football, and its phonograph is broken. The children
look up words in a dictionary with some pages miss-
ing, and they do extra research in an illustrated en-
cyclopedia published in 1950. Their world globe is
an old and rickety thing which still shows a colonial
Africa, needs Scotch tape to hold China in place, and
has no Pakistan or Vietnam.

The people down in the canyon meadows often
glance up with affectionate smiles when teacher
Carol Sorrell rings the bell (a real bell with a rope
dangling down from the green-shingled belfry) to
summon the children after lunch or recess. They are
proud of the little school, and they should be. Their
children are getting an extraordinarily good education.

They are not aware of the modern irony which the
Monarch School represents. In one sense, it is an
anachronism from America's socially decentralized
past, one of the dwindling hundreds of one-room
schools which linger on in the mountain hamlets,
prairie crossroads, and islands of the nation. But
many of the methods of learning which have
evolved, by necessity, in these modest and architec-
turally charming structures are today being adopted
by large and progressive urban school districts.

Wilson Riles of California, the new state superintendent of the nation's biggest and fastest-growing
school system, understands the ironic challenge. As
a young man, he taught in a one-room schoolhouse
in Arizona, with nine students of varied ages. "In
education," he says, "maybe we need to rediscover
the wheel. People need to learn from one another,

no matter how different they are. The one-room schools permit that, and the so-called modern schools are beginning to copy them. These little schools could represent the wave of the future in education."

Many educators tend to use more pedantic phrases to describe the changes going on in the schools. The self-labeled pioneers among them are also likely to be immensely pleased with themselves as they daringly risk what they regard to be "innovative systems" and "experimental programing": ungraded classrooms, flexibility and freedom in the use of class time, more independent study by pupils, and techniques which allow each child to "progress at his/her own rate of learning."

"Golly, I don't know about all that," says Everett Davis, the 75-year-old chairman of the Monarch School Board. "All I know is we got a pretty nice little school up there. That Carol Sorrell is a dandy teacher, and a couple of years ago we put in a new well—with a casing all the way down—so the kids could have indoor toilets and running water."

Mr. Davis fends off questions about educational philosophy. He notes with pleasure that a high proportion of Monarch's children make the honor roll when they go on to high school in Belt (27 miles away), but he talks with more animation and at greater length about the quality of the water pump installed with the new well for the school.

Monarch's teacher also resists philosophical or academic discussions about the patterns and portents of American education. Miss Sorrell—25 years old, realistically tough, and idealistically dedicated, both authoritative and gentle with her 17 pupils—says: "It's true that the urban schools are now picking up many of our methods. The children here have had a basically ungraded, flexible, independent study situation for years. There's no choice here, with kids at 10 different so-called levels of learning.

"Those 17 children and I are in one small room [it measures 19 by 25 feet] for almost seven hours each day. We are all involved with one another and we all learn from one another. We have to. I have only so much time and there's only so much space for all those children. I give each one of them as much individual attention as I can, but in one sense we are together all the time."

Miss Sorrell has a quick and versatile mind, possibly her most valuable asset as she tackles the tough daily task of teaching the awesome array of minds confined to the one room. In one moment, she must explain a simple arithmetic lesson to Dee Miller, a red-haired and petite 6-year-old who weighs less than 50 pounds and has an innocent curiosity about all things. In the middle of that instruction, she is interrupted by an intricate algebraic question from Kenny Permann, a husky and muscular 14-year-old who hefts 75-pound bales of hay on his weekend and summer job. In the next instant, she shifts to a chapter on common multiples for a group of 8-year-olds.

I observed the Monarch School routine for several days, to conclude that the children there have these learning advantages:

They are constantly exposed to a review of les-

sons they previously had and the challenge of material beyond their current "achievement level."
Each child overhears the lesson Miss Sorrell is giving to individuals or small groups she calls over to a card table set up at one side of the room. ("My official classroom," she calls it.) A child who is technically a fourth-grader, for example, can listen in on the lesson being given to the second-graders—or the sixth-graders.

They teach one another, and learn the lessons profoundly in that process. Because Miss Sorrell's time is spread so thin, she relies on a pattern in which the older children help teach the younger ones, the brighter students help the dull ones. At least half of the children regularly serve as teaching assistants, though no one calls them that. And they like the role. Ten-year-old Theresa Dirkson, after coaching and quizzing the 8-year-olds, said: "It's fun to play teacher, especially when I don't know the answers at first."

Despite the steady chatter of voices in the room, they learn to study independently and privately. They have to. Miss Sorrell can't give lectures to a class of such mixed ages. The children spend at least half their time alone with the textbooks and work sheets provided by the state, while Miss Sorrell moves from child to child for individual help. Dale Holzheimer, a conscientious and imaginative 12-year-old, kept his eyes glued to a social-studies text for a full half hour before raising his hand and waiting for Miss Sorrell to answer a question about taxation in the American colonies.

Almost every minute of their class time is fully

The Problems of
American Education

used in learning, directly or indirectly. There's quite a bit of pencil-sharpening and foot-shuffling in the first restless minutes of each day, but I saw almost no daydreaming or doodling. If a child is finished, or bored with his own lesson, his eyes and mind are distracted by another lesson being taught openly and audibly by Miss Sorrell or another child. "There's too much going on inside the class for the children to stare out the window or at the clock," Miss Sorrell laughs. "It's sort of like a seven-ring educational circus."

Though the time for individual instruction is limited, Miss Sorrell does give deep and personalized attention to each child's questions and needs. The big reason is that she cannot escape their unique needs through bland or blanket generalizations about a particular age group as she approaches each child, in the way that a teacher in a conventionally graded and separated classroom could. She is acutely responsive to each child in each moment. In the course of one minute and a half, I saw her become aware of and act on: Kenny Permann's confusion about the three branches of government, Theresa Dirkson's puzzlement about the causes of the Boston Massacre, Sheila Croff's mix-up of Confucianism and Chinese communism, Linda Schoberg's question about the difference between the Helots and the Persians, Dale Holzheimer's amazement about the amount of governmental revenue from Montana state liquor stores, Robby Permann's aimless fussing in his coloring book, and Dee Miller's need to go to the toilet.

The children work incredibly well together, and

they are touchingly tolerant of one another's differences. If they were not, Miss Sorrell knows, and perhaps all of them sense, the alternative would be chaos and cruelty in the 19-by-25-foot room. All of them kept hard at work through all the hours I observed them, but there was none of the aggressive competitiveness nor the tense and mean teasing I've noticed in dozens of other classrooms. Danny Mathes, one of the brightest, biggest, and oldest children in the school, spent 20 minutes gently, patiently, effectively helping a semiretarded little girl through her arithmetic lesson. When the whole class was involved in a social-studies discussion about what they would do if there were a nuclear war, no one ridiculed or put down 7-year-old Robby Permann when he said, "I'd hide behind a tree."

There are some intrinsic disadvantages for the children, aside from the paucity of modern educational equipment. The methods of evaluating their achievement are rigidly old-fashioned; the county requires Miss Sorrell to record letter grades for the children every six weeks. The children with specific learning handicaps get no skilled or specialized remedial help. The youngest children are gently treated in the classroom, but they are often shoved aside or bruised by the rough play of the bigger children during recess periods.

The learning benefits from the mixture of groups are inevitably diminished for the oldest children. Danny Mathes and Kenny Permann, the two eighth-graders, insist that they enjoy working with and helping the younger students, but they also admit that they are hungry for contact with others of their

221

own age or older in high school, and are more than
ready to leave the one-room situation.

The Monarch School is not literally a one-room
schoolhouse, though all the instruction is conducted in the single upper room. In Montana and
most of the other raw and rural regions of America,
the people call them "country schools." Most of
them range from one room to three. At best, as in
Monarch, the country school has the single
classroom, another room which serves as an apartment for the teacher (a "teacherage") and a basement room, too grandly called a "gym," that provides an indoor play area during the extreme Montana winters.

On the sloping two acres around the school, there
is a swing set with four seats, a teeter-totter with
two warped boards and a mini-merry-go-round
which is too rusty to move very fast. But the com-
pensations for the modest play equipment are vast.
A trail leads up from the school into the Lewis and
Clark National Forest, filled with lodgepole pine
and blue spruce, wild flowers in the spring and exciting ice and snow shapes in the winter, animal
tracks and bird sounds. On pleasant days, Miss Sorrell takes the children into the woods for two-hour
nature studies.

At 8:20 each morning, Harold Matye, a part-time
silver and lead miner, eases the school bus out of a
shed in town and begins the six-mile drive along
Highway 89 to meet the children, waiting at the
gates or the dirt roads in front of their homes. The
bus, a Bluebird body on a Ford chassis, seats 18 and
is of such bulbous shape that it looks like a yellow

Reform in the Public Schools

balloon bouncing along the highway. At exactly
8:45 A.M., the children pile out and run up the
school's stairway to hang their coats and stack their
lunch pails. ("Never been late," Matye says. "In
blizzards, I just leave earlier and drive slower.")

The children play in the gym for 15 minutes, most
of the boys tossing a leaking volleyball through a
netless and bent basketball hoop and the girls com-
peting with a jump rope improvised from a frayed
clothesline knotted together in three places.

"Okay, it's time," Miss Sorrell says at 9 A.M. She
speaks quietly, but with unhesitant authority, and
the children move in a orderly line upstairs and to
their desks, the little ones in front and the big ones
in the back of the classroom.

The pledge of allegiance is offered in hearty
voices to a gold-fringed flag hanging straight down
over a door in the rear of the room. Even on Monday
morning, there is no other warm-up or pacifying
prelude to the schoolwork. The older children find
their assignments on a sheet tacked to the bulletin
board, or written out by Miss Sorrell on the blackboard. She hands simpler work sheets to the two
youngest children, Dee Miller and Robby Permann.
Five children—third-graders, the largest age group
in the class—pull pencils and arithmetic texts from
their desks and move over to sit at the card table
with their teacher.

She spends 10 minutes with them, explaining the
day's lesson on common multiples, questioning all
of them to assure their understanding, answering
their questions and then ordering them to return to
their own desks to complete the lesson individ-

ually. Brief periods of instruction follow at the card table for the other, smaller "grade" groups. Dee, the only first-grader, and Robby, the one second-grader, get eight minutes at the card table. Kenny Permann and Danny Mathes are with Miss Sorrell for 14 minutes on their algebra lesson.

She remains seated at the little table for most of the hour, but her eyes and ears cover the entire room. Her voice slightly raised and her head turned only partly away from the students at the table, she calls out to different individuals in the class at appropriate moments: "Tommy Croff, if you've finished your lesson help Dee count by 10's up to a hundred. . . . Sheila, please give Robby a hand with his lesson now. . . . Theresa, if you understand that hard question now, explain it to the others. . . . Danny and Kenny, you two can work together over there now if you want. . . . Dale, I want you to work by yourself a while longer. . . ."

Miss Sorrell manages to keep them all at work and orderly, but she is not a stickler for rules or exact procedures. Every child knows that she is busy with others at the card table, but also accessible to them if they are truly stuck on a problem. At random moments, they come over to stand quietly next to her until she breaks off from her formal lesson to answer an individual question. A child rarely has to wait more than 10 or 15 seconds.

The most impressive aspect of the routine is the graceful manner in which one pupil helps another. I watched dozens of examples of such instruction. There wasn't the slightest expression of resentment by any of the children who were being taught by their schoolmates, nor the slightest hint of offensive superiority by any of the pupils who were acting as teachers.

When Miss Sorrell asked Tommy Croff to help Dee, he knew precisely what to do. Tommy is 8 years old, with curious, beautifully clear blue eyes, and is quickly intelligent and able to lead. But there was no bossy tone as he stepped over to Dee's desk and said, "O.K., Dee, we're going to work together for a few minutes."

Dee is a giggly little 6-year-old who thoroughly enjoys her mercurial moods. "O.K.," she said to Tommy, "but first I have to get the burrs out of my tights."

Tommy wasn't about to be diverted from the lesson. "Those aren't burrs; they're lint," he said firmly. "Let's go to the blackboard now."

Dee giggled with only slight guilt and quickly moved to the blackboard with chalk poised. She waited attentively and respectfully for Tommy's instructions, while he glanced over the arithmetic work sheet she had just completed at her own desk.

"You're having trouble with the multiples of 10," Tommy concluded. "Now write up to a hundred by 10's on the board."

Dee chalked "00" then "10," paused and frowned, forgot "20," confidently chalked "30 . . . 40 . . . 50," left out "60," raced through "70 . . . 80 . . . 90" and ended with a huge grin and a "100" three times the size of the other numbers.

Tommy watched her intently while she worked. He sat on the edge of a front desk, all business except for his legs swinging back and forth from the desk top.

"That's not very good," he said matter-of-factly, "but it's better than you did on your work sheet."

He hopped off the desk top, found a long piece of chalk, placed small commas between Dee's numbers, then with the full sweep of his arm scrawled huge check marks at the points of her mistakes.

Dee yelped with pleasure. "I only missed two . . . One is 20, I know, so don't tell me. What's the other?"

"Sixty," Tommy said. "Six and then a zero make a 60. Now read them all off, putting in the corrections."

Dee did it, they both had fun erasing the line of numbers and check marks, then she gazed at Tommy with an eager what-next expression on her face.

"Do it again, Dee," Tommy said firmly. "But don't try to go so fast this time. There's no hurry."

She included the "20" this time, but botched the "60" again, putting in an extra and out-of-place "80" instead. Tommy sighed, but was careful that Dee didn't hear the sigh or see his disappointment.

"Dee, you missed 60 again. You've got an extra 80 there. Do it again, but slow down at that part."

I was convinced that Tommy held his breath when Dee reached the critical point the next time. She paused a long time after "50," and an expression of intense hopefulness gripped Tommy's face. His legs were still. His lips moved to form a silent 60, and I sensed that he was consciously trying to will or pray Dee toward perfection.

Reform in the Public Schools

With labored scrawl and furrowed brow and the tip of her tongue poking through her teeth, Dee chalked "60" in the right spot. The nervousness drained from Tommy, his legs began swinging again and his hands clapped together once softly as Dee completed the fully correct lesson.

She turned around to see his reaction. "Okay, you got it right," Tommy said. "Now say all the numbers aloud."

Dee moved along the blackboard speaking each number as she reached it, adding a decisive and flourished accent at "60."

Dee was happy, but she'd had it with that lesson, wanted to shift to something else and looked dejected when Tommy drove in with a final question.

"Dee, what have you just done?"

"I dunno."

"Well, Dee, you didn't just write a bunch of numbers. You learned how to count in a special way. What is it?"

"By 10's?"

"Yes."

Tommy waited until Miss Sorrell had a free moment, and called her to the board. Dee had to repeat the whole thing for Miss Sorrell. Though restless now, she did it confidently and correctly.

Miss Sorrell's moment with Dee and Tommy was part of the crucial half hour she spent roving around the room after completion of the card table classroom periods. She stepped from desk to desk, to the blackboard where two other pairs of children were working, and back to individual pupils with hands in the air or pleas of "Miss Sorrell, I'm stuck." With a few words, usually phrased as a question full of half-hints, Miss Sorrell nudged each child over a separate hurdle in their independent study.

A 15-minute recess separates the math and reading-language periods. Miss Sorrell can't relax then. Most of the children run down to the basement gym to play, but others linger behind in the classroom (that day, 14-year-old Danny continued a game of chess with Miss Sorrell, and 8-year-old Judy Bauder stayed to talk privately about a personal problem).

The second half of the morning in the classroom is devoted to reading, phonics, writing, and other language skills. At noon, the children break for the lunch period—20 minutes to eat at their desks and 25 minutes of play in the gym on cold days or outside when it's warm. Miss Sorrell steps across the hall to her apartment to cook her own lunch, but the door remains open. ("They can come in whenever they want," she said, glancing around the roomful of colorful, upholstered furniture. "By the standards of their homes, this room is plush.")

Even while eating or cooking and deep in conversation with a visitor, Miss Sorrell is conscious of the children downstairs or outside. The babble below was, to me, an easily ignored murmur. But she could hear and immediately interpret the slightest and most distant change of tone, alerting her to a fight, a hurt child, or even the imminence of what she called "trouble coming."

Miss Sorrell is an outstandingly competent teacher. She did not once "speak down" to the chil-

dren while I was at Monarch. Instead, her vocabu-
lary was naturally rich with words uttered distinctly
but previously unknown to the children. Nor did
she contrive the sweet smiles and semibaby talk
which I've noticed with some teachers in other
schools. She could laugh with the kids over some
amusing incident in class, but she remained always
an adult with a tough job to do, and the kids seemed
to respect her more for that. It might be an exagger-
ation to state that Miss Sorrell loves the 17 Monarch
children; there's too little time and she isn't inclined toward sentimentality. But she is clearly involved with them throughout the seven hours each
day, and she cares very much about each of them.

"I'd like to teach in an urban school, perhaps the
sixth grade," she says. "But this is fun, and important, and I don't qualify yet for regular teaching."
(She has an emergency teaching certificate from
Montana authorities, requiring that she take education courses each summer until she has an A.B.
degree. She hopes to finish a year from now. Until
then, she is paid $6,100 a year.)

"The children and I are learning together. I don't
have any big philosophy about teaching, and I don't
have the time to prepare individual lessons for each
of them in advance. We just take a day at a time, almost an hour at a time. All I want to do is help each
of them learn as much as possible every moment of
the school day.

"It's not that hard to teach here. These children
don't have much in their lives. There's a lot of
poverty, lots of alcoholism in this canyon. For many
of the children, school is the best and most impor-

tant thing in their lives. I guess they feel respected here, because I really listen to them. That's easy to do though, because they are so naturally curious and creative.

"The best thing about these little country schools—and I've taught in two others before Monarch—is that we all learn from each other. We each want to learn each day. No one among us is better than anyone else.

"Each day, each hour, each child is an immediate challenge, but I have long-range hopes too.

"I'd like to see each of them become good . . . how do I put it? Well, just good people. Tolerant, kind and positive.

"I have some selfish hopes too. I'll get my degree, then I'd like to teach in an urban school for two years. Then medical school, and finally I'd like to be a psychiatrist, specializing in children. I've seen how solvable problems can limit or destroy lives. The children can be saved, with some careful help and concern. . . ."

Two of the children broke into the conversation then, near the end of the lunch hour. Miss Sorrell removed cans of soda pop they had requested from her refrigerator. Theresa Dirkson snapped one open too quickly; a brown and bubbly stream from the can splattered across the room and onto Miss Sorrell's sofa. She laughed. The two girls laughed, then Theresa cleaned up the mess, without any order or reprimand.

In the afternoon, there's an hour for social studies, another 15-minute recess, a half hour for music and dancing, and a final hour for science. Miss Sorrell does not adhere rigidly to a scheduled sequence of subjects. On some days she gives the children a lesson in French, which she happens to know, or they all join in an open discussion about a topic which has affected them (the surrounding complex of nuclear missiles, two of which are poised in underground silos in the Monarch canyon; women's liberation, a subject which they have heard their parents scream about at home; the rights of personal property, a subject suggested by an incident in which one boy's basketball was slashed by another's knife).

Some of the school's disadvantages are evident in the afternoon. The state of Montana provides good and up-to-date textbooks for social studies, but Miss Sorrell admits that it's not one of her better subjects, the children feel very far removed from a world of government and rapid social change and they see few newspapers or magazines. The Cascade County Bookmobile spends only a half hour once every two weeks in Monarch to offer them additional reading materials.

The sources for music are limited to a dusty old upright piano with a dozen dead keys and a few 45-r.p.m. records which came out of cereal boxes. The children dance (boys' choice, then girls' choice) as Miss Sorrell plays the records on a phonograph brought to school by one of the girls. The size and quality of the phonograph suggest that it came out of a somewhat larger cereal box.

The formal study of science requires equipment, but Monarch School has none. There are no test tubes, no chemicals, no Bunsen burner. Miss Sorrell can't even use the high-quality science-education films produced today; the school's projector doesn't work and there are endless bureaucratic delays after ordering the films from the state. Teacher and children improvise instead. They spent weeks working on a display of bryophytes and a big poster with excellent sketches of parts of the human body.

At times here, I was slightly depressed about the meager lot of Monarch's children: the lack of laboratory equipment, the paper clips instead of buttons fastening several of their shirts, the cushiony volleyball used for basketball practice (Monarch's team of Danny, Kenny, Dale, Marvin Croff, and Randy Permann was clobbered by the Neihart School team 63 to 29 the Friday night before I arrived.)

But there is no self-pity or complaining at all among the children, even though they are aware of poverty and can see the common luxuries of most of society on TV each night. They do not, however, passively accept their lot. The hopes and aspirations are there. Randy Permann wants to become a truck driver, and he makes it clear that he intends to be a really good truck driver, with mechanical skills and an understanding of the whole scope of commercial transportation. Cathy Croff intends to be a farmer's wife, but, with an early appreciation of the women's liberation movement, she's also determined to train horses on her own. Linda Schoberg expects to be an architect and Danny Mathes plans for college and an electrical engineering career. Judy Bauder shyly discloses that she wants to be an artist, then adds with conviction, "I have talent. And I practice."

The Monarch School and Miss Sorrell are giving them a good boost toward their goals. She knows that many of them will not be able to go to college, so she isn't filling their heads now with lofty and scary aspirations. She and the children are taking it one day at a time; all of them have an earthy, realistic attitude which seems to preclude the fearful kind of frustrations which mark many "advantaged" urban children.

The Monarch School has a value and its students are richly endowed with a quality which couldn't be matched by the most affluent and innovative school district. It's an attitude of helpful sharing, an atmosphere of respectful tolerance for the differences among individuals. Ranging from age 6 to 14, from toddler size to muscular height, from extremely intelligent to semiretarded, the Monarch children cannot possibly compete against one another. They are, by necessity and with Miss Sorrell's help, challenging their own individual limits in learning and achievement.

Much of the credit for the success of the Monarch School can go to Miss Sorrell, exceptionally talented and skilled as a teacher. But she emphasizes that the children benefit as much from the essentially ungraded classroom circumstances as from her efforts.

"With a poor teacher, or one who is indifferent or unhappy," she says, "the children in a one-room school still have a natural advantage over the kids in a big school which separates the kids into age groups. In any kind of school, the quality of the teacher is extremely important. But in the one-room school, the children will inevitably learn how to study independently and they will be naturally inclined to help and teach one another."

School systems throughout the nation obviously cannot copy all the natural methods of instruction which have evolved in the one-room schoolhouses, nor should educators seek to return to the comforting concept of the little red schoolhouse, with all its sentimental and back-to-basics appeal. Urban school districts, challenged by problems ranging from contemporary racial conflicts to the eternal difficulties of teaching masses of minds, just can't be that simple.

But they can learn—and are learning—some lessons from the success of the nation's one-room schools. The important lesson is that children learn best in informal, ungraded classroom situations, where they have abundant opportunity to study independently and work with one another. The teachers in the one-room schools don't have the time or inclination to compile statistics or conduct studies of the long-range influences on their pupils. But the indications, in Monarch and elsewhere, are that the children from these educational islands do as well or better in college and careers as the graduates of complex urban schools.

The one-room schools of America are fading away. They are, the professional administrators know and the taxpayers complain, less efficient and more expensive than large, complex schools. The two one-room schools in which Miss Sorrell taught

just a few years ago are both closed now. There's a
growing movement among some of the people of
Monarch canyon—mainly nonparents, supported by
one of the three members of the school board—to
consolidate with the Belt School District and send
the children to a big and modern school building 27
miles away.

"Our little school was built in 1915, and it's still
in good shape with the new well and all," Board
Chairman Everett Davis says. "We'll hang onto it
for as long as we can."

Miss Sorrell reluctantly but realistically admits,
"Consolidation is coming. The Monarch School
can't last more than another five years. It could be
closed and empty in another year or two."

Meanwhile, the Monarch children work hard and
dig for their education. There is no educational
silver spoon for them, ladling out skills and knowledge with all the sweet and easy-to-swallow ingredients of better-equipped schools. The children dig
into the task each day with impressive determination, with an ability to improvise, and with the necessity of cooperating with one another.

PART FIVE

Several of the earlier articles discussed mass higher education (Bush), the meaning of going to college for the affluent adolescent (Berger, Swados), and the impact of growing bureaucracy in large colleges and universities (Hacker). In this section, four articles take us deeper into major problems of American higher education at the end of a quarter century of post–World War II development.

One place "where the action is" now is the open-door community college, and the system that has committed itself one way or another to "open admissions." The first article, "Report Card on Open Admissions: Remedial Work Recommended," by Resnik and Kaplan, examines the first year of the new open-admissions policy of the City University of New York. Here are discussed the hard work, the dilemmas, the pulling and hauling involved when such a policy is effected in an established system long proud of its selectivity and quality. It will take some years to tell how well the policy will work in

The crisis of purpose and identity in higher education

the New York City system, but clearly the system as a whole will be transformed. There must be much remedial or "sub-college" work, to help the poorly qualified make up for lack of achievement in the years before college. The most exquisite dilemma in an open-door policy is whether to place the poorly prepared students in separate colleges or programs or tracks, risking charges of discrimination and cooling-out, or to throw them in with the better prepared and high-achieving students where they may be traumatized, demotivated, and flunked out by the brutal competition. There are no easy answers. It takes dogged effort to devise a new web of practices that will be educationally, morally, politically, and economically tolerable.

The second article, "A Kind of Higher Education," by Gene I. Maeroff, indicates what life is like for teachers and students inside an urban community college, with much attention paid to one particular two-year college—Bronx Community College

—within the New York City system. Here is the heaviest concentration of poorly-prepared students, compared with four-year colleges and universities, and the problems are immense. Some of the faculty, at least some of the time, think they are doing the most challenging and rewarding work in all of American higher education. But there is also worry that remedial programs cannot make up for the failure of students and schools in the elementary and secondary years, that standards inevitably blur and slip, and that the whole place could become an educational slum. For many of the students, in turn, the two-year college is the second or third—and probably last—chance to get things together for advancement to a bachelor's degree and a better job. And among them are late bloomers and other success stories that gladden the heart and, perhaps for all, make the place worthwhile. But for large numbers among the students, the open-door is inevitably a revolving door—easy in, but soon out or stalled in place. The math, the English, is finally too much, and the aspiration to complete college must be given up. Cruel disappointment is the fate of many: the community college is so sited in the educational structure that it must serve as a graveyard of hope as well as a path into higher education for those who otherwise could never enter. In Bronx Community College, we see the struggle in extreme form, with all the problems of racial disadvantage and aspiration loaded on top of the normal tensions of open-door colleges.

The third article, "A Crisis in Catholic Educations," by Daniel Callahan, is an explanation of how social change has affected the religious sector of American higher education. The founders of higher education establishments in this country were of Protestant denominations. Later in the nineteenth century, when large waves of Irish and European immigrants of Catholic background flooded into the country, the Catholic church followed suit, founding colleges and universities that devoted themselves to teaching Catholicism as well as the nonreligious aspects of general and vocational education. Thus, private American higher education has had deep religious roots. But the religious commitment has long been in decline, as students flowed into the fast-growing public institutions and as American higher education overall became a secularizing force. One religious college after another ceased to be religious or remained only nominally committed. The Catholic colleges, as a bloc, long held out against this trend, but the changes of the last twenty years have now thrown them into a veritable crisis of purpose. A "liberalization" has been underway in Catholic thought in general, and the Catholic institutions of higher education were bound to be caught up in much agonizing soul searching. Does it make sense to go on attempting to maintain a deeply religious atmosphere in a college? If not, should the Catholic orders get out of the "education business" altogether and use their scarce resources in some other way? Mr. Callahan offers a highly informative account of the history of these colleges and their current crisis of institutional identity.

The last article, "A Different Way to Restructure the University," by Irving Kristol, argues effec-

The Crisis of Purpose and
Identity in Higher Education

240

tively that American higher education in general
and the large university in particular have lost a
sense of purpose, and that this lack of purpose un-
derlies the student discontent and campus conflicts
of the last decade. What to do about it? Mr. Kristol
argues that fundamental reform will not come from
within, that none of the internal parties—trustees or
administrators or professors *or* students—has the interest, vision, and power to bring it about. Rather,
the established structure will best be opened up by
channeling federal funds directly to students in the
form of scholarships and loans, and then letting the
process of "consumer choice" lead to the development of institutions with different purposes. Some
students will want one kind of higher education,
which they will find in one kind of institution,
while other students will find what they seek elsewhere.

Reform, in fact, will come about in a multiplicity
of ways, with some paths undoubtedly devised by
reformers already within the system; but the general mechanism advocated by Kristol may well be
an important route. It fits the historical experience
of American higher education, with its combination
of private and public sectors, its freedom of choice
for students, and competition among institutions. A
"huge injection" of consumer choice would indeed
encourage some of the smaller and middle-sized
places to experiment in order to find the new purpose and institutional identity that would appeal to
some of the students most of the time.

In an age when a growing heterogeneity of individual and group needs and interest presses for

diversity and variety in institutional forms, American higher education is luckier than American elementary and secondary education. Educational policies designed to increase institutional diversity at the lower levels run head on into the tradition and structure of the public comprehensive school, but such policies at the level of higher education can find a more congenial setting.

In any event, the search is on for ways of forcing educational institutions to become self-conscious again about what they are, what they are doing, and what their roles in society should be. Many institutions will be forced into an identity crisis. Like individuals, they will not enjoy this state of affairs and will twist and turn in the agony of insecurity and confusion. Some will be permanently traumatized and stagger on as a pale shell of a fully alive social organism. Some will die from a lack of financial or moral nutrition. But most, like individuals, will grow in character from the experience of having to ask, and then to answer afresh, what one's existence is all about. Institutions, too, must have a sense of place. When they have it in full measure, they can serve us well.

Report card on open admissions: Remedial work recommended

SOLOMON RESNIK *and* BARBARA KAPLAN

As of last September [1970], 8,500 blacks and Puerto Ricans were registered as freshmen at the City University of New York, in a total undergraduate enrollment of 155,000. This figure represents, at least on the surface, something of a revolution. Last year's freshman class included less than half that number, or a total of 3,820 blacks and Puerto Ricans. We are witnessing, in other words, one of the most massive attempts in our history to provide a college education for members of minority groups, many of them from ghetto areas.

A major cause of this dramatic increase in black and Puerto Rican freshmen is CUNY's new open-admissions policy, which guarantees a place in the City University to every high-school graduate in New York City, regardless of his grades or the type of diploma he has. By working to insure an ethnic balance throughout the university, CUNY is mov-

ing toward the end of the *de facto* segregation that
has existed in the past.

The experiment has produced one of the most bitter educational fights in New York City in recent
years. Originally scheduled for 1975, the beginning
date was pushed up after a series of violent confrontations which at one point caused City College to
close down temporarily.

Now admissions may have to be cut back sharply
to fit the Procrustean bed of the city's overloaded
budget. The Lindsay administration warns that,
without more revenue for the city, CUNY may not
be able to enroll a freshman class next year at all.
While the intent of this threat is clearly political—to
pressure the legislature into approving more aid
and city taxes—even more realistic proposals by the
city might force the reimposition of limits on admissions and further shrink funds available for those
admitted in the first year of the policy.

Under the program, any student who has received
a diploma from a New York City high school in June
1970, or thereafter is eligible for admission to
CUNY, whether he has an academic, a general, or a
vocational diploma, and whether his average is 95
or 65. Such a policy is revolutionary in several ways.
For one thing, it does away with the traditional
requirement of a relatively high grade average, and,
for another, it eliminates the old requirement of a
certain number of academic high-school credits.
Less than 5 percent of the black high-school graduates earn academic diplomas, and it is easy to see
from this fact alone the dramatic effect open admis-

sions can have on the number of blacks eligible for college.

Nevertheless, open admissions has so far proved to be a boon to whites as well. The freshman class of about 34,500 includes 24,300 whites, a large number of whom would not have been eligible without open admissions. One of the largest groups to benefit is white Catholic students from working-class families, and thus the university's ethnic make-up has been changed in a second way. In previous years the great majority of students were Jews, predominantly from the middle class.

While every student is guaranteed acceptance into one of the branches of CUNY, the actual school he will attend depends on his high-school record. The most crucial issue is whether the student will go to one of the nine four-year senior colleges, which tend to concentrate on the liberal arts, or to one of the seven two-year community colleges, which have always had less stringent admissions criteria and concentrate on preparing students for jobs as dental technicians, hygienists, and the like. The community colleges do have an academic transfer program that enables a student after two years to attend one of the senior colleges, which are generally regarded as much more prestigious.

The Board of Higher Education's guidelines for open admissions require that the choice of both the school which the student attends and the particular program he enrolls in be made, as far as possible (but not entirely), by the student himself. The student's choice is limited by two criteria: his high-school average and his rank in his high-school graduating class. A high-school graduate who has an 85 or better average or is in the top 30 percent of his graduating class (70th to 99th percentile) will be guaranteed a place at the senior college of his choice. One who graduates with an 80 to 85 average or in the 50th to 70th percentile of his graduating class will be accepted by a senior college, but not necessarily his first choice. Those whose averages are below 80 and who are below the 50th percentile (i.e., in the bottom half of their class) are not eligible for senior colleges; they are automatically placed in one of the community colleges. Each student is placed in the highest category for which either his grade average or percentile ranking—whichever gives him a higher ranking—entitles him.

Once the student enters CUNY, the situation he encounters will depend on the particular branch he attends. The Board of Higher Education's guidelines require that various supportive services be provided, including financial aid, counseling, and remedial work. In fact, the amount and kind of help provided varies drastically from school to school.

The CUNY graduate of 20, of 10, or even 5 years ago, returning to his alma mater, would probably notice much that is different. CUNY is larger than it has ever been, and one sees long lines and crowds, and hears the grumbling associated with these things—in cafeterias, bookstores, student lounges. The larger numbers of black and Puerto Rican students now on campus have inevitably brought other changes in atmosphere. For example, the bulletin boards announce, in addition to traditional campus activities, meetings of various black and Puerto Rican organizations, and the college catalogues list an increasing number of courses oriented to minority-group issues.

The returning alumnus would find a great difference of opinion on the new conditions among students. Some, he would find, complain bitterly about overcrowding and see themselves almost as victims of open admissions. Others think the new policy has a stimulating effect on campus life. The alumnus would find this same split among faculty members, although their reactions tend to be couched in more academic terms. Some would be embittered and complaining about the lowering of CUNY's standards. A few would even be talking about quitting—although, as far as we know, open admissions itself has not yet been the cause of any faculty resignations.

For some faculty members, open admissions has been the cause of anxiety and uncertainty. Even many who favor the policy feel that their education and experience have not prepared them to teach open-admissions students and that, in order to be effective, they must go through painful retraining. Yet many professors speak animatedly about the challenges of the policy and the good that can come of it.

The result of this is that almost any discussion with a CUNY faculty member is bound to turn to open admissions. Words like "standards," "skill development," "relevance" are bandied about; the division that exists is reflected in veiled references by

The Crisis of Purpose and
Identity in Higher Education

the opponents of the policy to "those people," and
by proponents to unnamed "reactionaries."

Were the visiting alumnus to delve deeper, he
would see a university trying to implement a new
philosophy of education. The CUNY of the past
worked on the principle that the student had to
enter college with a certain level of skills and a certain amount of knowledge. The new CUNY, by taking on the added responsibility of helping a student
acquire the skills he needs to do college work, has
taken over some of the functions traditionally per-
formed by high schools.

The debate over open admissions, in other words,
is between two opposing views of the university's
role: The old, traditional view assumes college is a
privilege granted to a relatively few talented students, the B.A. degree is a rare and coveted prize,
and the university is under no obligation to reach
larger numbers of people; it is thus the responsibility of the student to meet, on his own, the rigorous requirements for graduation and a degree. According to the new view, it is the university's
responsibility to provide an education for as many
students as possible, though, ideally, not at the expense of standards. To do so, it must be active in
recruiting students and in helping them live up to
its standards. In place of the old "ivory tower," the
university is seen as a force in the struggle for social
equality.

CUNY's master plan provided for a total of 26,500
entering freshmen this year; the enrollment of approximately 8,500 students over that cannot be written off as just a mild reform. In this respect at least,

open admissions represents a triumph of the new desire to permit larger numbers of young people to attend college.

But the triumph is far from complete, and the statistics seem a bit less impressive on closer examination. Of the 7,000 blacks who entered CUNY this year as freshmen, approximately 3,500 could have been accepted under already existing programs such as College Discovery and Operation SEEK. Both programs have served as pilot projects for open admissions, bringing disadvantaged youth to college and providing them with the remedial help and financial aid that they need to get a degree.

Thus open admissions has so far helped only an additional modest number of blacks. As for whites admitted under the policy, many of them would have gone to college anyway. Their averages were too low under CUNY's old standards, but high enough to get them into one or another of the various private colleges in the New York area.

After only one full semester, it is too early to make a final judgment about open admissions. Still, we can begin to do the kind of evaluation that this ambitious social experiment deserves. We will see that wherever the new philosophy of education has guided decision-making at CUNY, the results have been promising. But CUNY is far from having made a complete transition to the new view, and the university's inability to do so has led to serious flaws in open admissions which we will examine in a discussion of four issues: (1) remedial programs; (2) academic standards; (3) racial goals, and (4) funding.

The Crisis of Purpose and Identity in Higher Education

I. REMEDIAL PROGRAMS

The success of open admissions involves more than just questions of quantity. To be successful, the policy must not only bring students to the colleges but also help them to earn a degree. Thus, a second major question arises: Is CUNY providing open-admissions students with a real opportunity for a good education? Or is it, as many feared, setting up not an open-door policy but a revolving door in which students are accepted—only to flunk out soon after?

The heart of this question is skill development. The failures of the New York City public-school system, especially in poverty areas, need no further documentation here. The practical result is that students from ghetto schools come to college with glaring academic problems: Their reading-comprehension level is often low; they have never been taught how to write a well-organized, critical paper, or to take notes or do research; they have had little training in critical thinking or in dealing with abstraction.

Remedying these deficiencies requires a total acceptance of the new view of education. However, torn between the old and the new views, CUNY has let each college decide how much remedial work to offer and the programs vary greatly, with some schools doing virtually nothing and continuing with traditional academic programs unchanged, others setting up token tutoring and workshop programs, and still others attempting full-scale skill-development courses.

In some schools, the student will simply be

placed in existing courses and left to shift for himself. In others, he is given a counselor who helps him adjust to a strange environment. Sometimes he is assigned a tutor to help him with academic problems, or will have the option of attending voluntary workshops in skill development.

This freedom permits wide experimentation. At the same time, the experiments have ranged from some with at least good potential to others that have already proved disastrous. While it is too soon for a precise evaluation of each school, one index of the great differences in effectiveness may be dropout rates. According to unofficial estimates by administrators, for example, the rate before exams in January was 8 percent at one school and almost 25 percent at another.

The most serious weakness of these programs is that they simply do not provide enough skill-development work. In at least one community college a quarter of the open-admissions class was excused, after taking a test, from any composition course. (By contrast, many of the senior colleges require *every* freshman—whether open admissions or not—to take such a course, and insist that a good number of students take two semesters of composition.) The irony here is that such exemptions are based not on evidence of good writing ability, but on the student's score in a reading test. Those who flunked the first time took the same test again during the semester, and, if they passed the second time (having seen the questions once before), were allowed to drop the course and were given credit for it.

The Crisis of Purpose and
Identity in Higher Education

Another example of a disaster was a "mini-course" set up at one college. The course, designed to teach students how to do research papers, was first given for a total of 10 class hours a semester (the usual college course involves 42 hours) but was soon reduced to 8 and then to 6 hours. Several teachers have pointed out that even 10 hours is not enough, and the 6- and 8-hour courses are close to useless. To make matters worse, the students had only to attend the lectures to pass the course; they were not required to write a paper at all. When a teacher in one section of the course did require a paper, the vast majority failed.

At a recent conference on open admissions, Dr. Melvin Taylor, principal of Benjamin Franklin High School, said, "Remediation is often a repeat, a rehash of educational techniques that have previously failed the students."

All too often, students are taught reading-comprehension and writing skills by traditional methods of boring exercises and multiple-choice questions which seem to have no relation to real college work or to anything that might be valuable and interesting to the student. Typical reading-comprehension assignments have included such scintillating topics as "Bombing the Paragraph" and "But What's a Dictionary For?"

To develop good writing skills students are asked to become excited about such topics as "My First Day at School" and "The Best Teacher I Have Known." Skimming techniques have been taught by going over recipes taken from a cookbook—the teacher apparently believing that reading a list of ingredients can be stimulating. These programs, following the traditional definition of remediation, ignore the crucial area of critical thinking.

Instead of the degrading exercises of the past, what is needed is a whole new approach in which students can work with intellectually challenging and relevant materials. This is a task worthy of the best minds in the educational system—but it is being done only in part.

Accustomed to functioning under the old system, some teachers and administrators adhere to educational theories geared to the traditional CUNY student who has gone to a middle-class high school that has done at least an adequate job of teaching him academic skills. However well-intentioned, such people have little conception of the leap that the new situation requires.

Equally at fault are many black student and faculty groups, which have tended to avoid the skill-development issue. Because they are primarily interested in developing a black consciousness, they have tended to direct their efforts toward establishing black-studies programs. While such groups often complain bitterly about the failures of the New York public schools, they too have done little to develop new concepts of remedial work. At times, they even deny the problem exists. One group, for example, claimed that the whole concept of remedial work was both irrelevant and racist.

At the beginning, of course, many of CUNY's approximately 13,000 full-time and part-time faculty felt a bit overwhelmed by the numbers of additional freshmen who were enrolled at the last minute in

The Crisis of Purpose and
Identity in Higher Education

the fall. The university did hire more teachers. Yet a common complaint among the administrators was that they were not given enough money to hire the necessary staff.

No program will succeed if it is not funded, and even minimal funds have been hard to come by—and will be even scarcer next year. Specialists in skill development emphasize the need for small classes, for experienced faculty, and for a low student-teacher ratio—all of which cost money. In at least one school, plans for a comprehensive skill-development program had to be scrapped in favor of a far more modest effort because of lack of funds.

Another obstacle is the conflict between the staff that supervises these skill-development courses and the traditional academic departments. The main issue here is usually whether academic credit should be granted for the courses. The old theory, adhered to by the traditionalists, is that remedial classes are basically high-school work which does not qualify for college credit.

Many people contend that the old concept does not apply anymore. The old definition of remedial work implied that the student had taken the same work in high school but had done badly. The fact is that the graduates of today's ghetto schools have not been taught many of these skills. It may thus be fair to give students credit for such work—just as the student taking French I (which is offered in high school) is given credit if he has had no prior work in French. Some argue, too, that credit is needed for purposes of morale, that it is too discouraging for a student to spend time on a course and receive no concrete reward for it. The traditional view, however, regards the question of morale as irrelevant.

Several academic departments have been willing to grant credit for remedial courses, but again the transition to the new is far from complete. Almost every administrator mentioned difficulties, especially those in the English and math departments. The resistance to granting credit is stronger at the community colleges, because the entire curriculum of such schools consists of only 64 credits (as opposed to 108 at the senior colleges) and many teachers argue that 9 or 12 credits for remedial work is too large a part of the total. Compounding the difficulty is the fact that the community colleges have the largest number of blacks from ghetto areas in the open-admissions program—and thus have the largest number of students who need remedial work.

One prediction can safely be made. In general, open admissions will mainly benefit students who have well-developed skills, whose poor record in high school was merely the result of lack of effort, and who will be able to do college work without the extra help if they only are given the chance. They will benefit less the student with very mild skills problems who needs only a little extra help to develop his academic skills. But for the student with weak skills—no matter how high his native intelligence—open admissions will prove least beneficial. Indeed, it may end up as a false hope and a cruel disappointment.

The failure to help these students would have far-reaching implications. Critics of open admissions

are already citing students' weak skills as evidence
of their lack of intelligence. The fault, however,
may lie not in the theory of open admissions, but
with the vacillating and half-hearted way that some
staff members have applied it.

II. ACADEMIC STANDARDS

Central to the theory is the belief that open admissions involves no lowering of standards for a
college degree. It assumes, rather, a lowering of the
standards for admissions only. A good skill-development program should prevent any compromise with
standards. The success of Operation SEEK demonstrates the fallacy of this particular argument against
the policy. Initially regarded with great fear precisely because it might bring down standards,
SEEK is now a source of pride to CUNY. Not only
has the original fear proved groundless, but in some
cases SEEK has led the way in curriculum reforms
which were later adopted throughout the school.

As of last June, CUNY was pointing with pride to
three SEEK students who had graduated from
Queens College with honors. Two had been on
parole when they entered college and the third was
desperately unhappy in a badly paying, menial job.
Of those three, two are now working for their doctorates at Harvard, both with Woodrow Wilson fellowships and full scholarships, and the third is in
the graduate sociology program at the City University. This past summer, one was director of a community center in Brooklyn, while another worked at
finishing up a novel which is scheduled for publication next year. Of the approximately 110 students

that began the SEEK program in 1966 at Queens
College, about 25 are expected to graduate (a striking number, since only two graduated from high
school with an academic diploma and none would
have qualified for admission to the college under
the old standards).

Even the most ardent proponents of open admissions do not ask that everyone be given a college
degree. The assumption behind the new view is
only that everyone has the right to a real opportunity for a college degree. This means, first, admit-
tance to college, and second, all of the help the
student needs to help him develop academic skills.
That is all we can do or be expected to do. If it is
done well, the student will be able to function up to
the level of his ability and desire. For some this will
mean a B.A. from a senior college, and for others an
A.A. (Associate in Arts) from a community college.
Not every entering freshman will be able to earn a
degree, but despite this the time spent in college
will be well worth it. Many former SEEK students
who didn't finish college, for example, are now in
well-paying jobs that they never would have been
eligible for without their additional schooling.

Still, the fact is that many teachers continue to
believe in the inevitability of lower standards, often
not from their concrete experience but from their
belief in the old view of the university. This attitude is all too prevalent at the community colleges,
which have traditionally felt somewhat inferior to
the senior colleges and thus have sometimes been
very defensive. Many staff members at these
schools regard open admissions as a further threat to

their status, and all too often they complain that it is not their job "to teach high school math and English."

Those teachers who argue that open-admissions students cannot perform in college could become the agents of a self-fulfilling prophecy, and there are already small groups of teachers who have adopted a kind of fatalism. We have no choice about accepting such students or not, they say, so we might as well just pass them and not be bothered about the problem. Basically such an argument is a rationalization for the teacher's unwillingness to deal with the problems. Where such an attitude exists, however, it can lead, ironically, to lower standards.

III. RACIAL GOALS

Adherents of the traditional view predict that the lower standards implicit in open admissions will drive many first-rate white, middle-class students away from CUNY. So intense were the fears at one point that programs were being set up to allow talented high school juniors to enter CUNY as freshmen in order to maintain an academic elite. But there is no evidence at all that CUNY is losing any of its good students; as several teachers have pointed out, open admissions is bringing in a number of "late bloomers," both white and black, who have high intellectual potential which they did not make full use of in high school.

On the other hand, the policy has not brought the even racial distribution throughout the branches of CUNY that was envisioned in the Board of Higher Education's guidelines. Ethnic balance was an

overriding concern when class standing was chosen
along with high school average as a criterion for assigning a student to one college or another. A black
student might have a low average and yet rank fairly
high in his own ghetto school.

While the ethnic balance of most of the schools
has improved to some degree, the community
colleges have been more affected than the senior colleges—and of the latter, only CCNY
seems to have enrolled an appreciably larger number of blacks.

There is another danger in using grade average
and class standing as the criteria for assigning students. The experience of the SEEK program has
shown that these are not reliable criteria. The good
student who is placed incorrectly in a community
college will not be harmed, since he can transfer to
a senior college after two years. But the student who
is placed in a four-year school and cannot handle
the work has no possibility of any kind of degree.

Is it possible for large numbers of black students
to coexist on a campus with white, middle-class
students? This is perhaps the most oft-stated question on campus and off. The fear of many who hold
to the old view of the university is that the abrupt
change is leading not to increased harmony and democracy but to virtual race war, and incidents of
black-white confrontations elsewhere in the
country are raised as a horrifying specter of what
might happen at CUNY.

At the moment, neither racial harmony nor civil
war seems likely. Racism is a problem, but not to
the extent some critics say it is. At one school, an in-

cident between a black student and a cafeteria worker led to a sit-in by the blacks. Many white students are delighted to relate stories of friends, or friends of friends, who were kept out of courses they wanted, or were cheated in some way, because of black open-admissions students.

The attitude of many white students that they had to work hard to get into college while the blacks did not can be interpreted, most generously, as simply an updated version of the Protestant ethic. Yet the racist aspect of the argument is clear from a look back at CUNY's history.

After World War II, veterans were accepted into CUNY as well as many other colleges throughout the country even if they didn't have all the proper credentials; there were few complaints. Similarly, several years ago, when the average required for admission to CUNY was lowered from the 90's to the 80's, many of today's opponents of open admissions hailed the change as a great reform, as a way of giving more students a chance to earn a B.A.

Open admissions has simply carried the principles of both earlier policies one step further, the only significant difference being that for the first time large numbers of blacks are eligible for college; in both earlier cases the majority of people affected were white. One is tempted to remember the statement of one professor, "I don't mind a trickle of black students, but this is a flood!"

Nevertheless, there is certainly not a civil war. Nor is the situation any worse than it was before open admissions—one need only remember the incidents at Queens College and at CCNY in 1969 to realize that racial tensions are not a product of open admissions alone.

Neither, however, is there much evidence of the greater racial understanding that many claim is developing. The vision of blacks and whites engaged in dialogues on the library steps, arguing, at times vehemently, but eventually coming to a deeper understanding of one another and walking off arm-in-arm has not materialized. What has happened, simply, is that old cliques and old friends have continued to stay together. Black students have formed their own groups, and their contact with whites is usually very limited. For proof of this, one need only glance at the cafeteria of any branch of CUNY. Almost invariably, the blacks are sitting together in one section while the whites remain in their own areas.

Yet the presence of more black students is having an impact on CUNY. The traditional contemporary civilization course has finally begun to deal with other "civilizations" besides that of the West, and academic departments are offering new courses on black topics. The coming of black open-admissions students has provided the impetus for more such changes and is beginning to have an impact on CUNY's white, middle-class students, many of whom have, until recently, been almost unaware of racial issues. Now, black students in class have shown them how racism and the unquestioning assumption of Western superiority are implicit in many of the books they read. This trend is a healthy one—and it reflects at least some willingness to create a new kind of university.

The Crisis of Purpose and Identity in Higher Education

IV. FINANCES

Finally, there are the very concrete financial issues. CUNY's budget of $328-million for 1970–71 included an increase over the previous year of $88-million—a good part of which went to finance open admissions. Yet the university has all along complained of a strained budget. Part of the problem is the newness of the policy. While original estimates for open admissions predicted an enrollment of 35,000 students, these estimates were later revised to 30,000 and money was appropriated on the basis of that figure. When the original estimate proved closer, a scarcity of funds resulted.

The shortage has two serious effects. First, as we already mentioned, it has led to some of the weaknesses in the remedial programs. Second, it has left most of the open-admissions students with an almost impossible burden. Since CUNY students live at home (the university has no dormitory space), pay no tuition, and are usually from the middle class, CUNY has felt (rightly or wrongly) that financial aid could be handled very easily with some student loans, part-time jobs, and so on. But open admissions has changed all that by bringing significant numbers of students from poverty areas. In theory, any student can come to CUNY, but if he has to work full-time to support himself, then the opportunity may be a meaningless one. It is asking a lot to expect a student to upgrade weak skills, carry a heavy program, and at the same time work long hours.

CUNY itself recognized this problem as early as 1966. When it started various programs for students from poverty areas, it provided a weekly stipend for each of them. Yet no such arrangement has been made for the neediest open-admissions students. There is no telling how many students have stayed away from college because they cannot afford it, and clearly many who are now in school will do less well because of money worries. A number of the open-admissions students feel that money was promised to them but never delivered, and resent the fact that SEEK students—who are chosen by lottery—do get stipends.

To make matters worse, the money that has been available for open admissions has not always been spent in the best way. Before the program started there was a frantic effort by the various colleges to rent, buy, and erect buildings that were considered necessary to accommodate the new students. Yet it is also fairly clear that CUNY is not using existing space as effectively as possible. The real problem concerns mainly nonacademic space: cafeterias, student lounges, study rooms, bookstores, and the like. Yet the available money is being spent not for these things, but for classroom space.

One source of the problem is, oddly, the use of computers to allocate classroom space. There is always a big difference between the computer-formulated list of empty rooms and the actual number available. In scheduling classes for SEEK, for example, administrators were repeatedly told that no more rooms were available. Yet investigation revealed many empty rooms that were listed by the computer as in use.

The Crisis of Purpose and
Identity in Higher Education

Moreover, there is no reason why more classes cannot be held in the evening hours or on weekends (the tradition of Saturday classes is a strong one at many private colleges)—provided allowances are made for students with religious objections and each student still has no more than five days of classes.

Many people argue that since money is already tight, there is no use even of thinking of any more ambitious plans for open admissions, however valid they may be. This argument is raised, for example, in discussions of proposals to expand recruiting and to set up programs for adults, for students with high potential who have no high-school degrees, and for parolees who have been released from prison and want to continue their education. All of these are valid plans in the spirit of the open-admissions guidelines, which say that CUNY "should offer programs that meet the needs of other segments of the community." But they are not taken seriously, and often the reasons given are financial. While the financial argument is a real one, especially in view of the current city budget crisis, if CUNY allocated funds more efficiently it could begin to implement at least some of these programs.

In the last analysis, the most important measure of success for the new policy will be the number of open-admissions students who graduate from college. If CUNY continues to cling to old patterns, the outlook is particularly bleak for exactly the students it held out the most promise to—black students from the ghettos. A cursory check of the college yearbooks indicates that of about 10,000 black stu-

---

dents that CUNY says were in attendance in 1966 only a very small percentage have graduated. The percentage seems particularly low in the senior colleges.

Without effective skill-development courses designed to make up for deficiencies in New York's public high schools, more open-admissions students will go out the revolving door before receiving a diploma. Unless this changes, we may ultimately have to choose between standards and numbers, and there is no way of avoiding serious consequences whatever choice we make. Should worst come to worst, it would probably be preferable to lower standards somewhat, since the alternative is far more undesirable. We cannot continue to deny a college education to thousands of students who have already been denied a good high-school education—especially at a time when a college degree is becoming a prerequisite for more and more jobs. But the better solution is to avoid this unhappy choice, and the only way to do that is to accept completely the new role implicit in open admissions. Only then will CUNY be able to turn its full energies to the problems involved.

Whether we like it or not, the highly complex, technological society of the twentieth century is forcing us to find ways to provide an education for larger numbers of people from all strata of society. Out of this need, and out of the movement for racial equality, open admissions and the new view of education it represents were born. Inevitably, conflicts arising in the social order have been brought into our educational institutions, and CUNY's problems

The Crisis of Purpose and
Identity in Higher Education

are comparable to those faced by every urban college. One thing is then clear: CUNY cannot go back to the old view of education; its survival will depend on how well it adapts to the new.

**The Problems of
American Education**

A kind of higher education

GENE I. MAEROFF

Prospering on a diet of academic leftovers, the community college—the stepchild of American higher education—had grown into a strapping, obstreperous adolescent that now, if only by virtue of size, commands the attention that it has frequently been denied in years past. The community, or two-year, college is a peculiarly American institution bastardized from the tradition of higher learning transplanted into New England's soil from Europe three centuries ago. Students attend the community college because of its proximity to their homes, the low cost, the chance to take technical and vocational courses that are not available in the typical four-year academic program, the greater opportunity for individual counseling and remedial studies and—more than anything else—because the community college is not particular about whom it accepts. Though its students are of varying abilities, it is, especially in the urban setting, the last refuge of the educational down-and-outer, the haven of the scholastic ne'er-do-well.

In contrast to the freshman at a four-year college or university, according to a national survey by the American Council on Education, the freshman at a two-year college did less well in high school, has a lower family income and has less-educated parents. He or she is more likely to live at home, to have a job while going to school and to have waited longer before starting college. He or she is also more likely to become a college dropout. While 78 percent of the students in four-year institutions return for their sophomore year, 66 percent do so in two-year colleges, the council found. "It may certainly be said that unfilled expectations are the rule rather than the exception among two-year students," says Dr. Alexander W. Astin, research director of the American Council on Education.

Despite its growth and emergence as a major new factor in higher education, the community college is still widely regarded as an institutional Johnny-come-lately, serving an untraditional student body. The community college is often misunderstood—even by its own faculty and students—and frequently is burdened with an adverse image. Authorized to confer no degree higher than the associate's, and usually leaving its doors open to anyone who wants to enter, the two-year college struggles to reconcile its existence with two popular concepts—that a genuine college should be at least somewhat selective, and that it should offer a four-year program.

A typical urban representative is Bronx Community College, which soon will have its own campus but, for the present, makes its headquarters on East 184th Street. It is around the corner from Loew's Paradise and a block and a half off the Grand Concourse, that expansive ribbon of 10-lane concrete along which the borough's blight is being propelled northward, a relentless encroachment of misery that has transformed the once-proud Bronx into the most impoverished of New York's 62 counties.

As irony would have it, the tan, five-story brick building used to house one of the sparkling jewels in the city's tarnished public educational system, the Bronx High School of Science, with its brainy, high-achieving youngsters who carried forth their ambitions to places like Harvard, M.I.T., and Yale. Now—Bronx Science itself having been relocated 21 blocks to the north—the building is home to a different type of school. While learning is still its first order of business, Bronx Community, with a majority of blacks and Puerto Ricans among its 12,700 students, reflects a changing city and different needs. Education at Bronx Community means biochemistry and the history of Western civilization, but it also may mean instruction in the repair of air-conditioners and the punching of computer cards, or even the kind of tutelage deemed necessary to bring undergraduates above an eighth-grade reading level.

Indeed, 70 percent of Bronx Community's entering students cannot read, write and, compute figures on a college level; 52 percent come from families with annual incomes of less than $7,500, and only

6.8 percent have fathers who are college graduates. Examples of the deficiencies many of them bring with them are legion. Two students paid to tutor in mathematics tell of having to teach some students how to add 5 and 3; a Yale graduate, teaching English part-time at the college, discovers that the only way he can lift the low reading level of some of his collegians is to use sixth-grade materials he borrows from his mother, an elementary-school principal.

Yet, given this lack of preparation, many of the students harbor a mystical faith that the magic of higher education will somehow alter and elevate them. "They come here thinking that it can change their lives and I agree with them," says George B. Davis, a young black novelist and former newspaperman, who lectures in the English department and coordinates Bronx Community College's black-studies program. "They are less sophisticated than students who go to four-year colleges, and their academic background is not as good. The level of class discussion is less abstract than it might be somewhere else, and many of them have trouble finding time to do homework assignments because they have part-time and full-time jobs. Their lack of preparedness is frustrating to a teacher. But many of them are bright and eager and have had high-school counselors who told them they weren't college material. They found themselves shunted into courses that did not prepare them for college."

Today, there are 2,866,062 students in 1,141 two-year institutions in the United States. There were fewer than a dozen two-year colleges in the nation at the beginning of this century. Most of them were privately supported, finishing-school-type institutions. Until the nineteen-fifties, so sketchy were the records pertaining to the development of junior colleges that the enrollment statistics from different sources conflicted. (In 1948, for example, there were either 211,000 students in 492 institutions, or 465,815 students in 648 institutions.) In the late fifties and early sixties, following the lead of California, junior colleges began to proliferate. By 1968, according to the Association of Junior and Community Colleges, there were 1,924,970 students in 1,038 two-year colleges.

Accompanying the change in junior-college enrollment came a change in appellation. The more frequent use now of the name "community" college reflects a desire by two-year college officials to play down the pejorative "junior"; it also reflects the fact that more than 95 percent of the two-year students are in publicly supported institutions. As a matter of fact, just this year, Miami-Dade Junior College in Florida—one of the biggest two-year colleges in the country, with an enrollment of 36,500—changed its middle name to "community" because, as one official put it, "We have just gotten too big to be 'junior.' "

Nevertheless, the redesignation of the two-year college seems not to have dispelled feelings of inferiority. Such is the image of the community college that when Dominican-born Gerard Lacay was a freshman at Bronx Community, he was so embarrassed about going there that he was ashamed to wear a sweat shirt bearing the college's name. "Do we tend to have an inferior status? The answer is unequivocally yes," says Dr. Herbert Robbins, psychology coordinator for the school's social-science department. "Four-year schools look down their noses at us and students in four-year schools think students in junior colleges must be inferior. In general, that's the kind of image that community colleges tend to project, and we would like to correct it."

Indicative of the attitude toward the community college is the anxiety that some people have felt since it became known last year that the state is planning to help New York University out of its financial difficulties by allowing City University to buy N.Y.U.'s Heights campus in the Bronx and turn it over to Bronx Community College. The purchase price is to be $62-million and an additional $35-million is to be spent on renovations. Concern has risen over what the community-college students might do to the magnificent Stanford White and Marcel Breuer buildings on the picturesque, 47-acre campus, and to the busts of the famous Americans that line the promenade of the Hall of Fame, high above the Harlem River. "They really believe the Visigoths are coming," says Paul Rosenfeld, a bearded associate dean at Bronx Community, who is handling the logistics of the move, which will occur this summer.

There are no known Visigoths at Bronx Community College, but there are many blacks and Puerto Ricans. For some people, accustomed to associating higher education with white faces, that is a fact of life that still takes some getting used to. Members of the Bronx Community faculty and administration have made a bold attempt to examine their own racial feelings in a series of overnight retreats held during the last year and a half at the Center for Humanistic Education near Albany. The sessions have sometimes led to tears and recriminations. "We've been dealing with the most difficult aspect of teaching—altering human behavior," says Dr. Richard A. Donovan, the college's assistant dean of the faculty, who has been the main figure behind the college's humanistic education efforts. "You have to remember that most of us have come out of achieving, middle-class, white, traditional graduate programs, and we were trained to teach people like ourselves. Now, we're trying to face up to the problems of teaching in a multi-racial society."

Bronx Community's predominantly white student body became a predominantly minority student body—a change accelerated by City University's open-admissions policy that, since 1970, has assured every high-school graduate of a place in college. In 1969, the last year in which it had a selective admissions policy, Bronx Community's enrollment was 54.8 percent white, 31.6 percent black, 11.3 percent Puerto Rican, and 2.3 percent "others." Last fall, the beginning of the third year of open admissions, the enrollment was 34.7 percent white, 45.8 percent black, 17.9 percent Puerto Rican, and 1.6 percent "others."

Community colleges, particularly in urban locales, tend to attract a larger proportion of minority students than do four-year colleges and universities. One reason is that tuition charges are invaria-

The Crisis of Purpose and
Identity in Higher Education

bly lower because, with their smaller per-student operating costs, community colleges are designed to accommodate those least able to afford higher education. Another reason is that open admission is the rule at most of them.

This pattern of low tuitions and open admissions has had much to do with raising the black enrollment in higher education throughout the country— a rise of 211 percent since 1964. It is estimated by the American Association of Junior and Community Colleges that almost 40 percent of all the blacks in institutions of higher education attend community colleges. Nevertheless, community colleges on the whole serve predominantly white students, for many of the institutions are situated in rural and suburban areas where there are few blacks. If blacks have gained by the spread of the community colleges, then whites have gained even more.

In the opinion of some observers, the role that the community college has been playing vis-à-vis the blacks is of questionable value. "The community college, generally viewed as the leading edge of an open and egalitarian system of higher education, is in reality a prime contemporary expression of the dual historical patterns of class-based tracking and of educational inflation," Jerome Karabel, a Harvard graduate student, wrote last November in *The Harvard Educational Review*. "The community college is itself the bottom track of the system of higher education both in class origins and [the] occupational destinations of its students. . . . As access to college was universalized . . . separate schools, two-year community colleges [were created to] provide an education for most students that would not only be different from a bachelor's degree program, but also shorter. The net effect of educational inflation is thus to vitiate the social impact of extending educational opportunity to a higher level."

At Bronx Community, students pursuing the associate's degree fall into two categories, transfer and career. The transfer program, which covers 58 percent of the students, prepares them to go on to a senior college for bachelor's degree studies. A student may lay the foundation for a four-year degree in business, engineering, liberal arts, science, even music.

Do community college students go on to four-year colleges? Bronx Community has just completed a study of what happened to the class that entered the college in 1970. It was found that 4 percent of the open-admissions students and 14 percent of the other students (who would have qualified for admissions under the more rigorous pre-open admissions standards) have obtained two-year degrees; approximately 95 percent of these went on to senior colleges. In addition, 45 percent of the members of the class that entered in 1970 are still enrolled at Bronx Community. Of the rest, a small percentage transferred to other colleges.

This is consistent with the pattern that shows community college students taking longer to complete their programs than comparable students in four-year institutions. The Carnegie Commission on the Future of Higher Education, in a 1970 report, found that, of the freshmen who enter a community college planning to go on to a senior college, about one-half end up in such institutions; furthermore, a majority of those who transfer eventually earn their baccalaureates.

Sometimes transferring isn't all that easy. It is common for some senior institutions to refuse to accept all of the credits earned by community-college graduates. The Carnegie Commission asserted in its report that relations between senior colleges and junior colleges still need a great deal of improvement. (The State University of New York has announced that by 1974 it will guarantee that every graduate of a transfer program in one of its 38 community colleges will have the right to be accepted into a senior college or university. The eight SUNY affiliated community colleges operated by the City University already make this guarantee.)

The nontransfer students at Bronx Community (the 42 percent enrolled in the career program) are equipped through their education to go directly into the labor market with no further schooling. Typical career programs are medical laboratory technology, legal secretarial skills, and data processing. Some of the career programs, such as electrical technology and nursing, though of a terminal nature, provide sufficient background for students to go on for bachelors' degrees if they so choose. (At least two Ivy League universities, eager to boost their minority enrollments in engineering, have encouraged Bronx Community College to steer engineering technology students to them.)

By far the most popular career program is nursing. Students even major in other fields waiting their turn to be admitted to the nursing program, which, with an enrollment of 1,180, is jammed full. Nursing students have their own 13-story building, which contains dormitory facilities, classrooms, and laboratories, adjacent to Bronx Municipal Hospital Center on Pelham Parkway in the northeast Bronx. The students, 96 percent of whom are women, seem intensely motivated. "For many of them, especially the blacks and Puerto Ricans," says Dr. Beatrice Perlmutter, head of the nursing program, "this changes their whole lives. It makes them professionals, where before they were nothing."

Nursing, though, is the exception. Bronx Community—like most such colleges—has trouble persuading students to go into the technical and vocational programs. They want to major in liberal arts and other fields that parallel those in four-year colleges and universities. If the community college is the bottom echelon of higher education, then technical and vocational programs are the bottom echelon of its curriculum. Bronx Community representatives have even been visiting high schools in the borough to try to talk students into entering the college's career programs.

"There is a selling job that must be done," says the school's president, Dr. James A. Colston. "It is a matter of prestige, and minorities have waited so long to get into higher education that now they've made it, they want to test themselves out at the bachelor's degree level." Dr. Colston, who gave up a life-time appointment as president of Knoxville College to accept the Bronx Community presidency, was thought to be the first black appointed to head a non-black college when he was named to his post in 1966, succeeding the founding president, Dr. Morris Meister.

Beyond those enrolled in the regular transfer and career programs, Bronx Community reaches more than 5,000 additional students through continuing education—330,000 hours of noncredit courses given at 63 separate sites for people of all ages who want to acquire the basic skills necessary to get jobs, to upgrade their skills, to get promotions and to fill leisure time. The continuing-education program is primarily paid for by government and foundation grants. For instance, the State Bureau of Manpower Development pays the college $245,000 to teach high-school dropouts to be auto mechanics; and the United States Department of Health, Education and Welfare pays $80,000 for counseling and instruction to prepare Vietnam veterans for college.

In addition to continuing education, there is another area of activity, sometimes controversial, in which Bronx Community and other two-year colleges may get involved. It is "community service," a gray area in which the college makes its physical and human resources available to surrounding neighborhoods. "Some people have thought the college should be satisfied to perform only an educational function because that is so important," says Eric Cox of the continuing-education staff. "But I think that in the same way that the land-grant college did wonders for agriculture, so can the community college do much to extricate our cities from the tremendous mess they're in."

Teaching at Bronx Community is conducted by a

full-time faculty of 540, supplemented by 400 moonlighters from business, industry, and other educational institutions. For faculty members, the biggest difference between working in a community college and a four-year college is the emphasis on teaching. Two-year colleges place much lighter stress on research, publishing, and scholarly ventures. A survey released this year by the National Center for Educational Statistics in Washington also found that junior colleges constitute the lowest-paying segment of higher education. The average salary of a university faculty member is $15,301; a four-year college faculty member $13,059; and a two-year college faculty member, $12,553. Community colleges in the City University are an anomaly because all of CUNY's teachers are represented by the same union, the Professional Staff Congress, which is affiliated with both the National Education Association and the American Federation of Teachers. There is virtually complete parity in pay for community college and senior college faculty in the City University.

Elsewhere in the country, though, community college faculty members not only tend to receive lower salaries than their colleagues in four-year institutions, but also, in general, have more modest academic backgrounds. Fewer of them have Ph.D.'s, and many come into community-college teaching from the ranks of high-school faculties.

The current glut of Ph.D.'s seeking jobs—and the attempt to upgrade community colleges—has changed this pattern somewhat. Nevertheless, the essential difference—the lack of orientation toward research and publishing by two-year-college faculty members—remains. Bronx Community has its handful of scholars, such as its plastics-technology expert, Dr. Sheldon M. Atlas, and its authority on Edgar Allan Poe (who was a Bronx resident), Dr. Burton R. Pollin. By and large, however, at a school where fewer than 20 percent of the faculty members have doctorates, what counts most is teaching and being able to relate to students.

Teachers like Dr. Leo Lieberman skillfully blend entertainment and information to command the attention of their students. Working in a crowded room with a Bible-as-literature class of more than 30 and a text—the Bible—that, in the hands of a more languid professor, would almost certainly be soporific, Dr. Lieberman can make an Old Testament patriarch seem as familiar to his students as the man who runs the corner candy store.

"Who is our next great character?" he asks without bothering to wait for a response. "Abraham. You remember the covenant he made with God. Seared into the flesh through circumcision. Well, in addition, God made another arrangement with Abraham. What was it? You are living on the Grand Concourse in the Bronx and what does God say to do? He says, 'Get thee out of the land you were born in and go to Scarsdale. Get thee out of thy country and from thy kindred and from thy father's house, unto the land that I will show thee.'" Slender and frenetic, he darts from one side of the room to the other, spouting quotations, firing questions. Students thumb quickly through their Bibles, searching for quotations, trying to keep up as he races through the cast of characters . . . Noah, Isaac, Esau, Jacob. Perhaps too much Broadway to please the purists, but it is a course many students may remember when the others have been forgotten.

Joseph (Gil) Riley leans less on showmanship, yet he also captivates his students, filling their heads with the essence of organic chemistry. A bruiser of a man who looks as if he had played middle line-backer somewhere (actually, what he played was basketball), Mr. Riley, now a Ph.D. candidate, got his undergraduate degree at North Carolina College, a black institution across the street from his boyhood home in Durham. Three years ago, he quit an industrial chemist's job, where he was making twice as much money, to teach kids at Bronx Community.

"I had always done some tutoring on the side," says Mr. Riley, "and I decided it's what I wanted to do most. I have a feeling I do pretty well with kids." He does. This particular day, he is wearing brown corduroy pants and a green sweater. No jacket or tie. He is standing behind a lab bench at the front of a tiered lecture hall, and talking about what happens when an electrical charge enters a ring. "Do you follow me?" the mustachioed Mr. Riley asks a student who is wearing a look of bemusement. "Ask me a question. Maybe I can help you."

"I lost you at the beginning," the student says, and Mr. Riley, lecturing from memory and without notes, patiently reviews what he said moments earlier. And so it goes, as Billy Pilgrim observed, until the hour has been consumed. One step back for each two ahead.

Student after student attests to the personal attention lavished by faculty members and staff at Bronx Community. "The teachers here like to help," says Joanne Turkfeld, a brown-eyed, dark-haired 21-year-old sophomore. "They treat you like a human being." Moreover, the individualized approach is fortified by a flock of full-time counselors and a battery of personalized tutorial services—assistance on a scale that is generally unavailable at a four-year college or university.

"Many students come to a place like this with the feeling that they have been academic failures in high school," says Dr. Cortland P. Auser, the 53-year-old chairman of the school's English department. "They are uptight, and before they can succeed they have to prove to themselves that they aren't failures. We should be sensitive and aware of their needs. It isn't a matter of diluting standards. The standards stay the same, but the approach changes."

Some critics are not so sure of that. They view the low level of prior achievement of so many of the students, and the remedial efforts to improve their performance, as a diminution of standards. "There should be a method of sifting the applicants and choosing those who are best suited to benefit from a college education," declares Samuel D. Ehrenpreis, deputy chairman of Bronx Community's history department and a veteran of 22 years of teaching in the CUNY system. "This is not a class or racial thing. There are numbers of whites from middle-class backgrounds who should be sifted out. No one should be admitted unless he can read and write on a 13th grade level. Unless these matters are corrected, standards are bound to slip. They have been slipping already. We will turn into an educational slum."

The change in the character of the student body since the advent of open admissions manifests itself in disparate ways. In the college's tiny 48,000-volume, 200-seat library, the emphasis is not on research but on helping young people who have seldom been in libraries to learn the skills needed to carry out their assignments. "In a university library," says Dr. Edwin W. Terry, the chief librarian, "the collection is what is important. Here it is service." This means that the job of a librarian at Bronx Community involves teaching students how to use a card file and how to write correct grammar in a research paper. It means, too, telling them politely but firmly about the difference between plagiarism and research.

At Bronx Community, remediation is supposed to be the bridge that carries improperly prepared students to the promised land of college-level courses. It is, in the opinion of some, however, a decrepit trestle that ought to be condemned. "Remediation has been a big flop," declares Richard Heller, a biologist, who has been among Bronx Community's leading boosters of open admissions. "It has been a crash program that has come crashing down around the ears of people who didn't design it well enough."

What is wrong with the remedial program, according to Diane Johnson, an articulate young black who grew up in Brooklyn's depressed Bedford-Stuyvesant section, is that the courses stop short of bringing the student to the college level. In addition, she says that there is little provision for dealing with the emotional and social needs of the students. "I had to take a whole year of remediation and, of course, there was no credit for the courses," Miss Johnson complains bitterly. "It's a damned shame. When I was in high school, I ranked 20th in my class, and then I got here and I was shocked by my low scores on the tests. I was being fooled in high school. The basic problems that most of us have here are the fault of the New York City public school system. It's not that we don't appreciate open admissions. We do. But the big thing is to find methods of remediation that don't penalize us any more than we have been already."

Penalties are something community college students would prefer to dispense with. Had they not been penalized in one way or another, many of them would never have gone to a community college. They arrive in search of success—though a large number will find only renewed failure—and, when the most abject of them discover success, it is sometimes a story of spectacular dimensions. "Even if only a minority of them make it through, it is that many more who have been saved from going down the drain," says Dr. Morton Rosenstock, the associate dean of Bronx Community's faculty. "I know it sounds like the Salvation Army, but when they make it, we have saved souls."

Peter Velez was saved, and he would be the first to admit it. A Puerto Rican-born high-school dropout, he returned to school at night to get his diploma when he was past 20. He thought about college and mentioned it to a counselor, who, upon looking at his grades, admonished him to forget the idea and get a job. He persisted, and, to get him off his back, the counselor told Mr. Velez that he would take care of getting him into college. "I didn't even know that I was supposed to do it myself, and when September came I found out, of course, that the counselor had done nothing." In February, Mr. Velez enrolled in Bronx Community, the only college that would have him. He dropped out after a semester and went into the Army for four years. Last year, at age 30, and the father of two, Mr. Velez, president of the college's student government, was graduated as valedictorian of his class with an A-minus average, winning three commencement awards. Today, the recipient of a scholarship, he is studying for a bachelor's degree in City College's engineering school. "What Bronx Community College did for me I can never repay," he says. "It was my crowning glory, a place where people went out of their way to help me. Without the chance that the community college gave me, I probably would have had to spend the rest of my life working in a factory."

A crisis in catholic education

DANIEL CALLAHAN

Even in a Roman Catholic Church revolutionized by the Second Vatican Council, surprises and shocks are still possible. When the surprise involves a nun, and the shock Catholic higher education, two stereotypes are assaulted at the same time. The most recent surprise came with the announcement by Sister Jacqueline Grennan, president of Webster College in suburban St. Louis and for many the very prototype of a new breed of nun, that she had asked for and received a release from her religious vows. The shock came with her simultaneous announcement that her order, the Sisters of Loretto, had applied to Rome for permission to turn Webster College over to a lay board of trustees, thus relinquishing ownership and control.

This was all too much for Bishop Fulton J. Sheen of Rochester, N.Y. Asked what he thought, he replied: "No comment. I am more interested in

Nathan Hales than Benedict Arnolds." A conservative diocesan paper, the *Brooklyn Tablet,* reported
the story under the head "Webster College Leaves
the Church," and a secular newsweekly entitled its
story "Another Nun Defects." While Catholic opinion was generally more guarded than Bishop
Sheen's remark, one Catholic college president saw
her plan as "extremist," and many others expressed
doubt that the move of Webster College would or
should provide a future pattern for other Catholic
colleges. One way or another, though, Sister Jacqueline (now Miss Grennan) by her initiative un-
derscored the existence of a major crisis in Catholic
higher education.

In part, the crisis is financial, reflecting in an
acute way the squeeze felt in recent years by private higher education, pressed from one side by rising costs and from another by the competition of
public education. At present there are some 363
Catholic universities, colleges, and junior colleges.
They range in size from St. John's University in
Jamaica, N. Y., with 12,000 students, to Assumption
College in Richardton, N. D., which in 1965 had 42
students. Some 60 of the colleges have fewer than
100 students, with an average of 58 students and 16
faculty members.

There have been no fewer than 96 new colleges
founded since 1939, a good number of them with
only the sketchiest financial base and a dubious financial future. Not only do the Catholic institutions
have to compete with public higher education and
the more prestigious private nonsectarian colleges—
a task for which they are ill-equipped—they also

have to compete with one another. There is just not enough money to carry on so many battles on so many fronts.

In part, also, the crisis is one of identity and purpose. Prior to the Second Vatican Council, the colleges had a reasonably clear sense of what they were trying to do. In theory, their aim was to combine a good secular education with a solid grounding in Catholic theology and philosophy. While there might be debate about the best kind of secular education, there was hardly any at all about theology and philosophy. The Catholic church, it was thought, possessed an impregnable and unchanging set of divine and human truths. The job of the colleges was to indoctrinate their students with these truths, thus shoring up their faith and protecting them from the dangers of a Protestant, secular America.

All the while, it was assumed that the ideal Catholic educator was a priest, nun, or brother. They were religious professionals, the laity mere amateurs. Moreover, these religious professionals were under the control of the bishops; thus there was little danger of contaminating Catholic Doctrine, much less bringing it under serious questioning.

The council and its attendant impact have dealt a series of devastating blows to this neat theory of Catholic Doctrine and education. The assault has come from many sides. Doctrinally, there has been a considerable loss of confidence in many old Catholic orthodoxies. The importance of the laity has been affirmed, even in theology and philosophy. The rapid growth of ecumenism has removed many

Catholic fears about American life and secular education. A strong drive for freedom within the
church, combined with a desire for a more relevant
expression of Christianity, has created an almost
revolutionary unrest within the religious orders.
Fewer and fewer members of the orders are willing
to be cast in the role of obedient purveyors of a fixed
body of dogma.

Miss Grennan's move catches well the flavor of
this unrest. She left her order, she wrote in a letter
to Joseph Cardinal Ritter of St. Louis, because of
her conviction "that nuns . . . have no business in
my kind of role." That role, as she sees it, is running
a college, a task which involves being "fully in the
public sector." While she still believes there is
much valuable work which nuns can perform, she is
also convinced that the structure and traditions of
religious orders are a major impediment to work in
the world.

She does not, she heatedly stresses, think of herself as a nun who has "defected." Instead, she
wants to see herself and her college freed from
some major restrictions. The most important of
these is the legal control of the church. "The very
nature of higher education," she has said, "is opposed to juridical control by the church. The academic freedom which must characterize a college or
university would provide continuing embarrassments for the church if her hierarchy were forced
into endorsing or negating the action of the college
or university."

The controlling phrase here is "juridical control,"
she says. She does not deny the value of a Christian

commitment on the part of a college; her own plans
for the future of Webster call for a continuing
"Christian presence." But it is a "Christian presence" which must be self-directing, responsible
only to its own communal conscience and goals.

Views like this do not endear Miss Grennan to all
members of the Catholic academic community.
Most Catholic administrators flatly deny that eccle-
siastical control curtails that freedom. They would
agree with Sister Margaret Claydon, president of
Trinity College in Washington, that "our faculty has
never had to compromise its academic principles
because of episcopal or religious pressure." And
many nuns, for that matter, are hurt by the suggestion that somehow their role as nuns and their role
as educators are irreconcilable. Sister Ann Richard
White, chairman of Webster's theology department,
said that while she respected the "personal decision" of Miss Grennan, she did not "feel that any
type of apostolate is incompatible with the basic nature of religious life."

But, increasingly, issues of academic freedom dog
the reforming steps of Catholic higher education.
Miss Grennan's diplomatically phrased concern
about "embarrassments for the church" has been
put more bluntly by Rosemary Lauer, one of the 21
teachers summarily dismissed in 1965 by St. John's:
"Until the official Catholic Church comes to see
that using the university to insure religious ortho-
doxy, to preserve people in the faith, is an uncon-
scionable violation of the nature of the university
. . . the Catholic Church and universities can't
mix."

For an older generation of Catholic administrators, an opinion like this is incredible. By and large, they feel that Catholic colleges have as solid a record of academic freedom as secular colleges (where, they are fond of pointing out, "freedom cases" arise all the time). For many younger professors, however, often fresh from secular graduate schools, the freedom proclaimed by clerical administrators is a good deal less than they want.

One lay professor of theology at a small men's college has pointed to a much-praised statement issued by the Rev. Victor R. Yanitelli, S. J., president of St. Peter's College in Jersey City, as an indication of the kind of problem someone like himself faces. In his statement, Father Yanitelli vigorously defended the right of a Rutgers professor, Eugene Genovese, to dissent as vigorously as he wanted from the administration's Vietnamese policy, arguing that the right of dissent was basic to democratic and academic freedom. In the same statement, however, Father Yanitelli said of his own university that "we demand that our Catholic professors and students be committed to the teachings of the Roman Catholic Church. After this there can be no limit on academic freedom other than intellectual honesty."

For the lay theologian this was just the kind of apparent double standard he could not bear. "A Catholic 'academic freedom' which doesn't allow me to dissent from the teachings of my church is no 'freedom' at all," he said. "They just can't seem to see that!"

It is something which Miss Grennan does see. In

a move which personified her approach to Webster's Christian character, she announced in 1965 that there would no longer be any prescribed requirements in theology (or, for that matter, in any field). "If one opts for a personally determined and directed probing," she said in an address to the student body, "then I submit that to prescribe a minimum requirement in theology is to denigrate it." She also made it clear that, for her, Catholic theology is not a matter of narrow doctrinal rectitude but "a search involving the insights and problems of persons from all fields and all faiths." She has put these convictions into practice by drawing heavily from a nearby Protestant school, Eden Theological Seminary, for lecturers in theology, and by making Webster's Religious Activities Committee fully ecumenical. She expects that Webster's new board of lay trustees will be equally varied.

Taken separately, few of these innovations are wholly original, even in Catholic colleges. The main difference between Miss Grennan and other Catholic educational reformers is the zest and intellectual showmanship she brings to her ambitions for Webster. A master of the dramatic statement, she speaks rapidly and passionately.

In an educational system often marked by pietistic rhetoric, her "worldly" bluntness was enough to set her apart. That she finally carried through on her ideas, changing both her own future and that of Webster as well, was, for some, final proof that their anxieties about her were well-founded. For others, it was only a vindication of their confidence in her.

The Problems of
American Education

At times, though, even her supporters have trouble understanding what she is trying to do. They admire the openness of her college, the freedom she gives students ("I'll let them do anything they feel they can live with," she says), her success in fundraising and in creating a distinctive image for Webster ("dynamic," "fun," "jumping" are only a few of the words which have been used to describe the atmosphere there). But they also wonder just what, in the end, her idea of a "Christian presence" at Webster will amount to. Those with a historical bent point out what happened to many Protestant colleges when they tried to get rid of their denominational sectarian traditions in favor of a more humanistic, nonsectarian atmosphere. They ended —Harvard, Yale, Chicago, for instance—as almost totally secularized institutions, their religious heritage living on only in the symbolic presence of a Protestant chaplain and an affiliated divinity school. What is to stop something of the same sort from happening at Webster in the years ahead?

Miss Grennan is aware of these worries, "There are no models for what I'm trying to do," she admits, "and I don't have a precise plan myself. It's a question of feeling our way, trying to make patterns out of what's happening.

"I'd like to train students to become tacticians, responsible tacticians—and this means training them to interrogate those in power. Students should scream at me. They should try to jar me. But they should also learn how to do this effectively and productively. That is what I mean by becoming 'responsible tacticians.' " In addition to having no fixed course requirements, students at Webster have considerable social freedom.

This is not the way Catholic colleges and their presidents have traditionally operated. For many decades the atmosphere in Catholic institutions was nervous, authoritarian, and paternalistic, more intent on "saving the faith" of their students than in producing scholars and leaders. When the first American bishop, John Carroll, founded the first Catholic college (now Georgetown University) in 1789, his goal was to provide for Catholics an alternative to the then-Protestant, anti-Catholic colleges which had hitherto been their only choice. His own aims for the college were scholarly enough, though shot through with the prevailing wisdom (in both Catholic and Protestant education) of "guarding and preserving the morals of youth."

As time went on, the motive of Catholic higher education shifted heavily to the morality side of the scholarship-morality equation. In great part this was a response to the outburst of anti-Catholicism which plagued much of nineteenth-century America, itself a reaction to the hordes of Catholic immigrants who began arriving after the eighteen-thirties. The immigrants, little enough intellectual in the first place, came to look upon the colleges as safe harbors for their children, well-guarded against the rough seas of a Protestant, secular, antipapist America.

Since Catholics still had to make their economic and political way in this America, however, the academic direction of the colleges also shifted heavily toward equipping their students with the utilitarian, professional skills needed to get ahead. First-rate scholarship, creative theology, engagement with the leading intellectual problems of the day, all came to have a minimal place. The important thing was to turn out safe, orthodox Catholics, well-armored to defend and hold on to their religion, but also prepared to compete successfully in the marketplace.

The colleges succeeded well enough in producing this kind of graduate. The few voices which complained from time to time about the dearth of Catholic scholars or about the anti-intellectualism of most Catholic college graduates were all but drowned out. In 1921 a leading Catholic editor bitterly wrote: "At the present time our lay leadership is well-nigh bankrupt. . . . Although we are one-fifth of the population, we do not furnish one-fiftieth of the higher intellectual life of the country." As late as the nineteen-fifties a distinguished Catholic historian, Msgr. John Tracy Ellis, could indict Catholic academicians for "their frequently self-imposed ghetto mentality which prevents them from mingling as they should with their non-Catholic colleagues, and . . . . their lack of industry."

The statistics bore out the charges, showing Catholic professors poorly represented in learned societies, notably weak in their output of books and articles, and undistinguished in sending their students on to graduate work. The lack of intellectual vitality in the colleges was abetted by rigid dormitory rules for the students, heavily censored newspapers, and close supervision of clubs and activities.

The Crisis of Purpose and
Identity in Higher Education

As for the students themselves, most came from lower- or lower-middle-class families, few of whose parents had ever been inside a college classroom. They had neither the background nor much inclination to challenge their Catholic culture, their professors, or the college administrations.

The situation of their teachers was not much better. Those who were priests or nuns were subject to the discipline and needs of their orders; if they stepped out of line they could be—and often were— silenced or transferred. Those who were laymen usually lacked doctorates, had large families to support and were, in any case, themselves ordinarily products of Catholic education. They rarely had either the imagination to think of reforming the colleges or, when they did, the academic bargaining power to push their demands through.

As if these weaknesses were not enough to debilitate Catholic higher education, there were also heavy financial pressures, some of them natural and others the result of poor planning and organization. The natural pressures came from the relative poverty of the Catholic community. For generations there were hardly any wealthy Catholic philanthropists able and willing to drop a few million dollars into weak endowment funds. Catholic equivalents of the Rockefellers, the Harknesses, the Vanderbilts (without whom Chicago, Harvard, and Yale would have been immeasurably weaker) just did not exist.

The few Catholics who did have money were, in any event, not much prone to give it or leave it to the colleges. As one exasperated president put it in the mid-fifties: "You're lucky to get a dormitory out of them; ask them to endow a professorial chair and they don't know what you're talking about."

The only other potential sources of funds were not much help either. The alumni on the whole were not so financially successful that they could do more than make token gestures of the $5 and $10 variety. The bishops, who controlled most of the church's general wealth, were more concerned with the parochial schools than with the colleges; they gave the colleges their blessings but no money.

Poor planning exacerbated these difficulties. To this day there has been no attempt to organize or co-ordinate Catholic higher education on a national basis. With few exceptions most of the colleges came into being as a result of the ambitions of the different religious orders or in response to local needs. It was almost unheard-of for the different orders to cooperate with one another. Milwaukee, for instance, has three Catholic colleges for women, each run by a different order, in addition to a coeducational university run by the Jesuits. Washington, D.C., has five colleges or universities. Westchester County in New York has six.

Besides the problem of financing, many colleges, especially the smaller, newer ones, have turned out to be increasingly hard to staff. The religious orders themselves, which own and administer all but a handful of the colleges, gave up hoping they could do so alone long ago. In 1940, members of religious orders outnumbered lay teachers 2 to 1. By 1965 the figures had been reversed, and with this drastic shift came even higher costs.

The Crisis of Purpose and
Identity in Higher Education

But the costs are not only in money. The only lay teachers many of the colleges can afford to hire are those without doctorates or those who do not or could not aspire to teach in stronger institutions. A survey of Catholic professors taken by Prof. John Donovan of Boston College in 1963 found that only 22 percent had their doctorates when they began to teach and that nearly 18 percent held only bachelor's degrees. (Miss Grennan's Webster College, for all its vitality, is close to the norm in this respect, with about 17 percent of the faculty holding Ph.D.'s.)

Figures of this kind, obviously enough, make academic distinction only a dream; most of the colleges consider themselves lucky to survive. Only a bare handful—universities such as Notre Dame, Fordham, St. Louis, Georgetown—can even pretend to be as good as the better non-Catholic institutions. It is not just that there is no Catholic Harvard or Berkley, but also that there are few as good as the much smaller Swarthmores, Reeds, and Sarah Lawrences.

Yet however weak academically many of the predominantly lay faculties may be, they are becoming strong enough numerically to challenge the control of the religious orders. Not surprisingly, these lay teachers have come to resent their usual exclusion from high policy-making positions. They feel they are too often treated as little more than the hired hands of a closed corporation—a corporation, moreover, intent on holding fast to its power at whatever the cost to good teaching, good academic policy, and good administration.

The Problems of
American Education

The general astonishment which greeted the summary dismissal of 21 teachers at St. John's University was not matched in Catholic academic circles. There it was seen only as a logical (even if particularly egregious) instance of what can happen when a religious order cares to assert its legal control.

The wiser orders, however, are coming to realize that there is a limit of how much informal pressure they can stand. Neither the morale of a faculty nor the public reputation of an institution can bear many incidents like that at St. John's. In addition, even lay teachers with poor academic backgrounds are becoming scarcer every year; they can now find the money to finish their graduate work while teaching in secular institutions. And if this is the case with that group, it is almost impossible to hope that the most talented lay scholars will be drawn to Catholic schools. Even if they can be lured at the outset of their careers they will flee the moment it becomes clear that their academic freedom is being threatened or that their voices will not count in forming policy. The recent announcement by St. John's that it is now prepared to submit its dispute with the ousted teachers to binding arbitration no doubt reflects nervous second thoughts about the impact of its actions.

Catalyzing these pressures on Catholic higher education are broader social and religious changes having a major impact on both the church and society. Among the most important are: (1) the general public demand for better colleges, a mood which has influenced Catholic educators to an extraordinary degree in the past decade; (2) the changing temper and values of the present student generation, a change which has brought more serious, more questioning, more rebellious students to Catholic campuses; (3) the ecumenical movement in the churches and the Second Vatican Council, which have together forced Catholic institutions to redefine their hiring policies, their relationship to church authority, their role in society, and their religious goals.

The response to this almost bewildering confluence of events and trends has been remarkably creative, even though uneven. While few colleges are prepared to follow the lead of Webster in turning over ownership entirely to lay trustees, many are preparing to give laymen a substantial degree of control. Almost simultaneously with Miss Grennan's announcement, at least six other institutions revealed plans to change the composition of their trustee boards.

Notre Dame, perhaps the strongest of the universities, will expand its present board of six priests to a twelve-man board, six priests and six laymen. While the new arrangement stipulates that the president must continue to be a member of the Holy Cross order, which has hitherto controlled the university, in most other respects the new board will assume total control. (Despite the stipulation about the presidency, many faculty members believe it quite possible that, within a generation the president will in fact be a layman.) Similar moves are underway at St. Louis University, which will shift from a thirteen-member, all-Jesuit board of trustees

to a board composed of eighteen laymen and ten
Jesuits; at John Carroll University in Cleveland; at
Holy Cross College in Worcester, Mass.; at the University of Portland and at St. Martin's College, in
Olympia, Wash., among others. In the near future,
many other institutions are expected to follow this
pattern.

No one is willing to say that these changes will
inevitably mean a drastic revolution. A common reaction among lay faculty members is wary hope;
they are not quite ready to believe that the religious
orders will quickly let go of their power. The fact
that so many clerical administrators have expressed
the view that a strong clerical presence is necessary
to insure the "Catholic" and "religious" character
of a college or university is enough to confirm the
lay wariness. A strong hint of this clerical view was
seen in a statement by the Rev. Theodore M. Hes-
burgh, president of Notre Dame, that, despite the
new board of trustees, it would remain the "exalted
mission" of the Holy Cross fathers to insure the
Catholic character of Notre Dame.

There is considerably less hesitation about the
other changes taking place in Catholic higher education. Academically, the colleges are profiting from
a more sophisticated, and often rebellious, student
body. Nearly half the fathers of the average Catholic
freshman class today have had some college education.

Recent statistics, moreover, show that Catholic
college graduates are now as likely to go on to further graduate work as Protestants (neither Protestants nor Catholics do as well as Jews in this re-

spect, though). These sociological shifts have well prepared the soil for the many changes in curriculum which have been tried in the past few years. Honors programs, a stiffening of study demands, revision of theology and philosophy requirements toward greater choice and flexibility, and a new emphasis on student freedom and initiative are only a few of the new directions.

Symbolically perhaps, the revamping of the theology and philosophy programs is most important. Long a source of bitter student complaints—for their mediocrity, irrelevance, and rigidity—these programs in particular are feeling the strong winds of the council. Less and less are Catholic students being taught a fixed set of Catholic "truths" in their theology classes and a packaged set of scholastic axioms in their philosophy courses. Scholasticism is giving way to existentialism, empiricism, and phenomenology.

Naturally, there is still some opposition to this trend. The University of Dayton, for example, recently saw a minority faction in the theology and philosophy departments accuse some of their colleagues of teaching "heretical" positions. That the charges were even investigated by the university seemed to many a throwback to an earlier era. That those investigated were eventually cleared of the charges and the minority faction slapped down was, however, taken as a sign of progress.

In terms of overall planning and organization of Catholic higher education, some important straws are in the wind. Many of the colleges have begun cooperative programs with other nearby Catholic colleges, exchanging faculty members and allowing student cross-registration in courses. A few have begun working out cooperative programs with nearby non-Catholic institutions. Fordham University, for instance, has a cooperative agreement with the Protestant Union Theological Seminary in theology and with Columbia University in engineering. Immaculate Heart College will shortly move from Los Angeles to become associated with the Claremont colleges.

While local developments of this kind do not necessarily presage a nationwide Catholic system, or any one dominant organizational plan, they indicate a growing recognition that few of the Catholic colleges can afford to retain their isolation, either financial or academic. One way or another, Catholic higher education is being forced to join the mainstream of American education.

There is also pressure on the colleges and universities to decide where they should go in the future. What is the point of a Catholic college, after all? At the moment there is uncertainty about the answer to this question. Jacqueline Grennan, however, has caught a predominant mood on the wing: "We have in the world today the most ecumenical kind of spirit, not only theologically but personally. . . . We live in an age of intense new probing in theology, probing not in a self-contained theological world or even in a self-contained Roman Catholic or Christian world but in an ecumenical world of search. . . . Webster sees a liberal education as the beginning search rather than the achievement of a minimum security requirement."

The Crisis of Purpose and
Identity in Higher Education

Where will this search lead? Miss Grennan cannot answer this question for her own college, nor will she try to answer it for the rest of Catholic higher education. "But look," she says, "you can't find patterns in what's happening until things begin to happen. We're just beginning all of us."

A different way to restructure the university

IRVING KRISTOL

I have the gravest doubts that, out of all the current agitation for a "restructuring" of the university, very much of substance will come. There are a great many reasons why this is so, among them the fact that practically no one any longer has a clear notion of what a "university" is supposed to be, or do, or mean. We are, all of us, equally vague as to what the term "higher education" signifies, or what functions and purposes are properly included in the categories of "student" or "professor." But in addition to such basic problems, there is a simple and proximate obstacle: all of the groups—professors, administrators, and students—now engaged in this enterprise of "restructuring" are deficient in the will to do anything, or the power to do anything, or ideas about what might be done.

Let us begin with the faculty, since they are indeed, as they claim ("Sir, the faculty *is* the university"), the preponderant estate of this realm. In most universities, it is the faculty that controls the educational functions and defines the educational purposes of the institution. It is the faculty that usually arranges the curriculum, makes staff appointments, etc. It is the faculty that has the moral authority, the mental capacity, and a sufficiently intimate knowledge of the realities of the educational system to operate upon it. Unfortunately, these virtues are far outweighed by an all too human defect—a limited imagination which leads to a lack of objective insight into its own position. What faculty members of our universities fail to see is that any meaningful restructuring will also have to include the faculty. And to ask the American professoriat to restructure itself is as sensible as if one had asked Marie Antoinette to establish a republican government in France. Whether or not it coincided with her long-term interests was immaterial; the poor woman couldn't even conceive of the possibility.

Now, I don't mean to suggest that there is anything especially shortsighted or selfish about the American professor. Some of my best friends are professors, and I can testify that they are every bit as broadminded, every bit as capable of disinterested action, as the average business executive or higher civil servant. Nor are they particularly smug and complacent. On the contrary, they are all keenly aware of the crisis that has befallen them, while many have long been discontented with their lot and full of haunting insecurities. Nevertheless, they do have one peculiar and notable flaw: being gener-

ally liberal and reformist in their political predispo-
sition, they believe themselves able to have a truly
liberal and reformist perspective on themselves.
This is, of course, an idle fancy. No social group really possesses the imaginative capacity to have a
liberal and reformist perspective on itself; individual members of the group may and do—but the
group as a whole cannot. Otherwise the history of
human society would be what it is not: an amiable
progression of thoughtful self-reformations by
classes and institutions.

So the beginning of wisdom, in thinking about
our universities, is to assume that the professors are
a class with a vested interest in, and implicit ideological commitment to, the status quo broadly defined, and that reform will have to be imposed upon
them as upon everyone else. If any empirical proof
were required of the validity of these assumptions,
one need only cast a glance over the various proposals for university reform that have been made by
faculty committees at Berkeley and elsewhere.

These proposals have one distinguishing characteristic: at no point, and in no way, do they cost the
faculty anything—not money, not time, not power
over their conditions of employment. They liberally
impose inconveniences upon the administration,
upon the taxpayers, upon the secondary schools,
upon the community. But they never inconven-
ience the faculty. They never, for instance, increase its teaching load. (On the contrary: after four
years of "restructuring" at Berkeley, professors
there now spend *less* time in the classroom than
they used to.) They never suggest anything that

would intrude on those four months' vacations; they never interfere with such off-campus activities as consultancies, the writing of textbooks, traveling fellowships, etc; they never discourage the expensive—but convenient—proliferation of courses in their specialized areas; they never even make attendance at committee meetings compulsory. This is precisely what one would expect when one asks a privileged class to reform the institution which is its very *raison d'être*. It is rather like asking corporation executives or trade union leaders or officials of a government agency, all of whom have been given lifelong tenure in their present positions, to "restructure" the institutions and redefine their positions.

I have touched upon this question of tenure because of its symbolic significance. Few professors, in conversation, will defend the present tenure system, whereby senior- and middle-level faculty are given a personal, lifelong monopoly on their positions. They will accept the criticisms of it by Robert Nisbet and others as largely valid. They will concede that it could be substantially modified—via long-term contracts, generous severance agreements, etc.—without any danger to academic freedom and with obvious benefits to everyone. They will agree that the "controversial" professor, whom tenure was supposed to protect, is today in great demand and short supply whereas the mediocre professor is its prime beneficiary. They may even admit that the presence of a tenured faculty is one of the reasons that the university has been—with the possible exception of the post office—the

The Problems of
American Education

least inventive (or even adaptive) of our social institutions since the end of World War II. They will
allow that tenure in the university, like seniority in
a craft union, makes for all sorts of counter-produc-
tive rigidities. But they will then go on to dismiss
the whole issue as utterly "academic."

To tamper with tenure, they argue, would produce fits and convulsions throughout their well-or-
dered universe. Nothing can or will be done, and
they themselves could not be counted on to try.
Even those economists who argue in favor of a free
market for labor everywhere else somehow never
think of applying this doctrine to themselves.

So when these same people announce that, to
cope with the crisis in the university, they are going
to "restructure" the institution, one has the right to
be skeptical. To suppose that they actually will do
any such thing is probably the most "academic"
idea of all.

Nor is the administration going to "restructure"
the university. It couldn't do it if it tried; and it is
not going to try because it doesn't regard itself as
competent even to think about the problem. University administration in the United States today
combines relative powerlessness with near-
absolute mindlessness on the subject of education.

That statement about powerlessness needs to be
qualified in one respect. Though a great many people are under the impression that the boards of
trustees are the "real" power structure of the university, this is in fact the one group over which the
administration does wield considerable influence.
The trustees of a modern university are rather like

the boards of directors of a modern corporation.
They represent a kind of "stand-by" authority,
ready to take over if the executive officers lead the
organization into a scandalous mess. (Having little
first-hand knowledge of educational institutions,
they will then usually make the mess even worse
than it was; but that's another story.)

They also may—repeat: *may*—intervene in certain
broad economic decisions, such as the construction
of a new campus, the launching of a major fund-rais-
ing drive, etc. But on the whole, and in the ordinary
course of events, they solemnly rubber-stamp whatever the administration has done or proposes to do.

And that's about the sum and substance of "administrative power." True, a determined administration can badger and bribe and blackmail the faculty into marginal revisions of the curriculum, just
as a determined administration can have some influence over senior appointments. But most administrations are not all that determined—like everyone else, university administrators prefer an
untroubled life. And even where they are determined, it doesn't make all that much difference,
from an outsider's point of view. Within the institution, of course, even small differences can cause
great anguish and excitement.

As for the administration's power over students,
that hardly seems worth discussing at a time when
the issue being debated is the students' power over
the administration. Suffice it to say that, where disciplinary power does exist on paper, it is rarely
used; and it is now in the process of ceasing to exist

even on paper.* In this respect, university administrators are ironically very much *in loco parentis*. They have about as much control over their 19- and 20-year-old charges as the parents do.

There might be something to deplore in this situation if one had reason to think that university administrators could wisely use power, did they have it. But there is no such reason, if what we are interested in is higher education. University administrators have long since ceased to have anything to say about education. By general consent, their job is administration, not education.

When was the last time a university president came forth with a new idea about education? When was the last time a university president wrote a significant book about the education of—as distinct from the government of—"his" students? Robert M. Hutchins was the last of that breed; he has had no noteworthy successors. Indeed, the surest way for an ambitious man never to become a university president is to let it be known that he actually has a philosophy of education. The faculty, suspicious of possible interference, will rise up in rebellion.

The university president today is primarily the chief executive of a corporate institution, not an educator. Unfortunately, he usually is also a poor exec-

* "Colleges are not churches, clinics, or even parents. Whether or not a student burns a draft card, participates in a civil-rights march, engages in premarital or extramarital sexual activity, becomes pregnant, attends church, sleeps all day or drinks all night, is not really the concern of an educational institution."—The president of the American Association for Higher Education as reported in *Time* (July 11, 1968).

The Crisis of Purpose and
Identity in Higher Education

utive, for various reasons. To begin with, he is almost invariably a professor, with no demonstrated
managerial experience. More important, there are
few meaningful standards against which to judge
his performance, as distinct from his popularity.
Since most university administrators have no clear
idea of what they are supposed to be doing, they
end up furiously imitating one another, on the assumption—doubtless correct—that to be immune
from invidious comparisons is to be largely exempt
from criticism.

Thus, at the moment, all administrations are
proudly expanding the size of their plant, their facilities, and their student bodies. An outsider might
wonder: Why should any single institution feel that
it has to train scholars in all disciplines? Why can't
there be a division of labor among the graduate
schools? Such questions are occasionally raised at
conferences of educators—but, since every administrator has no other criterion for "success" than
the quantitative increase in students, faculty,
campus grounds, etc., these questions spark no debate at all.

As a matter of fact, university administrators
never get much criticism—though, of course, they
are convenient scapegoats who are instantly *blamed*
for anything that goes wrong. The professors are just
too busy and self-preoccupied, and in the ordinary
course of events are perfectly content to leave the
government of the university to the administration—even when they have a low opinion of the administration. (This has been the story at Columbia
these past 10 years.)

The Problems of
American Education

It is interesting to note that, despite the fact that our best economists are all professors, there has been little public criticism from them on the grotesquely conservative way in which universities invest their endowment funds. It was not until the Ford Foundation's McGeorge Bundy made an issue of it, that the universities began to bestir themselves. Similarly, it was an off-campus man, Beardsley Ruml, who, some 15 years ago, pointed out that it was wasteful to leave campus facilities unused for months at a time, because of the vacation schedule. One would have thought that this idea could have passed through the minds of professors of management, or city planning, or something.

An interesting instance of the charmed life of university administrators is a recent report of the Carnegie Commission on the Future of Higher Education. Written by an economist, it delicately refuses to raise any interesting questions and limits itself to arguing for the need of ever greater government subsidies. After pointing out that the deficit in university budgets is largely incurred by the graduate divisions—a graduate student costs about three or four times as much as an undergraduate—the Carnegie report offers by way of explanation of the costliness of graduate education the following: "The conscientious supervision of a student's independent work is the essence of high-level graduate education."

"What this means in practice, as everyone knows, is that the only way universities can attract big faculty names away from other places is by offering them minimal teaching loads in the graduate division, and the only way it can attract the brightest graduate students away from other schools is by offering them attractive (i.e., expensive) fellowships." Whether or not it makes sense for each institution of higher learning to adopt such a competitive policy would seem to be an important problem; but the Carnegie Commission loyally refrained from exploring it. Nor did it show any interest in whether in fact there is "conscientious supervision" in graduate schools, and if so how extensive or effective it is. From casual conversion with graduate students, one gets the impression that such supervision is not all that common, to put it mildly.

In short and in sum: university administrations have neither the power, nor the inclination, nor the stimulus of informed criticism which would result in any serious efforts at "restructuring" their institutions.

And the students? They, alas, are indeed for the most part rebels without a hope of accomplishing anything except mischief and ruin.

In our society and in our culture, with its pathetic belief in progress and its grotesque accent on youth, it is almost impossible to speak candidly about the students. Thus, though most thoughtful people will condemn the "excesses" committed by rebellious students, they will in the same breath pay tribute to their "idealism" and their sense of "commitment." I find this sort of cant to be preposterous and disgusting. It seems to me that a professor whose students have spat at him and called him a "mother———" (it happened at Columbia) ought to be moved to more serious and more manly reflection on what his students are really like, as against what popular mythology says they are supposed to be like.

My own view is that a significant minority of today's student body obviously consists of a mob who have no real interest in higher education or in the life of the mind, and whose passions are inflamed by a debased popular culture that prevails unchallenged on the campus. We are reluctant to believe this because so many of the young people who constitute this mob have high I.Q.'s, received good academic grades in high school, and because their popular culture is chic rather than philistine in an old-fashioned way. Which is to say: We are reluctant to believe that youngsters of a certain social class assembled on the grounds of an educational institution, can be a "mob," in the authentic sociological sense of that term. (We are also reluctant to believe it because many of these students are our children, and we love them regardless of what they do. Such love is, of course, natural and proper. On the other hand, it is worth reminding oneself that members of lower-class lynch mobs have loving fathers and mothers too.)

The really interesting question is: How did they get that way? After all, we do assume that young people of a certain intelligence, provided with a decent education, will be more rational—and therefore more immune to mob instincts—as they near the end of their education than they were at the beginning. The assumption is plausible; but it also

The Crisis of Purpose and
Identity in Higher Education

patently fails to hold in many instances, and this can only represent a terrible judgment on our system of education.

How is it possible for a Columbia or Berkeley sophomore, junior, or even graduate student to believe in the kinds of absurd simplicities they mouth at their rallies—especially when, before entering college, many of these youngsters would have been quick to recognize them as nothing but absurd simplicities? How is it possible for a radical university student—and there is no reason why a university student shouldn't be radical—to take Che Guevara or Chairman Mao seriously when, in his various courses, he is supposed to have read Marx, Max Weber, de Tocqueville, has been examined on them, and has passed the examinations?

When I discuss this problem with my professor friends, I am informed that I display a naïve faith in the power of formal instruction as against the force of the *Zeitgeist*. And there is a measure of justice in this rejoinder. There can be no doubt that we are witnessing, all over the world, a kind of generational spasm—a sociological convulsion whose roots must go deep and far back and must involve the totality of our culture rather than merely the educational parts of it. It is fairly clear, for example, that many of the students are actually revolting against the bourgeois social and moral order as a whole, and are merely using the university as a convenient point of departure. Whether their contempt for this order is justified is a topic worthy of serious discussion—which, curiously enough, it hardly ever receives in the university. But, in any case, this

question ought not to distract us from the fact that
those radical students who are most vociferous
about the inequities of the university are the least
interested in any productive "restructuring."

On the other hand, not all of the rebellious students are all that radical politically; and it does
seem to me that, in these cases, it ought to be possible for a university education to countervail against
the mish-mash of half-baked and semiliterate ideologies that so many students so effortlessly absorb
within a few months of arriving on campus. My own
opinion, for what it's worth, is that the college and
the university fail to educate their students because
they have long since ceased trying to do so.

The university has become very good at training
its students for the various professions; and it is
noteworthy that, within the university the professional schools and divisions have been the least tur-
bulent. But for the ordinary college student—majoring in the humanities or in the social sciences—
the university has become little more than an
elegant "pad," with bull-sessions that have course
numbers or with mass lectures that mumble into
one ear and ramble out the other.*

---

* A special word is necessary about sociology departments, whose
students play a leading—perhaps critical—role in the current rebellion.
Sociology is an odd kind of hybrid: a profession many of whose
members are completely unprofessional in outlook, temperament, and
intellectual rigor. When I was in New York's City College in the late
nineteen thirties, most students majored in sociology because it was the
closest thing to a major in current social problems that the curriculum
offered—and majoring in such problems was what they really wanted to
do. In the end, most of them did become professional sociologists; and
if they remained interested in social problems and social reform, their

The Crisis of Purpose and
Identity in Higher Education

The entire conception of a liberal education—of the most serious ideas of our civilization being taught by professors who took them seriously—has disappeared, under pressure of one kind or another. The graduate divisions, with their insistence on preprofessional training, have done their part; but so has the whole temper of our educational system over the past decades, with its skepticism toward "great ideas" in general and toward great ideas of the past in particular.

I believe that, when students demand that their studies be "relevant," this is what they are unwittingly demanding. After all, what could be more "relevant" today than the idea of "political obligation"—a central theme in the history of Western political philosophy—or the meaning of "justice"? And, in fact, on the few campuses where such teaching still exists, the students do find it "relevant," and exciting, and illuminating.

But, whether I am right or wrong in this appraisal, the whole issue is, like so many others, "academic." The students think they are rebelling against the university as a "bureaucratic" institution, and they think it so powerfully that they are not likely to listen to anyone who informs them that they are really rebelling against a soulless institution—one that has been emptied of a great deal of its content. So those

interest was anything but simple-minded. But these days, though the motivation for majoring in sociology is still a heightened concern with social problems, the number of sociology majors is so large, the departments so amorphous, the curriculum so sprawling, that it is quite easy for a student to move through his courses with his passions never being seriously disturbed by a sociological idea.

The Problems of
American Education

319

who are not set upon destroying the university will be permitted to tinker at "restructuring" it. They will serve on committees that define the curriculum; they will help enforce a dwindling minimum of student discipline; they will be solemnly listened to instead of being solemnly preached at.

But you can't reform an institution unless you know what you want; and though our university students have always been encouraged to want the true, the good, and the beautiful, they have never been taught how to think about the conditions and consequences of such desires. To date, most of the reforms sponsored by students have been in the direction of removing their obligation to get any kind of education at all. It is not surprising that harassed administrators and preoccupied professors are quick to find such proposals perfectly "reasonable." *

So where are we? In an impasse, it would appear. Here we have a major social institution in a flagrant condition of crisis, and not one of the natural social forces involved with this institution can be relied upon to do any of the necessary work of reformation. In situations of this kind, the tradition is for the governmental authorities to step in and fill the power vacuum. And such, I think will again have to be the case this time.

* Jacques Barzun, in his book *The American University,* points out that it has long been common in many universities for students, at the end of a course, to hand in written critiques of its form and substance. He also points out that, if one surveys these critiques over a period of time, one discovers that the most recent will be demanding a return to what was rejected by students only a few years back.

**The Crisis of Purpose and
Identity in Higher Education**

320

That last sentence made even me, its author, shudder as it was written. The spectacle of state or federal legislators invading the campus en masse for solemn investigation or deliberation is the kind of tragic farce we can do without. And the idea of state legislators or congressmen trying to impose educational reforms by legislation is as fantastic as it is horrifying. Still, the fact remains that there is a genuine "public interest" at issue here, and there is no one except government who can be asked to defend it. Fortunately, I believe that for once we are in luck, in that the particular circumstances of the moment permit government to act in an indirect, noncoercive, prudent, yet possibly effective way.

The first such particular circumstance is the fact that the very idea of "higher education" has become so devoid of specific meaning that there is little danger of government, or anyone else, imposing some kind of orthodox straitjacket on the prevailing chaos. There just aren't any such orthodoxies available. Indeed, the very reason we have a crisis in the universities is because all such traditional notions about the function and ends of higher education have, during these past three decades, become otiose.

The real problem at the moment is that no one—not the faculty, not the administration, not the students—has any kind of clear idea of what any "institution of higher learning" is supposed to be accomplishing. It is even beginning to be suspected by many that such phrases as "the university" or "higher education" have acquired different and contradictory meanings, that the vast number of young people now moving onto the campuses are too diverse in their interests and talents to be contained within the old category of "university students," and that the root cause of our distemper is our failure to sort out all these meanings and people, and to make suitable institutional adjustments.

In other words, the situation seems to be such that what we need is a huge injection of pluralism into an educational system that has, through the working out of natural forces, become homogeneous and meaningless at the same time. No one can presume to say what the future pattern of higher education in America should be like. Not until we have far more experimentation—not until we have tried out different kinds of "universities" for different kinds of "students"—can we even hope to know what the real options are. In the ordinary course of events the prospects for this kind of pluralism would be so dim as to be utopian: None of the existing institutions can be counted on to cooperate except in a ritualistic and rather hypocritical way. But this leads me to the second "particular circumstance," which gives the prospect an honest dimension of reality.

This second particular circumstance is the fact that government—especially the federal government—is going to be pouring more and more money into the universities. This is inevitable, and I am willing to persuade myself that it is desirable. But it is neither inevitable nor desirable that the money should flow through the conventional channels—i.e., directly from the public treasury to the bursar's

The Crisis of Purpose and
Identity in Higher Education

office. Understandably enough, college presidents cannot imagine it proceeding otherwise—higher education is "their" province, and they feel strongly that the money should be "theirs" to expend as administrative discretion and wisdom prescribe.

But the citizens of this republic have a claim to assert that higher education is "their" province, too; and they have a right to insist that public monies be expended in such a manner as might overcome the crisis in our universities, instead of deepening it.

What I would therefore like to see—and the idea is one that is slowly gaining favor with many observers; it is not original with me— is something along these lines: (a) state expenditures for higher public education should be frozen at the present level, and all increases in this budget should take the form of loans to qualifying students—these loans being valid for out-of-state institutions as well as in-state ones; * (b) federal grants to institutions of higher learning (excepting research grants) should be slowly phased out entirely, and this money— together with new appropriations, which are to be expected—should also be replaced by loans to the qualifying student. This means, in brief, that our universities should have a minimum of direct

---

* Ideally, the entire state budget for higher education should, in my opinion, take the form of student loans. But so radical a measure has little chance of getting through—the state universities would lobby it to death. Besides, so radical a measure is not really necessary. With a ceiling on their budgets and with inevitably increasing costs, the state universities will be constrained gradually to compete for students in terms of the education they offer, as against the low fees they charge, and their position will become a little less privileged with every passing year.

The Problems of
American Education

access to public funds to spend as they see fit, since their vision in this matter has turned out to be too imperfect. It also means that students will have more of the only kind of "student power" that counts: the freedom to purchase the kind of education they want, on terms acceptable to them.

There are potential benefits and risks attendant on this proposal, and they merit a listing. But, first, one must face the frequently heard objection to student loans—that their repayment may place too great a burden on a student, especially the student from a poor family, after his graduation. This objection can be surmounted. To begin with, not all students would need loans, and many would need only small ones. There are plenty of well-to-do parents who would still want to pay for their children's education. In addition, repayment plans can be—have been—calculated so as to be proportionate to the student's average income during his working life, and to exempt those whose average income would fall below a fixed level; and the burden on both student and taxpayer (for a subsidy would still be necessary, especially for women) could be made perfectly tolerable.

If one wished to be more egalitarian, one could augment a loan program with a part-scholarship program for those from low-income families. When all is said and done, however, the university graduate is the prime beneficiary, in dollars and cents, of his education; he ought to be the prime taxpayer for it. There is no such thing as "free" higher education. Someone is paying for it and, as things now stand, it is the working class of this country that is paying

The Crisis of Purpose and
Identity in Higher Education

taxes to send the sons and daughters of the middle class—and of the wealthy, too—through state colleges. (Some 60 percent of the students at Berkeley come from families with incomes of over $12,000.) It is not an easily defensible state of affairs, though we are now so accustomed to it that it seems the only "natural" one.

Now, as to benefits and risks:

1. A possible benefit that might realistically be expected that college students would take a more serious and responsible view of their reasons for being on the campus. To the extent that they would disrupt their own education, they would be paying for this out of their own pockets. As a consequence, there would certainly be less casual or playful or faddish disruption. One does get the impression that for many students the university is now, like the elementary and high schools, a place of compulsory attendance, and that the occupation of a campus building is a welcome lark and frolic. If these students were called upon to pay for their frolics, some of them at least might go back to swallowing goldfish. This would be bad for the goldfish but good for the rest of us.

2. Another potential benefit is that the large state universities, denied the subsidy which permits them to set very low tuition rates for state residents, would find it difficult to grow larger than they are; the college population would probably become more widely distributed, with the smaller and medium-sized institutions in a position to attract more students. This would be a good thing. It is clearly

foolish to assemble huge and potentially riotous
mobs in one place—and to provide them with room,
board, a newspaper, and perhaps a radio station to
boot. This violates the basic principle of riot control. We should aim at the "scatteration" of the
student population, so as to decrease their capacity
to cause significant trouble. I would also argue
there are likely to be some educational gains from
this process.

3. An obvious risk is that a great many of the radical and dissenting students would use their money
to attend newly founded "antiuniversities." And
many of the black students would veer off into black
nationalist institutions of higher learning. Something like this is bound to happen, I suppose,
though to what extent is unpredictable. It would,
beyond question, create bad publicity for the whole
student loan program. On the other hand, it would
take the pressure off existing institutions to be both
universities and "antiuniversities"—as well as "integrated" and "black nationalist" universities—at
the same time. The degree to which such pressure
has already been effective would shock parents,
state legislators, and public opinion generally, were
the facts more widely known.

Quite a few of our universities have already decided that the only way to avoid on-campus riots is
to give students academic credit for off-campus rioting ("field work" in the ghettos, among migrant
workers, etc.). And at Harvard—of all places!—there
is now a course (Social Relations 148), which
enrolls several hundred students and is given for
credit, whose curriculum is devised by the S.D.S.,

whose classes are taught by S.D.S. sympathizers, and whose avowed aim is "radicalization" of the students.

4. As a corollary to this last risk, there is the possibility that more new, "good" (in my sense of that term) colleges would also be founded. I'm not too sanguine about this—a fair portion of the academic community would surely look more benevolently on a new college whose curriculum made ample provision for instruction in the theory of guerrilla warfare than one that made a knowledge of classical political philosophy compulsory. Besides, it would be much easier to find "qualified" faculty for the first type than the second. Nevertheless, it is conceivable that "traditionalists," as well as the academic hipsters, could take advantage of the new state of affairs. And among the students they attract there might be quite a few blacks who are not really interested in studying Swahili or Afro-American culture or "black economics," but who—as things are now moving on the campus—are pretty much forced to do so by their black nationalist fellow students.

5. The greatest benefit of all, however, is that the new mode of financing higher education will "shake things up." Both university administrators and faculty will have to think seriously about the education of the students—and about their own professional integrity as teachers. This shake-up is bound to have both bad and good consequences. Some universities, for instance, will simply try to reckon how they can best pander to what they take to be student sentiment, and many professors will

doubtless pay undue attention to their "popularity" among students. On the other hand, it is reasonable to assume that you can't fool all the students—and their parents—all of the time; and if students are paying for their education, most of them will want to be getting their money's worth.

So, at long last, the academic community, and the rest of us as well, will have to engage in sober self-examination, and address ourselves to such questions as: What is this "college" of ours, or this "university" of ours? What is the "higher education" we offer? What do we parents expect from a particular "institution of higher learning" when we send our children there? The answers will certainly be too various to be pleasing to everyone. But at least they will be authentic answers, representing authentic choices.

It would be ridiculous to expect that, during this period of "shake-up," calm will descend upon our campuses. As I have already said, the roots of the student rebellion go very deep, and very far back. I recall Leo Rosten observing long before Columbia that, so far as he could see, what the dissatisfied students were looking for were: adults—adults to confront, to oppose, to emulate.

It is not going to be easy to satisfy this quest, since our culture for many decades now has been ploughing under its adults. But I agree with Mr. Rosten that this is what is wanted, and I am certain it will not be achieved until our institutions of higher education reach some kind of common understanding on what kind of adult a young man is ideally supposed to become. This under-

The Crisis of Purpose and
Identity in Higher Education

standing—involving a scrutiny of the values of our civilization—will not come soon or easily, if it ever comes at all. But we must begin to move toward it—and the first step, paradoxically, is to allow a variety of meanings to emerge from our existing, petrified institutions of higher learning.

SUGGESTED READING

Ahlstrom, Winton M., and Robert J. Havighurst, *400 Losers: Delinquent Boys in High School* (San Francisco: Jossey-Bass, 1971).

Boocock, Sarane, *Introduction to the Sociology of Learning* (Boston: Houghton Mifflin, 1972).

Bronfenbrenner, Urie, *Two Worlds of Childhood: U.S. and U.S.S.R.* (New York: Russell Sage Foundation, 1970).

Cicourel, Aaron V., and John I. Kitsuse, *The Educational Decision-Makers* (Indianapolis, Ind.: Bobbs-Merrill, 1963 [paperback]).

Clark, Burton R., *The Distinctive College: Antioch, Reed, and Swarthmore* (Chicago: Aldine Publishing Company, 1970).

———, *The Open Door College* (New York: McGraw-Hill, 1960).

Cottle, Thomas J., *Time's Children: Impressions of Youth* (Boston: Little, Brown, 1967 [paperback]).

Crain, Robert L., *The Politics of School Desegregation* (Garden City, N.Y.: Doubleday, 1969 [Anchor Books paperback]).

Dunham, E. Alden, *Colleges of the Forgotten American* (New York: McGraw-Hill, 1969).

Goslin, David A., *The School in Contemporary Society* (Chicago: Scott, Foresman, 1965 [Keystones of Education Series paperback]).

Hefferlin, J. B. Lon, *Dynamics of Academic Reform* (San Francisco: Jossey-Bass, 1969).

Janowitz, Morris, *Institution Building in Urban Education* (New York: Russell Sage Foundation, 1969 [paperback]).

Jencks, Christopher, and David Riesman, *The Academic Revolution* (Garden City, N.Y.: Doubleday, 1969 [Anchor Books paperback]).

Koerner, James D., *Who Controls American Education?* (Boston: Beacon Press, 1969 [Beacon paperback]).

Kroll, Arthur M., ed., *Issues in American Education* (New York: Oxford University Press, 1970 [paperback]).

Kruytbosch, Carlos E., and Sheldon L. Messinger, eds., *The State of the University: Authority and Change* (Beverly Hills, Calif.: Sage Publications, 1970 [paperback]).

Lieberman, Myron, *The Future of Public Education* (Chicago: University of Chicago Press, 1962 [Phoenix Books paperback]).

Miller, Harry L., and Marjorie B. Smiley, eds., *Education in the Metropolis* (New York: Free Press, 1967 [paperback]).

Rogers, David, *110 Livingston Street: Politics and Bureaucracy in the New York City School System* (New York: Random House, 1969 [Vintage Book paperback]).

Schafer, Walter E., and Carol Olexa, *Tracking and Opportunity: The Locking-Out Process and Beyond* (Scranton, Pa.: Chandler Publishing Company: An Intext Publisher, 1971 [paperback]).

Schrag, Peter, *Village School Downtown* (Boston: Beacon Press, 1968 [Beacon paperback]).

Silberman, Charles E., *Crisis in the Classroom* (New York: Random House, 1970 [paperback]).

Veblen, Thorstein, *The Higher Learning in America* (New York: B. W. Huebsch, 1918).

Yamamoto, Kaoru, ed., *The College Student and His Culture* (Boston: Houghton Mifflin, 1968).

**The Problems of
American Education**

INDEX

334

Index

Index

Index

NOTES ON THE EDITOR

BURTON R. CLARK is professor of sociology at Yale University. Born in Pleasantville, N.J. he received his B.A. and Ph.D. degrees at the University of California at Los Angeles. He has taught at Stanford University, the Graduate School of Education at Harvard University, and the University of California at Berkeley, where he was affiliated with the Center for the Study of Higher Education and the School of Education. He is the author of *Adult Education in Transition: A Study of Institutional Insecurity; The Open Door College; Educating the Expert Society;* and *The Distinctive College: Antioch, Reed and Swarthmore.*